Trauma and Affect

Artur Żmijewski, *80064* (2005), film still.

Ernst van Alphen

VIS-À-VIS

Valiz

Trauma and Affect

(Mis)Understanding Pain in Art and Culture

Contents

Part 2: Transmissions of Affect

Introduction

Understanding Trauma and Affect

From Holocaust Studies to Genocide Studies to Gaza Studies

It was in the 1990s that Holocaust studies and in its wake, trauma studies, came about. Until that decade not many people addressed the Holocaust in research because listening to the traumas of survivors was no priority. It took almost four decades to rebuild the ruins of Europe and the new State of Israel had to be created; instead of victims to listen to, heroes were needed as inspiration or role models.

Of course, more and more historical facts of the Holocaust became known due to testimonies, memoirs, and historical research, but all that was especially inspired by the obscene desire to know everything about horrible, destructive Nazi Germany. This explains how, already soon after the Second World War had ended, the Holocaust became the moral benchmark for absolute Evil. It was especially the Nuremberg trials held between November 1945 and October 1946 that were of great importance in the consolidation of the Holocaust as this Evil. Prominent leaders of Nazi Germany were prosecuted for war crimes, crimes against humanity, and crimes against peace.

One of the effects of the notion of the Holocaust as a universal moral benchmark of Evil is that one is not allowed to compare the Holocaust with other genocides, because that would make the Holocaust less unique. This taboo, still prevalent in the field of Holocaust studies today, is of course based on a misunderstanding of what is done when comparing: comparison does not erase differences but makes one become aware of what events or situations have in common as well as how they differ. But there is one thing that makes the Holocaust differ from other genocides: it is the only one that has the status of universal moral 'standard' of absolute Evil. Comparison could result in the conclusion that other genocides deserve the same status and that may not happen, until now.

In the last ten years, scholars became more and more aware that the taboo that does not allow to compare the Holocaust with any other genocide is difficult to defend, so more and more institutions specialized in war and Holocaust studies added genocide studies to their official title. The NIOD in Amsterdam, for example, changed their name and became the Institute for War, Holocaust, and Genocide Studies. It is perhaps shocking, but all these scholarly discussions have become dated and trivial with the genocide in Gaza and the settler colonization of Palestine that goes on NOW. The atrocities that take place on a daily basis in these places are horrendous. And what makes it worse is that this genocide is performed by Israeli Jews who legitimize their acts by having been the victims of genocide themselves. One can try to understand this dialectic psychologically by arguing that victims of violence often become perpetrators of violence. But the special status of the Holocaust is not based on psychological criteria but on moral ones. With what is going on since 2023 in Israel and Palestine, especially Gaza, the Holocaust can no longer be used to legitimize the politics of Israel. There is now a new benchmark of absolute Evil and that is Gaza. When Israeli politicians and the leaders of the US, Germany, the Netherlands, the United Kingdom, and some other European countries legitimize the genocide by referring to how Jews were victimized in the past and more recently, the Holocaust can no longer be an absolute benchmark of Evil. When victims of the Holocaust, meaning Israeli Jewish politicians and the people who support them, perform a new Holocaust they have created a new benchmark and that is Gaza.

Why This Book Then?

I wrote the chapters in this book over the last twenty-five years and I decided to collect them because what they have to offer in thinking about trauma and affect is theoretically and conceptually still very important. But most of the essays, especially those on trauma that deal with victims of the Holocaust, are a dated issue as I just argued, because there are nowadays other victims that need our care and attention. Two years ago, I explained in the contribution 'Nostalgic Archiving: Productive or Monstruous?' to the Spanish journal *A*Desk* why I had stopped writing on Holocaust and trauma; I did that because already then, I felt very uncomfortable by how insights of Holocaust studies were used to legitimize Israeli politics. I declined the status of 'honorary Jew' which had been bestowed on me because of my work in Holocaust and trauma studies. But all this does not mean that the essays collected in this volume are not relevant anymore.

My contribution to Holocaust and trauma studies is not historical, but theoretical and conceptual, meaning that their value is not limited to the history of the Holocaust or the special moral status it once had. What I try to understand in these essays is how trauma comes about, how it remains with us in our bodies, and as a result, how it is reenacted. Although it is ironic to say that my cases, through which I elaborate these arguments, were victims of the Holocaust and I can hardly say that this is now irrelevant because it could have been as well victims of Gaza.

Although all the horrors taking place now are beyond imagination, I remain hopeful. That means that I am confident that within a few years there will be new Nuremburg trials, although probably in another place. In those trials, the Israeli politicians and Western politicians who continued to support them, responsible for this shameful and extremely deadly episode in human, but especially Palestinian history, will be prosecuted for war crimes, crimes against humanity, and crimes against peace, exactly the same crimes Nazi criminals were prosecuted for. I seriously hope that the insight offered in this book will help the judges to come to their verdicts.

Now More Specifically, This Book

All the texts collected in this book deal with trauma and affect. Why is it important and useful to have these essays in one volume? Both concepts have become increasingly important in the criticism of art and literature and of culture at large since the 1990s. In those years a turn to trauma and a bit later also to affect has taken place. Whereas the movement of structuralism was exclusively focused on signification and the question 'what does it mean', poststructuralism developed an increasing attention for the limits of signification and for processes that cannot be understood in terms of signification. In short, dealing with culture and with cultural objects, practices, and processes, it is often not enough to ask: What does it mean? Other urgent questions have become: How does it work and what does it do?

Roland Barthes' notion of *punctum* is a prime example of a phenomenon that we can now, after the turn to affect, see as the work of affect instead of the product of signification. When a viewer of a photographic image is hit or 'wounded' by a photographic detail, thus, for example, making her or him aware of the fact that the photographic world belongs to the past and is no longer alive, something happens between that viewer and the image that cannot be accounted for in terms of meaning, but of being affected. Barthes formulates the affective nature of the punctum as 'that accident which pricks me (but also bruises me, is poignant to me)'.[1] In explaining the methodological framework for his phenomenology of photography, he is very explicit about the kind of power intrinsic to photography he is setting out to explore: 'Affect was what I didn't want to reduce; being irreducible, it was thereby what I wanted, what I ought to reduce the Photograph to.'[2]

This turn to affect has, however, also resulted in a situation in which the term affect is being used in a great variety of ways, and in a great variety of disciplines and domains. The same is the case with the term trauma; minor events, for example having a flat tire, are sometimes called traumatic. It has become the equivalent of something annoying.

Although the gain of the turns to affect and trauma is great and should not be underestimated as a paradigmatic change or even revolution, it has also resulted in great

1 Barthes, *Camera Lucida* (1981), 27.

2 Barthes, *Camera Lucida* (1981), 21.

3 Rose, 'Trading Spaces' (2012), 208.

confusion. Taking part in a roundtable discussion on the interaction between art and architecture in October 2012, American art historian Hal Foster made the following devastating remark:

> When I hear the word *affect* I reach for my Taser. An unfair reflex, I know, but *affect* seems to me a prime medium of ideology today—an implanted emotionality that is worse—because more effective—than false consciousness.[3]

His assessment draws attention not only to the so-called 'affective turn' that has taken place over the last two decades, but also more importantly to the overuse and exhaustion of the term that has emerged in its wake. For when concepts become fashionable, they usually lose their meaning, impact, and operationality. And although they may be used as buzzwords to promote the right discourse, from a conceptual point of view they lose their power. The clarity of the concepts affect and trauma has dissolved into uses of these terms in only suggestive ways, that do not really contribute anymore to a better understanding of affect as phenomenon. This makes it more and more difficult to employ affect and trauma as useful, critical concepts. What we need at this moment is a reframing of the landscape of cultural affect studies, affect theory, and trauma theory. Instead of accepting this depletion of these terms, I prefer to critically assess the concepts of affect ass well as trauma in their many uses and give them back their critical edge.

As already said, the concept of trauma has suffered from inflation when minor, annoying events are called traumatic. On top of that, the distinction between trauma and memory has been dissolved as if everything that happened in the past is (potentially) traumatic. This is demonstrated by the common use of the term traumatic memory that suggests that trauma is a kind of memory. However, in this collection of essays it will become clear that trauma blocks the possibility of memory. When something could not be experienced when it happened, it cannot be memorized and remains within the body as trauma. It does not return in the form of memory but as re-enactment. Whereas memory is by definition mediated, a re-enactment of an event implies that no mediation has taken place and it returns in its full immediacy, as if it happens for the first time.

Although the concepts trauma and affect should not be confused, they have an important characteristic in common. Images, texts, media, and social practices do not only work on the basis of signification, on what they mean. Trauma, in its manifestation of re-enactment, but also affective transmission triggered by images and other media, can only be understood when we develop conceptual frameworks that go beyond theories of signification and meaning production. In many respects, this implies a kind of epistemological revolution, a movement that can be traced back to post-structuralism and its preoccupations with the limits of signification and processes that cannot be understood in terms of meaning and representation.

Although for some scholars traumatic re-enactment is a form of affect, I will not argue this in the chapters of this book. But what they have in common is that both phenomena point to how images, texts, and media also work performatively. This performative quality cannot be understood in terms of meaning production or (mimetic) representation or its negation (abstraction). In the first part of this book, devoted to trauma, I will first explain how trauma originates in the past and what explains its re-enactment in the present. This rather precise assessment of trauma, of how it originates and manifests itself, is necessary in order to give it back its critical power as a concept. As will become clear in the chapters that follow, my notion of trauma implies that many horrible events are not at all traumatic, whereas even very positive, pleasant events can be traumatic.

In this introduction I will not further elaborate my notion of trauma, because I do so already at length in the first chapter 'The Limits and the Need of Representing the Holocaust'. The other chapters of the first section, titled 'Caught by Images: On the Role of Visual Imprints in Holocaust Testimonies' and 'Neither "Post-" nor Memory: Second Generation Testimony, Transmission of Trauma, and the Concept of Postmemory', demonstrate this notion of trauma and its re-enactment through the work of a variety of visual as well as literary artists: Charlotte Delbo, Toni Morrison, Carl Friedman, and Andrey Zvyagintsev. Most of these 'cases' are examples of Holocaust representation. That does not mean, however, that the concept of trauma can only be used for an understanding of the aftermath of the Holocaust. In the chapter 'Legacies of Stalinism and the Gulag' I argue that the Gulag has been in some respects even more traumatic than the Holocaust, not only for the survivors but especially for later generations. I will close-read the Russian film *The Return* by Andrey Zvyagintsev, which he made in 2003, in order to show how the aftermath of the Gulag manifests itself in the present. Although my cases are restricted to very specific catastrophic events, the Holocaust and the Gulag, the concept of trauma as developed in these chapters is hopefully also useful for an understanding of the aftermath of the Spanish civil war and of the military regimes in Latin America, among which those in Argentina, Chile, Brazil, and Peru.

In the second part of this book, devoted to the transmission of affect, I will first give an overview of the most important notions of affect in order to better understand the diverse ramifications of this concept. The other chapters are again 'cases that demonstrate how one can use the notion of affect that looks for specific elements, forms, aesthetics that triggers affect'. In order to explain what that means, the triggering of affect by form, I will spend the rest of this introduction to the mapping of different affective transmissions. Hopefully that will be helpful in understanding how the term affect can be used, and what kind of affective triggering one is interested in.

Mapping Affective Processes

Instead of accepting this depletion of the term, I prefer to critically assess the concept of affect in its many uses and give it back its critical edge. I find it useful to focus on what precisely affects do, how they operate within aesthetic forms and cultural practices and what can, in fact, be done with them. This volume develops affect as a highly productive concept for both cultural analysis and the reading of aesthetic forms, insisting on their performative force. Shifting the focus from individual experiences and the human interiority of personal emotions and feelings towards the agency of cultural objects, this collection of essays examines how affects operate, trigger and are, in turn, triggered by various aesthetic forms, social arrangements, and media strategies.

In order to show more clearly how affects work, we must also return to the originators and disseminators of the concept and see what motivated them to propose it. The works of French philosopher Gilles Deleuze and American psychologist Silvan S. Tomkins were the sources of inspiration for an understanding of how texts, images, media, and social practices work beyond signification. In many respects, this turned into an epistemological revolution, a movement that can be traced back to poststructuralism and its preoccupations with the limits of signification and processes that cannot be understood in terms of meaning and representation.

The turn to affect has also resulted in a situation where now the term has entered common usage and is employed by many different disciplines and domains.[4] Whereas originally it was mainly used in psychology and, due to Deleuze's influence, also in philosophy, it has now become an important concept in queer studies, feminism,[5] media and communication studies,[6] cultural theory and analysis,[7] art theory,[8] film studies,[9] literary studies,[10] postcolonial studies,[11] cognitive science,[12] anthropology,[13] social sciences,[14] and even economics.[15] The gain from the turn to affect has been considerable and the paradigmatic shift it has brought about should not be underestimated. However, at the same time, the clarity of the concept has been diluted to the point that now the term seems to be mainly used in suggestive ways. In short, we have lost sight of what affect really means: as a phenomenon, as a critical concept, and as an analytic tool. So, at this decisive juncture we need to reconfigure the landscape of cultural affect studies and affect theory.

No matter how useful, it is no longer accurate to distinguish the two main strands within the turn to affect: one inspired by the work of Baruch Spinoza, as explained, elaborated and put to analytic use by Deleuze and further discussed by Brian Massumi,[16] versus another inspired by the work of Tomkins and his best-known follower Eve Kosofsky Sedgwick.[17] In other words, our understanding of affect has traditionally been based on two competing frameworks:

4 A very good overview of cultural affect theory is provided in the introduction to Gregg & Seigworth (eds.), *The Affect Theory Reader* (2010). For more on the turn to affect, see Clough & Halley, *The Affective Turn* (2007).

5 Ahmed, *On Being Included* (2012); Ahmed, *The Cultural Politics of Emotion* (2004).

6 Karatzogianni & Kunstman (eds.), *Digital Cultures and the Politics of Emotion* (2012); Papacharissi, *Affective Publics* (2015).

7 Bal, *Of What One Cannot Speak* (2010); Ngai, *Our Aesthetic Categories* (2012).

8 Bennett, *Empathic Vision* (2005); Didi-Huberman, *Confronting Images* (2005).

9 Carroll, in Plantinga & Smith (eds.), *Passionate Views* (1999); Shaviro, *Post-Cinematic Affect* (2010); Duncan, *The Emotional Life of Postmodern Film* (2016).

10 Gumbrecht, *Atmosphere, Mood, Stimmung* (2012); Hogan, *Affective Narratology* (2011); Wehrs & Blake, *The Palgrave Handbook of Affect Studies and Textual Criticism* (2017).

11 Ahmed, *On Being Included* (2012).

12 Damasio, *Descartes' Error* (1994); Panksepp, *Affective Neuroscience* (1998); Schmitz et al., 'Emotions Outside the Box' (2011).

13 Stewart, *Ordinary Affects* (2007).

14 Brennan, *The Transmission of Affect* (2004); Blackman, *Immaterial Bodies* (2012); Berlant, *Cruel Optimism* (2011); Mühlhoff, 'Affective Resonance and Social Interaction' (2015); Wetherell, *Affect and Emotion* (2012).

15 Frey & Stutzer, *Happiness and Economics* (2002); Altman (ed.), *Handbook of Contemporary Behavioral Economics* (2015).

16 Massumi, *Parables for the Virtual* (2002b).

17 Sedgwick, *Touching Feeling* (2003).

the philosophical-aesthetic versus the psychological. And now, to muddy matters even more, these two conceptual currents have been intermingled to such a degree that it is rather impossible to decide what sets each apart.

One important critique of the scholarship that employs affect as an analytical concept enables us to rethink affect studies and comprehend more precisely the diversity and abundance of approaches used by various modes of cultural analysis. In her book *The Forms of the Affects* published in 2014, film theorist Eugenie Brinkema criticizes the kinds of thinking and writing the affective turn has brought about. In their place, she proposes and elaborates upon a different notion of affect.[18] Denouncing affect scholarship for completely disregarding textuality and close reading in favour of vague embodiment and for privileging the affected subject—meaning the affected critic or theorist—with its personal emotions and feelings, Brinkema writes:

> If affect as a conceptual area of inquiry is to have the radical potential to open up ethical, political, and aesthetic avenues for theoretical inquiry, then, quite simply, we have to do better than documenting the stirrings of the skin.[19]

According to Brinkema, the affective—and, more often than not, 'affect-laden'—turn has shifted attention away from affects themselves and onto the production of something immediate, visceral and corporeal in the theorist.[20] As a result, it has become a re-establishment of interiority, one that was condemned in the 1930s by the so-called 'new critics' William K. Wimsatt and Monroe C. Beardsley for producing an 'affective fallacy'. Brinkema argues that affect is wrongly seen as personal, something without form or meaning. She picks apart the notion that affect is intentional, a mere device

18 Brinkema, *The Forms of the Affects* (2014).

19 Brinkema, *The Forms of the Affects* (2014), 37–38.

20 Brinkema, *The Forms of the Affects* (2014), 27.

21 Brinkema, *The Forms of the Affects* (2014), 38.

22 Spinoza, in Curley (ed.), *A Spinoza Reader* (1994).

23 *Oxford English Dictionary*, 3rd edition (2010), s.v. 'trigger'.

for the generation of intensities in the critic. Thus, established as the affected subject, new readings and questions can in fact never arise. If affect theory re-establishes the interiority of a subject, then the subject can only ever talk about what she or he already knows. Only by speaking of what is not yet known, about what is not yet interiorized, can new thought develop. Brinkema redirects the affective turn under the name of radical formalism. For her, affects can have form and should therefore not be understood in terms of expressivity or interiority, but rather as formal dimensions, such as, in the case of cinema, as lines, colours, light and rhythm. Affects should not be placed inside the subject and interpreted from a position of interiority, they should be studied as forms, since 'forms are auto-affectively charged, and [...] affects take shape in the details of specific visual forms and temporal structures'.[21] By focusing on the forms of affect, we restore agency to form.

The nature of the agency of form is, however, not exactly clear. Suggesting that affects have form may even imply that form and affect relate to each other as signifier and signified—rather like how Saussurean structuralism would view the two sides of a sheet of paper. But when Brinkema explains that 'forms are auto-affectively charged' and 'affects take shape' in forms and temporal structures, it becomes clear that an affect stands for a process, a production, or, to use Spinoza's term, an action.[22] Affect, then, is not an object, an ontologically stable unit, but a stage in a process of triggering; in other words, form is what triggers affect.

But what does the verb trigger exactly mean? And how does it differ from signifying processes? According to the *Oxford English Dictionary*, the verb 'to trigger' means to activate, to stimulate, to initiate a change of state, or to spark off.[23] To trigger is thus defined as a process that produces, generates, provokes and, eventually, opens. In contrast with signification and representation, it does not convey meaning of a pre-given referent. When we consider affect as a process, the activity of triggering becomes twofold; while in Brinkema's work, it is form as a trigger, or better forms that trigger affects, the resulting affects, in turn, work as triggers in their own right. Affects can trigger thoughts, feelings, emotions, moods, and bodily responses. By rethinking affect as a triggering process, one might conclude that the major theorizations of affect focus on different phases in the affective process. Whereas scholars like Deleuze and Tomkins focus on affect as a productive trigger of thought and/or emotion, Brinkema explains form as a trigger of affect. As a result, we can distinguish three stages of the affective process:

1. Form as the trigger of affect
2. Affect as the intensity, sensation, or resonance in which this triggering results
3. Affect as the trigger of thought, emotions, imagination, bodily responses

In his philosophical treatise *Ethics* published in 1677, Spinoza makes a distinction between the last two phases: *affectus* and *affectio* (usually translated as affect and affection), where affectus is action and affectio passion.[24] The action of affect can be seen as the second phase; affect as intensity. Its qualification as an action informs the third phase, whereby intensity triggers passion. We can outline the whole process as follows:

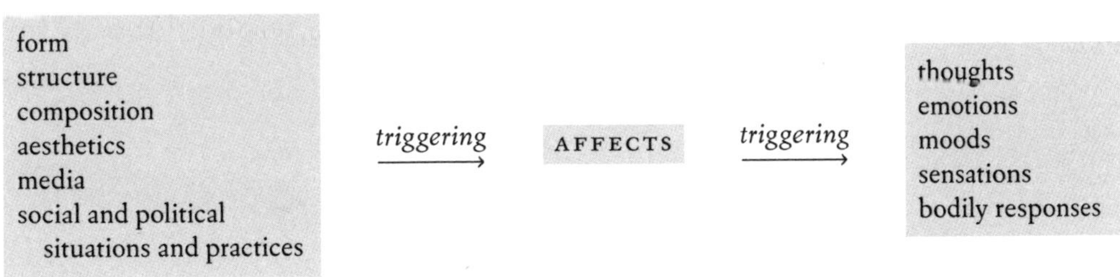

24 Spinoza, in Curley (ed.), *A Spinoza Reader* (1994), 154.

On the basis of this scheme, the most important theories of affect can be mapped. This enables us to understand what distinguishes various theories from each other, since they focus on different phases in the affective process or emphasize the other results or objects that affects trigger.

In the chapters devoted to affect in this book, however, I will especially explore the possibility and productiveness of the idea that affects have legible forms. By doing so, I will go beyond the idea that affect is an energetic intensity effecting a reaction in a reader or viewer. Of course, when affects have been triggered they effect such a reaction in the viewer. But inspired by Brinkema's idea that affects are triggered by specific forms in texts or images, I will try to read the aesthetic forms of Andrew Wyeth's canonical painting *Christina's World* that activate this triggering process.

Conventionally one acknowledges certain subject matter as resulting in strong affects in the viewer or reader. The arousal of the viewer by pornography or increasing tension in the viewer by representations of extreme violence can be understood in terms of specific themes, the realistic representation of sex, and violence that trigger affect. The chapters 'Playing the Holocaust: Playacting and Toys' and 'The Performativity of Provocation: The Case of Artur Żmijewski' should be understood as examples of a specific subject matter that more or less automatically triggers affect, namely the Holocaust. The visual artists I discuss in these two chapters are very much aware of the affective burden they address with their works, but in order to provoke reflection beyond affective responses resulting in strong emotions they develop strategies that process affect into critical thinking.

Part 1

Notions of Trauma

The Limits and the Need of Representing the Holocaust

Redefining the Notion of Experience

> I am other. I speak and my voice sounds like something other than a voice. My words come from outside of me. I speak and what I say is not said by me. My words must travel along a narrow path from which they must not stray for fear of reaching spheres where they'd become incomprehensible. Words do not necessarily have the same meaning. You must hear them say, 'I almost fell. I got scared.' Do they know what fear is? Or 'I'm hungry. I must have a chocolate bar in my handbag.' They say, I'm frightened, I'm hungry, I'm cold, I'm thirsty, I'm in pain, as though these words were weightless.[1, 2]

1 Delbo, *Auschwitz and After* (1995), 264.

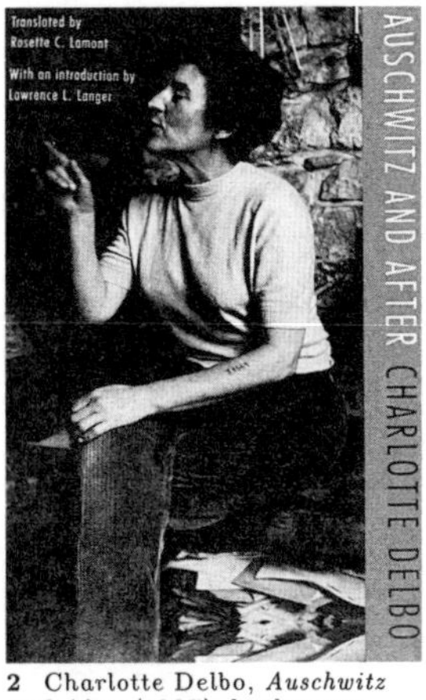

2 Charlotte Delbo, *Auschwitz and After* (1997), book cover, transl. from French.

The past of the Holocaust brings with it a general semiotic problem that confronts not so much the historians of the Holocaust or artists or writers, but in the first place the survivors. What survivors of the Holocaust often have in common is the incapacity to express or narrate their past experiences. The uniqueness and extremity of the Holocaust cannot be represented. This semiotic problem is the background of the widespread conviction that the Holocaust is unrepresentable.

The Holocaust's unrepresentability has, then, no moral significance, in the sense that it is dangerous or reprehensible to represent it, but its representation is technically impossible. The problem of this silence as I will discuss it here is fundamentally *semiotic* in nature, not *ethical*.

In the face of this semiotic problem, an historical approach to the Holocaust appears to be the least inadequate. Historical discourse is then seen as more basic, as closer to experiences that cannot, or hardly, be reached or expressed. From this perspective the imaginative discourses of art and language are seen as secondary discourses which can only work upon the historical discourse which is more primary. The privileging of historical discourse on the Holocaust is, therefore, motivated by an issue that cannot be understood as too limited, too ideological a conception of either the historical or the imaginative. In this first chapter I am especially interested in the question of the cause of the semiotic problem, and its implications for other semiotic processes. Is it caused by an intrinsic restriction or limitation of language, or by the extremity of the events which make out Holocaust experiences? If the latter were the case, it would legitimate or justify a privileging of the historical approach to the Holocaust, because it is historical discourse which sets itself the task to making the past present. But if the semiotic problem of the unrepresentability of the Holocaust originates in a discursive limitation in the technical sense, the realm of the imaginative might be a solution instead of a liability and even provide some privileged access, because it is there that the characteristics of the symbolic order are creatively challenged.

But even so, the alternatives are not so clear. I will argue that it is not language, nor the events or history of the Holocaust as such which cause the unrepresentability of

Holocaust experiences. More generally, it is rather language as a function of history, that is, as a precondition of experiencing history, which was disrupted during the Holocaust. To understand this, we first need to focus on, and perhaps redefine the notion of experience.

Semiotic Incapacity

The standard view has it that within the symbolic domain representations of the Holocaust are a case apart because in representing the Holocaust, symbolic language falls short in its mimetic possibilities. The historical reality which has to be represented is beyond comprehension. Faced with the extremity and uniqueness of this piece of history, according to this view the limitations of representation are intrinsic to language. This view implies that it makes no sense to develop new forms of representations, or a new rhetorical mode, as, for example, Hayden White has advocated.

An illustrative example of this view can be found in Dresden's book on Holocaust literature, *Vervolging, Vernietiging, Literatuur*[3] (*Persecution, Annihilation, Literature*[4]). But he has expressed the same view already in his earlier essay 'Souvenir inoubliable'. In this essay Dresden claims that war and Holocaust memories do not differ from other memories in structure; they only differ in content.

> The memories have the same structure as always, although their content is totality different. They are fixated, one can talk about them, they have become verbalized by many. Hunger winter, executions, persecutions, camps, gasifications, they seem now, in terms of structure, more or less like the perspective a tourist has. More

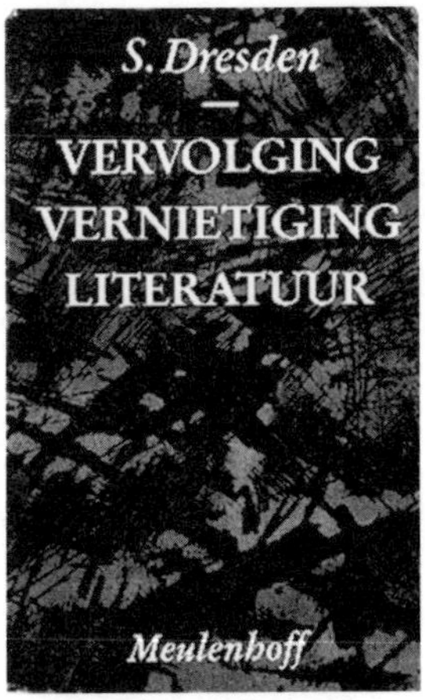

3 Sem Dresden, *Vervolging, Vernietiging, Literatuur* (1992), book cover, original Dutch version.

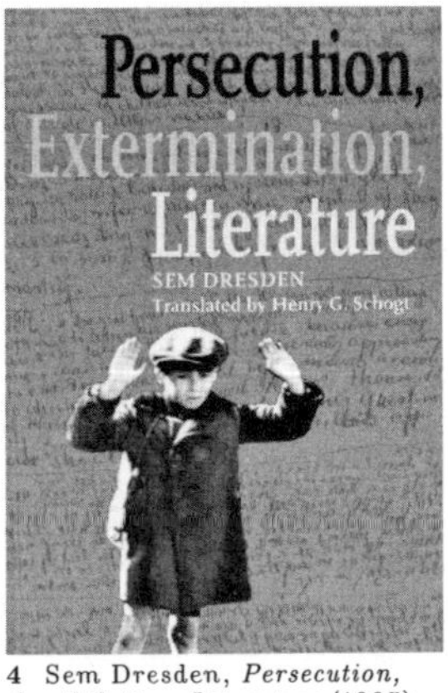

4 Sem Dresden, *Persecution, Annihilation, Literature* (1995), transl. from Dutch.

> or less, however. For, their content is of such nature, that they hinder and make impossible the total verbalization.[5]

Because of the extreme horror of the historical reality, language falls short. Quantitative notions that describe the extent of the historical reality are used as explanations. The semiotic problem, then, is caused by a feature of the *object of representation*. The means of representations remain undiscussed. The cause of Holocaust's unrepresentability is not examined on the level of representation, but on the level of history. Dresden is explicit in this regard. When he says that Holocaust memories have the same structure as all memories, he locates the problem of representation completely in the object of representation, the content of experience: history as an exterior reality outside the realm of representation.

A side-effect of this view is that the Holocaust is provided with metaphysical dimensions: the Holocaust becomes the absolute Evil. The Holocaust as the absolute symbol of Evil, is, then, as unrepresentable as Jahweh. Such a metaphysical status of the Holocaust is undesirable and even dangerous, because it ultimately makes it impossible to see it as a moment, albeit apocalyptic, in *human history*. When the Holocaust becomes the embodiment of a negative metaphysical principle, it becomes very difficult to raise the question of the responsibility for it and the causes of it. In the words of Ringelheim:

> The Holocaust is then seen as ontologically separate from human history; at the same time, it is used to make 'relatively trivial' other events or other people's experience prior to, during, or even after the Holocaust.[6]

In the following pages I will argue, however, that the problems with which representations of the Holocaust are

5 Dresden, 'Souvenir inoubliable' (1992), 8 (my translation).

6 Ringelheim, 'Thoughts About Women and the Holocaust' (1990), 142.

struggling are more adequately located in the process and mechanisms of representation itself. By doing that I by no means want to relativize the extremity of the Holocaust as a historical event. I presume, however, that in principle, representation does offer the possibility to give expression to extreme experiences.

But representation itself is historically variable. Sometimes there can be situations or events—and the Holocaust is prototypical for such situations—which are the occasion of experiences that cannot be expressed in the terms which the language, or broader, the symbolic order, offers *at that moment*. With this emphasis I want to stress the fact that for me representation is not a static, timeless phenomenon, of which the (im)possibilities are fixed once and forever. For every language user, representation is an historically and culturally specific phenomenon. Languages, whether literary, artistic or not, are changeable and transformable. This supposition implies that to answer the question of the causes of the unrepresentability of the Holocaust, it is better not to focus on the limits of language or representation as such, but on the features of the forms of representation that were available to Holocaust victims/survivors to articulate their experiences. When the survivors of the Holocaust are not, or hardly, able to express their experiences, that difficulty can be explained by the fact that the nature of their experiences is in no way covered by the terms and positions that the symbolic order offers to them. It is exactly this discrepancy which has to be investigated, because it is in that discrepancy that the cause of the Holocaust's unrepresentability lies. In short, the problem is not the nature of the event, nor an intrinsic limitation of representation, but the split between the living of an event and the available forms of representation with/in which the event can be experienced. This is where the cause of the Holocaust's unrepresentability must be examined.

So far, I have used the notions 'experience' and 'the expression or representation of an experience' as if they involve two separate moments. First, we experience something, next we try to find an expression for that experience. Such a conception would imply that experiences are not discursive, that they arise without connection to the symbolic order. The experience of an event or history is, however, dependent on the terms which the symbolic order offers. It needs these terms to transform living through the event into an experience of the event. For, to be part of an event or of a history as an object of its happening is not the same as experiencing it as a subject. The notion of experience implies already a certain degree of distance to the event. Hence the experience *of* an event is already a representation of it and not the event itself. I contend that the problem of Holocaust survivors is precisely that the lived events could not be experienced because language did not provide the terms and positions in which to experience them. This defines them as *traumatic*. The Holocaust has been so traumatic for many, precisely because it could not be experienced; because a distance to it in language or representation was not possible. In this view, experience is the result or product of a discursive process. That is why, I propose, the problem of Holocaust experiences can be formulated as the stalling of this discursive process. Because of this stalling the experience cannot come about.

This implies, in fact, that the problem of the unrepresentability of the Holocaust has already arisen *during* the Holocaust itself and not after it, when survivors tried to provide testimonies of it, literary, artistic or not. Or, to put it differently, the later representational problems are a continuation of the impossibility during the event itself to experience the

Holocaust in the terms of the symbolic order then available. Lawrence L. Langer's study *Holocaust Testimonies* (1991)[7] offers many examples of this stalling of the discursive process of experience. Langer discusses the oral testimonies of Holocaust survivors which were recorded on videotape by the Fortunoff Video Archive for Holocaust Testimonies[8] at Yale University. Langer shows how the problems these survivors have in their self-experience are closely bound up with the forms in which they are able to remember the Holocaust.

In what follows I will use his findings to show more concretely what kind of representational problems arise in efforts to experience the Holocaust (as yet). Langer's goal is to show which forms of memory the Holocaust has assumed, and how the self of the survivors is determined in a fundamental way by these forms of memory. He distinguishes five different forms of memory and as a consequence of those, five different personality structures. He distinguishes 'deep memory' (the buried self), 'anguished memory' (the divided self), 'humiliated memory' (the besieged self), 'tainted memory' (the impromptu self) and 'unheroic memory' (the diminished self).[9]

Within the scope of this chapter I am not so much interested in the relation between memory and self, but in the discursive basis of the unrepresentability of Holocaust experiences. Therefore, the distinctions I will make concern different kinds of obstacles which can stand in the way of experience-and-representation. I will distinguish four kinds of representational problems, two of which concern the subject position of the survivors; the other two concern narrative frames which are used to tell the Holocaust. Each of them involves a discrepancy between the reality of the Holocaust history and the positions and terms which the symbolic order provided to experience this reality. These four problems are:

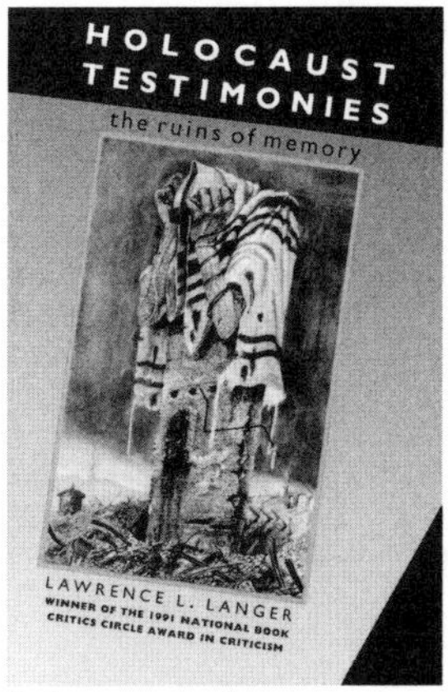

7 Lawrence L. Langer, *Holocaust Testimonies* (1991), book cover.

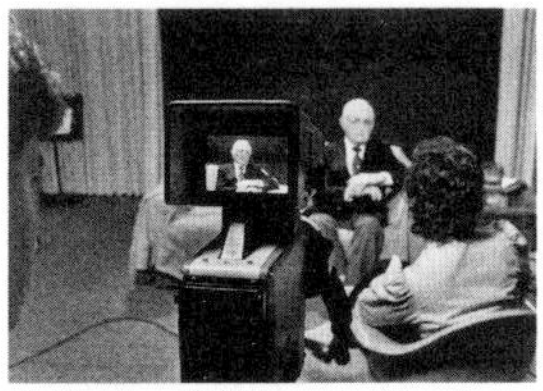

8 Fortunoff Video Archive for Holocaust Testimonies.

9 Langer, *Holocaust Testimonies* (1991), 49. Langer's *Holocaust Testimonies* is a valuable book because of the careful attention he pays to the testimonies. I don't agree, however, with the unmediated status he applies to testimony. Experience and testimony are for him authentic because unmediated, whereas he meets literary representations of the Holocaust with suspicion because those are the result of mediated conventions. I fully agree with LaCapra's critique of Langer: 'Langer's view obscures the role of rhetorical conventions in oral discourse and the interaction between "literary" writing and speech' (LaCapra, *Representing the Holocaust* (1994), 194). Another insightful critique of Langer is offered by Dekoven Ezrahi, 'Representing Auschwitz' (1996).

1. Ambiguous actantial position: one is neither subject nor object of the events, or one is both at the same time;
2. Total negation of any actantial position or subjectivity;
3. The lack of a plot or narrative frame, by means of which the events can be narrated as a meaningful coherence;
4. The plots or narrative frames which are available or which are inflicted are unacceptable, because they do not do justice to the way in which one partakes in the events.

Ambiguous Subjectivity: Between Responsibility and Victimhood

In his chapter 'Anguished Memory' Langer discusses testimonies of survivors who have 'split' their selves in reaction to what happened to them in the camps. The only way to allow memories of this past is by ascribing the memories to someone else. One of the survivors describes this mechanism as follows: 'I'm thinking of it now … how I split myself. That it wasn't *me* there. It was somebody else.'[10] In some of the testimonies it becomes clear what the causes can be for this splitting of the self. Langer tells about the testimony of Bessie K., who found herself in 1942 as a young woman with a baby in the Kovno ghetto in the situation in which labourers were being selected. Because of the fact that children were not admitted (and were killed immediately), she hid her baby in her coat as if it concerned a bundle of possessions. When her baby began to cry, it was taken by the German soldiers. Until 1979 she has never been able to tell anybody about the loss of her baby. Her testimony makes clear, however, that her incapacity to talk about her loss was caused at least in part by the limitations of the language that was available. Now she talks as follows about the dramatic event:

10 Langer, *Holocaust Testimonies* (1991), 48.

> I wasn't even alive; I wasn't even alive. I don't know if it was by my own doing, or it was done, or how, but I wasn't there. But yet I survived.[11]

The language falls short of enabling her to experience a position where subjectivity and objecthood are ambiguous and undecidable. Bessie K. is still confused, because she does not know if she had any responsibility for the loss of her baby, or if she was the victim of that situation. If she had not hidden her baby in the bundle of clothes, would she not have lost it? She does not know which actantial role she has had in the event. Was she the subject, which means that she had an active actantial role in the loss of her baby, or was she only the object, which implies that she underwent the event passively, as a victim?

Bessie K.'s bewilderment is caused by the fact that she does not know the answer to this question. In the testimony of Alex H. this kind of bewilderment manifests itself rather as uncertainty.

> [...] It is difficult to say, talk about feelings. First of all, we were reduced to such an animal level that actually now that I remember those things, I feel more horrible than I felt at the time. We were in such a state that all that mattered is to remain alive. Even about your own brother or the closest, one did not think. I don't know how other people felt... It bothers me very much if I was the only one that felt that way, or is it normal in such circumstances to be that way? I feel now sometimes, did I do my best or didn't I do something that I should have done? But at that time, I wanted to survive myself, and maybe I did not give my greatest efforts to do certain things, or I missed to do certain things.[12]

11 Langer, *Holocaust Testimonies* (1991), 49.

12 Langer, *Holocaust Testimonies* (1991), 65–66.

When we translate the testimony of Alex H. in actantial terms, we can say that he is not sure if he has been enough of a subject. Has he made enough of an effort to help others? While Bessie K. is afraid that she might have had too active an actantial role—but she does not know it—, Alex H. does not know if he has had it enough. In both their cases, this uncertainty results in an ambiguous, battered feeling of subjectivity. They feel themselves neither subject nor object. Another example is the French member of the resistance Pierre T. After his resistance group had killed a Nazi-officer, the Nazis executed twenty-seven people of his village as a reprisal. His doubts concern the actantial role he has had in the execution of his fellow-villagers. Is he co-responsible for it, or is he victimized by this measure of the Nazis?

Earlier, I argued that experiences, hence, also self-experiences, can be seen as discursive processes. But what do the battered feelings of subjectivity of Bessie K., Alex H., and Pierre T., and their difficulties in talking about what happened to them, have to do with language? In what sense precisely are forms of representation at least partly the cause of their confusion?

As I mentioned before, Hayden White has argued for the necessity of developing a new kind of language, 'a new rhetorical mode' in order to be able to talk about the Holocaust. The reason he puts this necessity forward helps me to analyze the problems survivors like Bessie K. and Alex H. are struggling with, in a way that treats the difficulty as discursive. This is why Hayden White proposed to attempt to find a mode of expression analogous to the 'middle voice', which would allow a different subject position in relation to the event. The active as well as the passive mode situate the agent or actant outside the action as such. The agent is subject or object of it. The middle voice on the contrary situates the agent inside the action. The agent takes part in the action or event without being either subject or object of it. The agent is being affected by the action, although without being directly the object or subject of it.[13]

For me it is hard to imagine how we can develop a new rhetorical mode on this basis. Nevertheless, White's proposal contains an adequate diagnosis of the kind of problems of Holocaust survivors described in this section. They had difficulty in experiencing the events they were part of, because they only had language at their disposal which offered them two possibilities. As speaking subjects they must ascribe to themselves the role of either subject or object in relation to the events. But the situation of the Holocaust was such that this kind of distance to the action was not possible. One took part in a history which did not provide unambiguous roles of subject or object. This is one of the reasons why the situation of the Holocaust was not 'experienceable' and hence later, not narratable or otherwise representable.

13 Basing himself on Lang, *Act and Idea in the Nazi Genocide* (1990), White argues that we need a rhetorical mode that offers a subject position which is neither active nor passive. He refers to classical Greek as an example of a language which has not only an active and passive mode but also a so-called 'middle voice'. The three different voices imply different actantial relations (of the agent) to the action or event. Whereas the modern Indo-European languages only offer the possibility of the active and the passive mode, classical Greek offers with this 'middle voice' a different subject position in relation to the event. For an actualization of the middle voice, see Boletsi, 'From the Subject of the Crisis to the Subject in Crisis' (2016).

Denied Subjectivity: About 'Nothing'

In the previous section I discussed cases in which it was not clear for Holocaust survivors which role they had in the events they ended up in: subject or object? Although their actantial role was experienced as fundamentally ambiguous, it was not their subjectivity as such which was under pressure. I will now discuss the consequences for representation of situations in which the subjectivity of the inmates of the camps was reduced to 'nothing'. In these situations, the survivors did not even experience their role in it as that of an object. Their existence as human beings was totally denied.

14 Langer, *Holocaust Testimonies* (1991), 85.

They played no actantial role whatsoever, which put their subjectivity as such in jeopardy.

In Western culture the individual subject him/herself is held responsible for his/her own destiny to an important degree. One is responsible for how one acts. It is precisely because of this individual responsibility that it is possible to form one's own subjectivity by means of consciously-chosen behaviour. When one does not make any conscious choices, one is in fact not one hundred percent a subject. This view of subjectivity has great implications for those who had to live in the camps. Constantly they had to endure situations which would normally, in the society they came from, require taking action and asserting oneself. When a family member, a friend, or even a total stranger is being ill-treated or killed, one is supposed to intervene. The failure to do so corrodes one's subjectivity. In the camps, however, inmates were constantly in the situation of not being able to intervene, while the situation asked for it. This had consequences not so much for those who were being ill-handled or killed (they were going to be killed anyway), but for those who had to watch it.

These consequences are in fact caused by the close link between subjectivity and ethical norms:

> The concept of 'you cannot do nothing' is so alien to the self-reliant Western mind (dominated by the idea of the individual as *agent* of his fate) that its centrality, its *blameless* centrality to the camp experience continues to leave one morally disoriented. The very principle of blameless inaction by former victims is foreign to the ethical premises of our culture, where we sometimes confuse such inaction with cowardice, or indifference.[14]

The most extreme consequence of this impossibility to act is not even a feeling of impotence, but, much more radically, one of lack of interest. One is forced to abjure the concept of subjectivity which associates passive looking on with morally weak or not fully-grown subjectivity. In order not be disqualified all the time as a full subject, the only solution was to give up the concept of subjectivity, which was the ground for such a disqualification.

The abjuring of this conception of subjectivity because of the moral issue at stake is clearly the issue in the testimony of Joan B. She worked in the kitchen of a labour camp. When one of the inmates was on the verge of giving birth, the camp commandant gave the order to boil water:

> 'Boil water. But the water wasn't to help with the act of giving birth. He drowned the new-born baby in the boiling water.' The appalled interviewer asks, 'Did you see that?' 'Oh, yes, I did,' the witness imperturbably replies. 'Did you say anything?' the dialogue continues. 'No, I didn't'.[15]

Later, Joan B. gives the following comment:

> I had a friend [...] who said that now when we are here, you have to look straight ahead as if we have [blinders] on like a race horse... and become selfish. I just lived, looked, but I didn't feel a thing. I became selfish. That's number one.[16]

Langer remarks rightly that in the camp situation 'selfish' has no longer the meaning of being ungenerously indifferent toward others. Selfish must be read as 'self-ish': in order to survive all norms and values regarding fellow human beings must be ignored. It is exactly this necessary and purposeful ignoring and abjuring of a system of values which kills subjectivity at the very moment that one chooses life.

15 Langer, *Holocaust Testimonies* (1991), 123.

16 Langer, *Holocaust Testimonies* (1991), 123.

In the fifties and sixties these kinds of situations have been presented as existential choices that have to be made and that exemplify life, the human condition, in general. The testimonies Langer discusses make clear, however, that this is a highly romanticized view, because there were no choices to be made. The situation was defined by the *lack* of choice. One just followed humiliating impulses which killed one's subjectivity but safeguarded one's life. In the words of Langer: 'It is indeed a kind of annihilation, a totally paradoxical killing of the self by the self in order to keep the self alive.'[17]

Yet, subjectivity is not a fixed, universal category, but a social construction. That is why one can wonder if this corroding of subjectivity was equally annihilating for everyone. Myrna Goldenberg's remark in her article 'Different Horrors, Same Hell: Women Remembering the Holocaust' that the camp situation was less immediately deadly for many women than for most of the men can be understood from this perspective.[18] In Western patriarchal society masculine subjectivity depends much more extremely on the construction of an independent, initiating subjectivity. When subjectivity has to be abjured, masculinity is impaired in its essence.[19]

This gender difference in constructions of subjectivity can even explain the fact that men died much sooner in the camps than women. Goldenberg points out that life in the camps was usually much harder for women than for men. Adult men were treated relatively better, because they could be better used in the labour camps. Nevertheless, in 1943, for example, three times as many men as women died in Ravensbrück. Goldenberg suggests that this can be explained by the fact that men were less able than women were in 'killing the self in order to survive'. Women could more easily renounce their subjectivities, because in the cultures they

17 Langer, *Holocaust Testimonies* (1991), 131.

18 Goldenberg, 'Different Horrors, Same Hell' (1990), 153.

19 On testimonies by women survivors, see also Lothe, *Time's Witnesses* (2017).

came from the independence and strength of their subjectivity had been limited anyway.

> [...] and being less dependent on inflated egos, as men were, when these egos cracked and were swept away, women recovered faster and with less bitterness.[20]

This view confirms the constructedness of subjectivity as much as its crucial importance in the ability to experience.

So far, I have described the mechanism of survival which forced inmates to kill the self in order to keep the self alive. But how can this mechanism be responsible for the unrepresentability of the Holocaust experience? It is not so much the content of the experience that causes this problem, but the fact that the capacity to narrate is lacking. When one had to kill the self, one is no longer able to tell. It is the voice which has disappeared by abjuring subjectivity. While one lives on, one's voice has been struck dumb. In the words of one of Delbo's fellow deportees: 'I died in Auschwitz, but no one knows it.'[21]

The lack of a 'voice' is clearly expressed in the testimony of Joan B. quoted earlier. In the literal sense of the word Joan B. has recovered her subjectivity and voice. For she does testify of her camp experiences. The way she does this, however, shows no expression of her subjectivity at all. She records the factual events without any concern or compassion. She repeats the recorded happening in an almost mechanical way. Watch her language:

> 'He drowned the newborn baby in the boiling water.' The appalled interviewer asks, 'Did you see that?' 'Oh, yes, I did,' the witness imperturbably replies. 'Did you say anything?' the dialogue continues. 'No, I didn't.'[22]

20 Goldenberg, 'Different Horrors, Same Hell' (1990), 153.

21 Delbo, *Auschwitz and After* (1995), 267.

22 Langer, *Holocaust Testimonies* (1991), 123.

Although Joan B. speaks (again), she speaks with a minimum of expression. It seems as if a voice without subjectivity is speaking. Or to formulate it more pointedly: it is not Joan B. who is speaking, it is just her mouth. On a literal, superficial level Joan B.'s testimony weakens the conviction that Holocaust experiences cannot be represented. For, there is narration going on. But it is precisely this testimony which makes clear why so many Holocaust survivors are not able to tell about the events of which they were part. Although they survived, their selves were killed in Auschwitz. A killed self has no experiences, not to mention narratable memories.

The Holocaust as Narrative Vacuum

Events never stand on their own. We experience events not as isolated happenings, and happenings cannot be experienced in isolation. Events always have a pre-history, and they are themselves again the pre-history of events which are still going to happen. I don't want to suggest that this continuity is present in reality. Reality is rather a discontinuous chaos. It is, however, the form in which we experience and represent events that turns events into a continuous sequence. We experience events from the perspective of narrative frameworks in terms of which these events can be understood as meaningful. When somebody has passed a final exam, the meaning of this event is derived from an anticipation of events which are expected to follow: further study, jobs, a career. When somebody dies, it is a dreadful event, exactly because all expectation of coming events is now closed off. Death gets its negative meaning from this lack of a narrative framework which makes it possible to anticipate future events.

In the account of this narrative issue, I have used the term framework instead of context. The last decades there has been important discussions about the status of 'context' in those disciplines in which history is an element. Is context a factual given which can be reconstructed, or is it the product of interpretive acts? It is necessary to dwell on this discussion because it puts the difficulties of narrating Holocaust experiences in a perspective, and this perspective decisively changes the parameters of the discussion.[23]

Jonathan Culler has phrased the problematic clearly. Whereas the term 'context' contains the noun 'text' the prefix cuts it fundamentally off. 'Context' appears to escape the need for interpretation but this is an illusion:

> But the notion of context frequently oversimplifies rather than enriches discussion, since the opposition between an act and its context seems to presume that the context is given and determines the meaning of the act. We know, of course, that things are not so simple: [...] context is not given but produced; what belongs to a context is determined by interpretative strategies; contexts are just as much in need of elucidation as events; and the meaning of a context is determined by events. Yet, whenever we use the term *context* we slip back in the simple model it proposes.[24]

In other words, context is itself a text consisting of signs in need of interpretation. The allegedly positive knowledge history yields is itself a product of interpretive choices. Varying on Derrida's statement that 'No meaning can be determined out of context, but no context permits saturation', Culler affirms: 'Meaning is context bound, but context is boundless'. This textualization of context is no reason to set the relationship between text and context aside as too open, ambiguous,

23 For a more extensive discussion of Culler's significant proposal, see Bal, *Narratology* (2017).

24 Culler, *Framing the Sign* (1988), xiv.

25 Culler, *Framing the Sign* (1988), *xiv*.

or arbitrary. On the contrary, special, keen interest in that relation focuses on its greater complexity. When context is no longer conceived as a causal chain of single events but as the product of a textual process, contextual 'facts' become signs. And structurally, signs are not single. Signs are by definition iterative, they function in a plurality of contexts. Texts, works of art, but also 'events' in the more literal sense of the word, are thus 'made' by a multitude of recipients, in different times, in different ways.

This poststructuralist view extends the idea of causality to the notion that texts become elements in chains of meaning production. Such meaning productions are not only geared differently; the text or artifact has a different status within them. No longer a product of a cultural-historical context that precedes it, it is now itself a producer of semantic relations. This is how the poststructuralist tenet can be understood according to which texts *constitute* identity and culture. In this active conception lies the importance of the concept of *frame* as a replacement of *context*. Culler formulates the advantage of the former over the latter:

> It reminds us that framing is something we do; it hints of the frame-up ('falsifying evidence beforehand in order to make someone appear guilty'), a major use of context; and it eludes the incipient positivism of 'context' by alluding to the semiotic function of framing in art, where the frame is determining, setting off the object or event as art, and yet the frame itself may be nothing tangible, pure articulation.[25]

The frame, in other words, consists of the pressure exercised by the social-historical situation, on the one hand, on the production of events, art and literature—not a contingent con-text but an active combination of forces; on the other hand, on the way in which members of a culture deal with events, or texts in a historically specific situation; the pressure they exercise to produce specific meanings.

It is exactly this impossibility to activate a narrative framework as an anticipation of coming events which characterizes Holocaust experiences from a narrative point of view. Edith P. formulates this impossibility as follows:

> You don't think what goes through your mind. You say to yourself, 'Well, here I am in Auschwitz. And where am I, and what is going to happen to me?'[26]

Edith loses the capacity to reflect on the situation in which she finds herself. She explains the loss of that capacity as follows. We can say 'when I get married', or 'when I die', or 'when somebody dies whom I love', 'when I will have a child', or 'when I will find a job'. With these kinds of expressions, we automatically create theoretical possibilities of what is going to happen. It requires no effort:

> imagining oneself into those situations because we know how to think about them—they have precedents in our own or other people's experience. But no one has ever said 'when I get to Auschwitz, I…'; therefore the mind remains blank.[27]

In Auschwitz it was not possible, Edith explains, to know what kind of events could be expected. You never knew either if you were partaking in the middle, the beginning or the ending of a sequence of events. The inmates could not know this because 'mental process functions not in a vacuum but in relation to something that happened previously, that you had felt, thought, read, seen, or heard about.'[28] Life in the camps in all its aspects had no precedent.

26 Langer, *Holocaust Testimonies* (1991), 103.

27 Langer, *Holocaust Testimonies* (1991), 103.

28 Langer, *Holocaust Testimonies* (1991), 104.

If the experience of an event could be immediate, if this event were not itself discursive, this missing of precedent would not be a problem, on the contrary. In that case it would be their total 'newness' and unexpectedness thanks to which events could be absorbed intensely. But this turns out not to be the case. Because the Holocaust situation did not fit into any conventional framework, it was almost impossible to 'experience', and therefore later to represent it.

The Holocaust as Negation of Narrative Frameworks

So far, we have seen situations that could not be experienced because there were no conventional narrative frameworks in terms of which camp reality could be worked through. The events seemed to be enacted in a kind of vacuum. Now I want to pay attention to a different kind of discontinuity between reality and discursive experience, one which closely relates to the problem discussed above. In many testimonies the unrepresentability of what happened during the Holocaust is explained not by the lack of narrative frames but by the inadequacy of frames which are inflicted on the victims by the surrounding culture. Whereas there were no frames available for life in the camp while one was living in the camp, that situation seemed to have changed when the Second World War had come to an end and the inmates of the camp still alive were liberated. Then the moment of liberation followed the situation of imprisonment. Now a narrative frame offered itself within which the events in the camp situation could be given meaning retrospectively.

According to Langer this narrative framework structures almost all the testimonies in the Fortunoff Video Archive. The interviewer imposes the frame by the kind of questions he or she poses and by the order in which the questions are being asked. Again and again the interviewers begin with questions like: tell something about your childhood, your family, your school, your friends. In short, they begin with reconstructing the normal life of the survivor which preceded the total disaster of the Holocaust. Although the reconstruction is performed by the survivor her/himself, the activity as such is directed by the interviewer. After the reconstruction of the period which preceded the Holocaust, questions are being asked which are about life during the war, life in the ghetto, the deportation, camp life. In conclusion the interviewer asks questions like: tell me about the liberation. The last part of the interview stimulates the survivors to tell their further life as a happy ending, a comforting closure to a horrible crisis. The narrative framework which is imposed is the conventional story of a peaceful youth and beginning, which is cut off by a dreadful event or crisis, but which ultimately comes to a happy end.

Many of the survivors have, however, great difficulty in accepting the liberation as a closure of what happened to them in the camps. Langer quotes the response of one of the victims who was asked about how he felt after his liberation: 'Then I knew my troubles were *really* about to begin.'[29] The traditional historical plot requires that a situation of a conflict or crisis be followed by a solution, a denouement. This Holocaust survivor refuses, however, this conventional mould for his life. With the liberation his camp experiences have not come to an end; on the contrary, after the liberation they only became more intense. Narrative frameworks allow for an experience of (life) histories as continuous unities. It is precisely this illusion of continuity and unity which has become fundamentally unrecognizable and unacceptable for many survivors of the Holocaust. The camp experience

29 Langer, *Holocaust Testimonies* (1991), 67.

30 Langer, *Holocaust Testimonies* (1991), 173.

continues, whereas the camps only persist in the forms of Holocaust museums and memorials. The most elementary narrative framework, which consists of the continuum of past, present, and future had disintegrated.

> 'So there's no tomorrow, really,' observes the interviewer to this witness. 'No there isn't,' he replies. 'If you think there is, you're mistaken.'[30]

One of the causes of traditional narrative frameworks' failing can be explained by the fact that the 'selves' of many inmates of the camps have been killed. As I explained earlier, it was necessary to kill the self in order to live. But by means of which conventional plot or narrative framework can this be told? In terms of no traditional narrative continuum is it possible to have died in the past and to continue living in the present. This gives an additional layer of meaning to Delbo's statement 'I died in Auschwitz, but no one knows it.' 'No one knows it' posits narrative conventions as cultural, social. It means, then, no one is able to ac*know*ledge it, to give the knowledge back to her.

This implies that the basic feeling of being dead, or of continuing living as a dead person, is not narratable. The addressees of such a story will read such narration necessarily as being true only as a manner of speaking. For, the narrator of this story is still alive while he or she tells it. But a figurative reading does not acknowledge the problem of the unrepresentability of the experience of many survivors. On the contrary, it denies it. The conflict between a lived reality and the inadequacy of available narrative frameworks disappears. The figurative reading is based on the idea that *in language* a similarity is highlighted between a remembered negative camp experience (the compared) and the concept of death (that what is compared to). But death is much more real than an abstract notion that functions as the comparant in a comparison. Something has really died, not in a figurative, but in the most literal way. Many testimonies make clear that life in the camp is not being remembered at all. There is no distance from something that once happened and cannot be remembered. Many survivors still live *in* the situation of the camp, which precludes the possibility of a distance from it. It is precisely because for them the past of the Holocaust continues, that narrative frameworks which makes use of the sequence past, present, and future are inadequate.

The Experience of the Other Hell

The unrepresentability of the Holocaust is thus caused not by the extremity of Holocaust experiences as such, but by the fact that this horrible history was not figuratively, but literally *unknown*. The symbolic order did not offer terms, positions or frames in which the Holocaust could be experienced, because these events had no precedent whatsoever. A remark by Hayden White formulates this difference tersely: 'It is not the difference of the experience, but the experience of a different "history" which is hard to represent.'[31]

31 White, 'The Structure of Historical Narrative' (1972).

The close connection between representability (the possibility to experience) and discourse also becomes clear when we compare Holocaust testimonies with the testimonies of SS soldiers. The SS soldiers who fought at the front, especially in Russia during the fight for Stalingrad, also met extremely violent and destructive events. Two Dutch writers, Armando and Hans Sleutelaar have interviewed some Dutch former SS soldiers. These interviews contain elaborate descriptions of horrible events which were performed as well as endured by these soldiers.

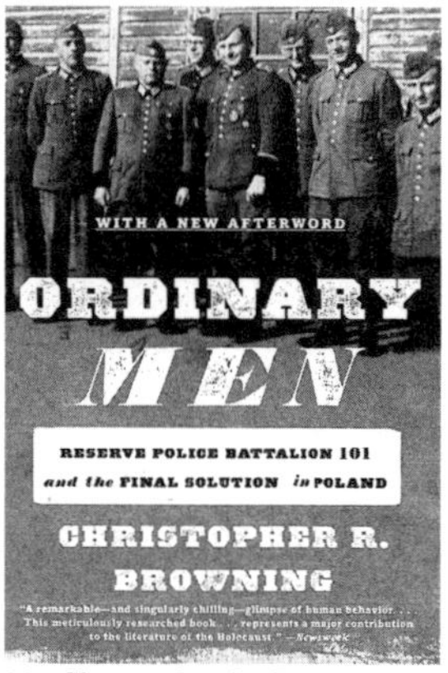

32 Christopher R. Browning, *Ordinary Men* (1992), book cover.

In his remarkable book *Ordinary Men* (1992)[32] Christopher R. Browning has dealt with the behaviour and experiences of extreme violence of another group of perpetrators: the battalions of the reserve police which never saw any battle or encountered a deadly enemy. Their contribution to the war was to 'clean' the ghettos by killing the Jews or by transporting them to the camps. They had to carry out 'the final solution'. Their behaviour and experiences are in a certain way even more extreme than those of the SS soldiers at the front because the events in which they partook could not be naturalized by the traditional concept of war. They did not fight against an enemy. They annihilated a race. By seeing the Jews as a dangerous race, the Jews were dehumanized, transformed into objects, which facilitated their killing.

It seems senseless to me to develop a gradual scale on which the extremity of the horrible experiences of soldiers or other 'ordinary men' are set off against the extremity of the camp situation. From a moral perspective there can be no discussion at all: the experiences of the inmates of the camps is more horrible, simply because of the fact that they were totally victimized, while the SS soldiers, especially Dutch volunteers, had *chosen* a profession in which they could end up in horrible limit-experiences. But this moral difference based on responsibility has little bearing on the possibilities to work through the events in which the persons were involved. This concerns not a moral but a psychological and, as I have tried to argue so far, a representational perspective. Even so, the difference is striking.

It is remarkable that these voluntary SS-ers talk quite easily, sometimes even with eagerness about their experiences. Consider the following example:

> Try to imagine yourself: a battlefield with ten thousand dead bodies. Russians and Germans. A tank-battle followed. And when the tank battle is over, and you find yourself on such a battlefield!.. What do you think, what kind of chaos you saw there? I do not have to tell you anything. When you continue thinking about... That is not possible.
>
> I have seen it often enough. Tank battle. Wounded persons. Killed persons. Again forward. Through the mud. For you had to go forward! You had to seek cover in the mud of cadavers/dead bodies! Do you understand this? Sometimes you pulled a couple of dead bodies to each other to make a shelter out of them. You pulled three or four of them together. Yourself behind them. That is totally normal at the front.[33]

33 Armando & Sleutelaar, *De SS'ers* (1990), 63 (my translation).

In these interviews, events which are extremely gruesome for the soldiers are at first sight made understandable by integrating them in the framework of the war or of the front. This SS soldier even does it very explicitly. He says: 'That is totally normal at the front'. When they see the events in the context in which they happened, they do not have to linger on the extremity of violence and destruction.

Consider for example the way one SS soldier reflects about a cruel event he had to witness. A Russian partisan was killed after the SS-ers had used him for a day to carry four boxes with munition. The soldier is puzzled by the fact that the partisan was very eager to carry the load, although he was probably sure that he would be killed afterwards. He sees this as a sign of the human inclination to cling to life till the bitter end. He was and is, however, not at all touched by this event. This is what he says next: 'One could say now: "a horror". But things like this are in a war totally normal.

I think that the under-officer (who performed the execution) has slept very well afterwards.'[34]

The same SS-er recalls another event in which one of his fellow SS-ers was executed because of theft. The whole battalion had to line up to witness the execution. The ease with and the way in which the SS-er experiences this execution of one of his comrades is again significant:

> Something like that is normal. That man has to be sentenced to death and you know that. I didn't know anything about the pre-history. They didn't tell you that. [...] It was not such an important case. Important of course for him upon whom it had fallen. Those things happen at both sides. I cannot say that it made an enormous impression on me.[35]

This soldier was able to normalize and work through cruel events by means of a 'master plot' of war. His symbolic order provided him with a general understanding of what is 'normal' in wars. This enabled him to naturalize extreme events to the proportion of something which is not striking at all. Later he tells of an episode at the beginning of the war when he was not yet an SS soldier, but he helped to carry wounded persons from the train to a hospital in the German city of Essen. Then he was deeply impressed.

> That is how I came in closer touch with the war. That is total horror... There were heavily and less heavily wounded people, there were people of whom members had been amputated who came from the field hospital. That made an enormous impression on me. That has always stayed with me. But I was strongly nationalistic and a strong nationalistic disposition can help to bridge this.[36]

34 Armando & Sleutelaar, *De SS'ers* (1990), 306 (my translation).

35 Armando & Sleutelaar, *De SS'ers* (1990), 304 (my translation).

36 Armando & Sleutelaar, *De SS'ers* (1990), 306 (my translation).

This time it is not war as a conventional master plot, but rather an ideology of nationalism which enabled him to deal with extreme situations.

In none of these interviews a traumatic return of events is mentioned. Some former SS-ers were bothered by nightmares for a short time, but these were always of a passing nature, as in these testimonies:

> When I came back in '49, I had nightmares. My wife was frightened by it at night. I still had nightmares of it. You don't get rid of it that soon. Now I have a dream once in a while, or something like that, but nightmares, no I don't have them anymore.[37]
>
> And then you found your comrades, sometimes your intimate comrades, fallen. That remains with you. Not eternally! Not forever![38]

You never get the impression that the subjectivities of these men are killed or corroded. On the contrary. Regularly a tone of bravura and restrained pride can be heard from their testimonies. Their use of language still expresses a self-confident subjectivity.

The testimonies of the former SS-ers do not show serious problems with working through the horrible events they had been part of. Maybe some of them did have them, but they were able to solve these within conventional narrative frameworks. Within the argument of this chapter this can be explained by the fact that their symbolic order offered plenty of possibilities to understand these limit-experiences as meaningful. In general, one can identify their symbolic order as the Nazi ideology of national-socialism. But for the soldiers that ideology manifested itself in much more direct and concrete form in a specific construction of masculinity.

37 Armando & Sleutelaar, *De SS'ers* (1990), 60 (my translation).

38 Armando & Sleutelaar, *De SS'ers* (1990), 18 (my translation).

39 Armando & Sleutelaar, *De SS'ers* (1990), 306 (my translation).

In his seminal study *Male Fantasies* Theweleit has analyzed how the Nazis' construction of masculinity consisted of a cultivation of sadistic aggression as well as of masochistic discipline and self-sacrifice. The construction of masculinity in which the SS soldiers were submerged offered them narrative frameworks as well as subject positions which enabled them to work through the extreme destruction which they inflicted on others, or had to go through themselves. Christopher R. Browning comes to similar conclusions in his *Ordinary Men* concerning the question how the men of Reserve Police Battalions were psychologically able to carry out 'the final solution'. His conclusion is that these Germans were acting less out of belief in the anti-Semitic Nazi ideology or out of deference to authority or fear of punishment than from motives as insidious as they are common: careerism and peer pressure.

The Nazi construction of masculinity as analyzed by Theweleit is the most predominant framework present in all the SS soldiers' testimonies. Most of them did not know anything of the ideology of national-socialism including its anti-Semitism. They were just attracted by the ideals of discipline, order, strength and purity as means to give shape to their masculinities. The SS construction of masculinity, more extremely and strictly based on discipline than any of the other divisions of the Nazi army, enabled the SS soldiers to survive psychologically the events they performed or endured. In the words of one them:

> You were hardened. Stone-hard. Retrospectively you think, how is it possible that you could stand something like that. It is thanks to the discipline and the hardships which they had you to endure wantonly.[39]

The situation of the inmates of the camps differs here fundamentally. The extreme forms of destruction and annihilation they were confronted with, could not be understood or dealt with by means of any narrative framework. Whatever ideology or religious background they adhered to, in the face of the reality of the Holocaust, these frames were beside the point, powerless. As a consequence, the Holocaust became an event which could not be experienced by many of those who had to live in this reality. The crisis of representation as caused by the Holocaust is usually presented as a form of being speechless after having faced a metaphysical evil. It was rather, however, the abyss of difference between the lived history and the frames which normally enable us to experience the events in which we are involved, that has silenced many of those who had to live in the Holocaust.

Emplotting the Holocaust

This close connection between discursive possibilities and experiential collapse sheds new light on the binary opposition between historical and imaginative representation. So-called historical literary genres like the diary or the memoir cannot be considered unmediated access to an historical past. Event and interpretation cannot be disentangled without violating the situation, because interpretation takes place as part of the event. My analysis of Holocaust testimonies in this chapter implies a radicalization of this view. We can now say that event and experience of the event cannot be disentangled either, because experience of the event is the only access to the event. And experience is not a *transposition* of the event to the realm of the subject; it is an interpretive *transformation* which depends on the symbolic order to take place. And it is precisely this discursive process of experience which was disrupted in the Holocaust.

This conclusion compels us to reconsider the status of Holocaust historiography. For there is no reason to assume that only those who lived the historical reality of the Holocaust had no transparent, immediate access to it and that historians, who write later about that historical reality, can do that without the intrusion of a framing activity. If even the inmates of the camps depended on narrative, discursive frameworks to experience, to make sense of the reality in which they had ended up, then it is almost arrogant to think that historians of the Holocaust can do their work without framing.

But where does the framing take place, or, how can we recognize that activity in this academic discipline? That Holocaust historiography needs framing acts to make sense just as much as other historical endeavors, as has been demonstrated convincingly by Friedlander under the rubric of different emplotments of the Holocaust. This historian has attempted to grasp the essentials of the new German debate about the Holocaust by means of an analysis of the emplotment of the extermination of the Jews in those debates. First, he defines the elements of the traditional historical representation, in order to be able to outline some aspects of the challenge and subsequently, to consider the implications of the new German approaches in terms of public memory.[40]

The differences in interpretations of Nazism as such notwithstanding, a common understanding has been established concerning the place and interpretation of Nazi crimes, in other words, concerning historical responsibility. Structurally, within the traditional image and narrative of historical responsibility for the extermination of the Jews, three collective actors are identified: perpetrators, bystanders, and victims.

One version of this plot, the so-called 'liberal view' of the

40 The volume edited by Friedlander, *Probing the Limits of Interpretation* (1992), to which many of the aforementioned historians have contributed, is very valuable because it contains diverse positions, critical of one another, but all within the same 'questioning' mode of critical historiography. The books by Friedlander *Reflections of Nazism* (1993a) and *Memory, History and the Extermination of the Jews of Europe* (1993b), provide detailed discussions of the repercussions of several ways the Holocaust and Nazism have been framed. Also, Young's book on Holocaust memorials *The Texture of Memory* (1993) provides an analysis which derives its strength and value from the insight that the memory of the Holocaust is constructed in the act of framing it.

Nazi period, frames nazism and the Holocaust with liberal theories of totalitarianism and leads to a particular emplotment. From this point of view, Nazi Germany is essentially understood as a political and ideological deviance from the Western liberal model. One of the implications of this liberal framework is the difficulty of differentiating between Nazism and Stalinism. The specificity of nazism, especially its anti-Semitism as it has been leading up to the Holocaust, is difficult to address. The framework of liberalism leads to an emphasis on the ideological origins, as well as the political and criminal dimensions of nazism.

In this framework the plot is obvious. The perpetrators are clearly identified: Hitler himself, such organizations as the SS, the Nazi party and its periphery, including its bureaucratic infrastructure and instruments. The bystanders are characterised by partial knowledge of the crimes committed and by more or less sustained indifference and passivity. They include German society at large, characterized, with limited exceptions, as 'a society widely impregnated with prejudice on the one hand and increasingly enthusiastic adherence to the *Volksgemeinschaft* ideal on the other.'[41] The victims range from political opponents imprisoned in concentration camps, people killed in the 'euthanasia' program because of (mental) illnesses, Gypsies, Slavs, homosexuals, to the ultimate category: the Jews.[42] After the war this emplotment of the Holocaust has shaped official German memory, as well as Western memory in general, a memory which continuously frames, and thus naturalizes it. It results in a narrative which recognizes a basic historical responsibility both anchored in the pre-Hitler past and having found its expression in the events of the Third Reich.

Next, Friedlander distinguishes a *structural* emplotment of the Holocaust. This emplotment dominates traditional

41 Friedlander, *Memory, History, and the Extermination of the Jews of Europe* (1993b), 25.

42 Friedlander, *Memory, History, and the Extermination of the Jews of Europe* (1993b), 26

left-wing interpretations and the new left historiography of the sixties. The theoretical framework now leads to a characterization of Nazism not as totalitarianism, but as fascism. It puts much emphasis on the dynamics of institutions and social structures and relatively little emphasis on the importance of ideology and personalities within the Nazi system.

This framework leads to an emplotment of the Holocaust which is at first sight not very different from the totalitarian emplotment produced by the liberal framework. The difference lies only in the category of the perpetrators. In the structuralist emplotment, the perpetrators are imagined as a complex interaction of subgroups. This makes it extremely difficult to pinpoint where the responsibility lies, as each partial decision flows from some partially perceived context.[43] The consequences of the structural emplotment are the following:

> One may argue that such a view of the perpetrators considerably widens the field of responsibility and encompasses many more elements of German society within the tortuous criminal processes; on the other hand, it bolsters the argument that the very fluid and nebulous aspect of these processes made any kind of opposition extremely difficult. In any case, we are faced with a somewhat paradoxical image of mass murder of a totally unprecedented kind being enacted without any clear representation of a primary locus of responsibility.[44]

Another difference between the framework of liberalism and the framework of Marxist structuralism is brought to the fore by the similarities with other socio-political phenomena. While the totalitarianism emplotment of the liberal framework systematically compares the crimes of Nazism with

43 Friedlander, *Memory, History, and the Extermination of the Jews of Europe* (1993b), 27.

44 Friedlander, *Memory, History, and the Extermination of the Jews of Europe* (1993b), 27–28.

those of Stalinism, the Marxist framework induces vaguer but nonetheless explicit comparisons between the criminal policies of fascist regimes.

While the liberal framework and the subsequent emplotment of totalitarianism predominated the historical debate of the fifties, the Marxist framework did so in the late sixties and early seventies. In the eighties, however, a conservative, revisionist approach took hold of the debate in Germany. This approach, advocated by historians like Ernst Nolte, Andreas Hillgruber and Joachim Fest, questioned the specificity of Nazi crimes, in order to liberate German identity from the identification with the historical responsibility for the Holocaust. The responsibility of the Nazis for their crimes is not denied, but a shift in emphasis is caused by emplotting nazism as a defensive reaction to the Red Threat of the Soviet Union. At the same time Nazi crimes are 'balanced' against the responsibility of the Red Army (and the Allied Forces) for crimes committed on German soil.

In terms of emplotment, this anti-communist framework leads to the following narrative. There are now two categories of perpetrators: the Nazis and, facing them, a mixed representation of Soviets and Allied forces in so far as the latter had destructive plans for Germany in mind. Friedlander shows how the emplotment in Ernst Nolte's text even consists of a reversal of the traditional schema. Nolte even goes so far as to argue that the Nazis became perpetrators out of anguish at the idea of being themselves potential victims of the Red Terror:

> He who does not want to see Hitler's annihilation of Jews in this context (communist annihilation) is possibly led by very noble motives, but he falsifies history. In his legitimate search for the direct causes, he overlooks the

45 Nolte quoted in Friedlander, *Memory, History, and the Extermination of the Jews of Europe* (1993b), 34.

> main precondition without which all those causes would have remained without effect. Auschwitz is not primarily the result of traditional anti-Semitism. It was in its core not only a 'genocide', but was above all a reaction born out of the anxiety of the annihilating occurrences of the Russian revolution...[45]

This would imply that the Nazis, the traditional perpetrators of the other narratives, become potential victims, and the traditional bystanders become actual victims. The effect of this new, sinister emplotment is a displacement of the *source* of all evil, displaced at one more remove, in the past of the past. The historical responsibility is displaced, and cannot be situated any longer within an exclusively German context.

Friedlander's readings in terms of emplotment represent, in my opinion, a radical break-through in historiographic discussions. The unescapable conclusion is that historization is never done in the domain of 'objective history'. Historization can only be done by framing the event. The framing of the event is the moment that the moral and political responsibility of the historian shows itself: it is the moment that history is made relevant for the concerns and interests of the historian. Frames are never inherent to the object of framing. They are, ultimately, legitimized by the (hidden) agenda of the historian, determined by sets of *a priori* values. This implies that collective memory is not in the service of objective historiography, but that historiography is in the service of collective memory.

This confrontation of different emplotments of the Holocaust also has repercussions for the way we evaluate and judge theories, in this case theories of Nazism and the Holocaust. After having assessed the referential adequacy of a certain approach, evaluation in the end is predicated upon the performative effect of a theory. How does that theory constitute contemporary collective memory? What kind of (political) values are served by it? When historical truth is being exchanged for performative effect, this does not mean that we end up in total relativism.

The legitimacy of performativity as the ultimate norm for judging a frame, is unescapable in the case of Israeli emplotments of the Holocaust. For a long time, the Holocaust was inserted in the historical sequence of Jewish catastrophes leading to the redemptive birth of the state of Israel. It is beyond question that this Zionist interpretative framework has played a decisive role in building the new Jewish state. The redemptive closure of this narrative started to crack open, however, with the Eichmann trial. At that occasion stories became alive again and challenged the reassuring certainties and their resulting effects. This demise of closure resulted in a growing sensitivity for individual testimonies of the Holocaust which challenged the socially imposed codes of interpretation. The more time passed since the extermination of the Jews of Europe, and the more Israel was forced to legitimize the size of its territory instead of its birth, the less compelling the initial interpretative frameworks became for Israeli historical consciousness. According to Friedlander, no relevant emplotments, and I would add, no frameworks producing relevant meanings have appeared in their stead.

The need for such frameworks remains acute, however, for without meanings assigned to them, trauma-inducing events cannot be remembered. The issue, then, is not to decide which frame will win the contest of meaning, but *that* meaning be produced in the service of memory. The ultimate importance of memorizing the Holocaust is situated not in the past events themselves, but in the past events in relation to our contemporary and future concerns. In the words of James Young:

> We should also ask to what ends we have remembered. That is, how do we respond to the current moment in light of our remembered past? This is to recognize that the shape of memory cannot be divorced from the actions taken on its behalf, and that memory without consequences contains the seeds of its own destruction.[46]

James Young's book on Holocaust memorials, *The Texture of Memory*,[47] is another recent example of a critical perspective based on the idea that the understanding of past events depends on the construction, or framing, of memory. Young describes a large number of memorials and museums in Germany, Poland, Israel, and the United States. He reinvigorates the memorials with the stories of how they have come about, and with stories about the responses and discussions they have provoked. By doing this he explores the kinds of meaning created at those sites and the kinds of principles around which Holocaust museums organize their memory-telling.

In all cases it becomes clear that memory is never shaped in a vacuum. As Young expresses it: 'the motives of memory are never pure.'[48] Both the reasons given for Holocaust memorials and the kinds of memory they generate can never be reduced to the past events. In every nation's memorials and museums, a different Holocaust is remembered, often with conflicting political and religious goals. Depending on where and by whom the memorials and museums are constructed, the sites remember the past according to a variety of national myths, ideals, and political ends.

46 Young, *The Texture of Memory* (1993), 15.

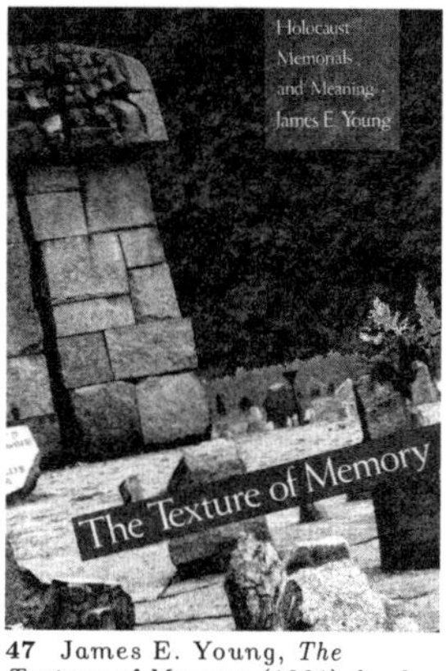

47 James E. Young, *The Texture of Memory* (1994), book cover.

48 Young, *The Texture of Memory* (1993), 2.

Young's crucial question in the above quotation is easier to answer in light of the testimonies of the survivors which I analyzed in the first part of this chapter. The ultimate end to which the survivors have tried to tell their story is to work through at last the horrors they had to live through and to integrate themselves *with their past* in our present. I will return to the importance of testimony when I discuss Boltanski's art as a humanizing and transactive practice. But in the context of the writing of the history of the Holocaust, Young's question will never allow a definite answer because it should be asked again and again. Changes in time and in context require each time a new engagement with what we can learn from the remembrance of the Holocaust.

The unrepresentability of Holocaust experiences has a discursive basis and histories of the Holocaust are necessarily the product of emplotment, which implies a framing activity performed by a subject living in the present. Individual experience as well as the more collective endeavour of history writing happen within the conditions of the discursive or symbolic realm. This may seem a disenchanting conclusion for those who believe in an objective transmission of history by means of transparent language. But first of all, the ontological question of the reality of the events—did it happen?—must be firmly distinguished from the epistemological question of access to it in order to make sense of it. Yes, it happened. And Nazi Germany did it. Nolte's attempt to insert a framework that shifts the responsibility away from Germany and back to an earlier threat, attempts to capitalize on the frequent confusion of these two philosophical domains. That is why his view, sinister as well as implausible, is also intellectually objectionable, based on sloppy, or rather perverse reasoning: he disguises an ontological certainty under a cloak of epistemological doubt. Moreover, I would like to emphasize the positive side of the 'dependency' on discursive frameworks and framing acts. It is thanks to this dependency that testimony as well as history writing is relevant beyond the production of knowledge of the past. It is because discursive frameworks belong to the present, and framing acts take place in the present that memory of the past—knowledge of history—can have consequences for our contemporary and future world.

Caught by Images

On the Role of Visual Imprints in Holocaust Testimonies

What I saw with my wide-open eyes.[1]

The Trouble with Seeing

> Someday you be walking down the road and you hear something or see something going on. So clear. And you think it's you making it up. A thought picture. But no, it's when you bump into a rememory that belongs to somebody else.[2]

Toni Morrison's novel *Beloved*[3] here writes about the importance and reality of what she calls 'rememories', and what students of the Holocaust call, with a contradictory term, 'traumatic memories'. The key word here is 'pictures'. In an interview, Morrison insists on the *visual* quality of these images:

> What makes it fiction is the nature of the imaginative act: my reliance on the image—on the remains—in addition to recollection, to yield up a kind of truth. By

1 Borowski, *This Way for the Gas, Ladies and Gentlemen* (1976), 174.

2 Morrison, *Beloved* (1987a), 36.

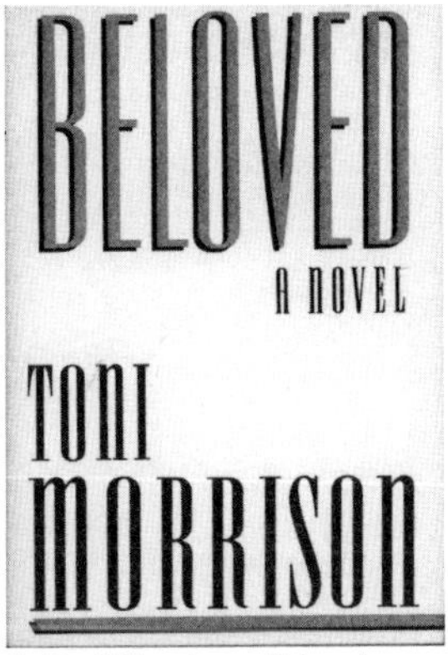

3 Toni Morrison, *Beloved* (1987), book cover.

4 Morrison, in Zinsser (ed.), *Inventing the Truth* (1987b), 111–112.

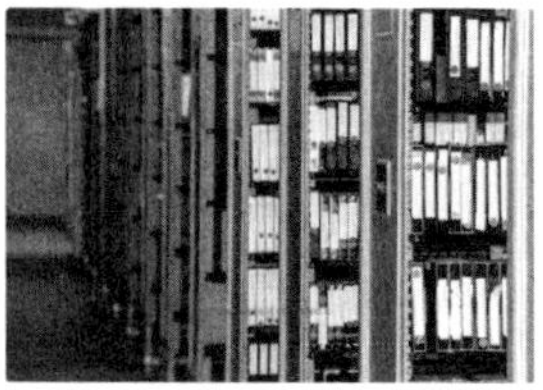

5 Fortunoff Video Archive for Holocaust Testimonies.

'image', of course, I don't mean 'symbol'; I simply mean 'picture' and the feelings that accompany the picture.[4]

It is my conviction that current interest in specifically visual art related to the Holocaust and other traumatic historical events, finds in these statements by Morrison its *raison d'être*: both its explanation and its theoretical justification. Morrison is a writer, not a visual artist. Yet she insists on the founding, grounding function of specifically visual images in the 're-membering', the healing activity of memory that present-day culture, facing the disappearance of the eye-witnesses, is struggling to articulate and implement. Paradoxically, it is most clearly and convincingly through creative written texts, commonly called 'fiction', that this visuality and its truthfulness can be assessed. This chapter, then, follows the theoretical reflections on the need and difficulty of representing the Holocaust with specific reflection on the 'picture' and the feelings that accompany the picture.

We have seen how Joan B., one of the Holocaust survivors whose testimony was video-taped by the Fortunoff Video Archive for Holocaust Testimonies,[5] recounts how she worked in the kitchen of a labour camp and saw how the camp commandant drowned a newborn baby in boiling water. Later she acknowledges that she didn't say anything, and didn't feel anything either. Although Joan B. has seen what has happened to the newborn baby, her act of looking seems to involve no more than the recording of a visual impression. One of the epistemological implications of seeing, namely apprehension, to discern mentally, to attain comprehension or grasp, seems to be lacking in her act of seeing. That which was visually distinguishable has been imprinted on her memory like an immutable photograph, but the traces of that visual imprint seem never to have been emotionally experienced, let alone worked through. She recounts an event which is no more than a visual recording. In her narration of it, the event seems not to have had any emotional or ethical dimensions.

Joan B.'s testimony is emblematic for the profound way the Holocaust has disrupted the conventional notions of seeing, of the visual domain in Western culture. Since the Enlightenment the observation of the visual world has had a privileged epistemological status: it is a precondition and guarantee for knowledge and understanding. Being an eyewitness of something implies more or less automatically apprehension and comprehension of the observed situation or event. This link between seeing and comprehension, however, has been radically disrupted in the experiences of Holocaust victims. As I will argue, it is because of this disruption that 'to see' and the description of visual imprints have such a central role in the testimonies of Holocaust survivors. But these eye-witnesses' testimonies of visual imprints concern events that cannot be processed in the same manner as those recounted in the eye-witness account in a police report. In Holocaust testimonies the visual functions more as the unmodified return of what happened, instead of as a mode of access to or penetration into what happened; instead of being the raw material to be processed into understanding. Even after all this time, that first step has still not been made. Yet, the image is there; it refuses to budge.[6]

Perhaps it is due to this strong, yet problematic nature of vision in the face of a disaster of the magnitude of the Holocaust that so much intense debate concentrates on visual art that represents it. Films such as Roberto Benigni's *Life is Beautiful* (1997)[7] and, before it, Steven Spielberg's *Schindler's List* (1993)[8] are criticized in terms of the 'authenticity' of the representation, and blamed for lacking in that regard. These films are unfavourably compared to the classic *Shoah* (1985),

6 For an extensive analysis of why Holocaust experiences have disrupted the abilities to remember, see Alphen, van, *Caught by History* (1997). Especially chapter 2, 'Testimonies and The Limits of Representation'.

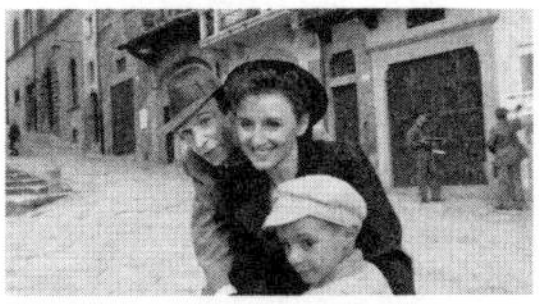

7 Roberto Benigni, *Life is Beautiful* (1997), film still.

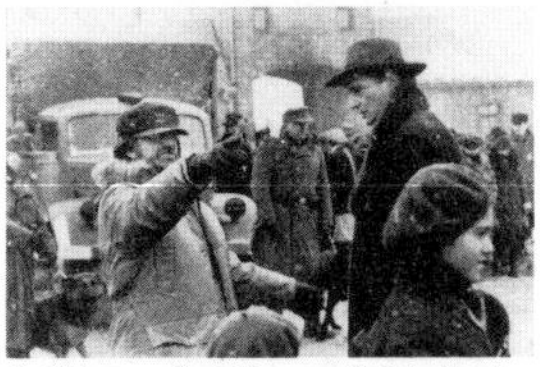

8 Steven Spielberg, *Schindler's List* (1994), behind-the-scenes shot.

Claude Lanzmann's documentary film recording testimonies of survivors, comparable to Joan B. cited above. Lanzmann's witnesses *were there*, hence, their eye-witness accounts are *authentic*. They *saw* with their own eyes what happened, and the images are imprinted forever on their retinas. Benigni and Spielberg mocked this obsession with authentic vision by having the events represented by *acting*, the quintessential art of feigning, faking, cheating, and pretending. It is as if art itself is suspect in the face of the cultural need for authenticity.

Given how strongly vision has been bound up with truth and authenticity in the Western imaginary from the Renaissance on, it comes as no surprise that visual art is the domain where the question of historical truth in the face of a truth that is unbearable, appears to be played out so strongly today. Shakespeare's *The Rape of Lucrece*[9, 10] is entirely structured around the opposition between vision as 'true' and language as a fallen state of man, in which deception is the order of the day. But already there, the opposition falls apart. And so it does today. An intense discussion is going on, at the moment that eye-witnesses become rarer and fiction is one of the few remaining options to keep the memory of the events alive. Visual artists such as Christian Boltanski and Armando, to name two discussed in this book, struggle to come up with strategies of representation that supplement the documentary mode that is no longer possible. And whereas the thrust of their work is obsessively singular in this attempt, the term 'authenticity' does not apply to it at all. Insofar as their work is primarily visual, a case might be made, however, for the *separation* or *distinction* between the question of authenticity and vision *per se*.[11]

But that distinction does not require giving up the primacy of vision. Instead, my thesis will be that it might be

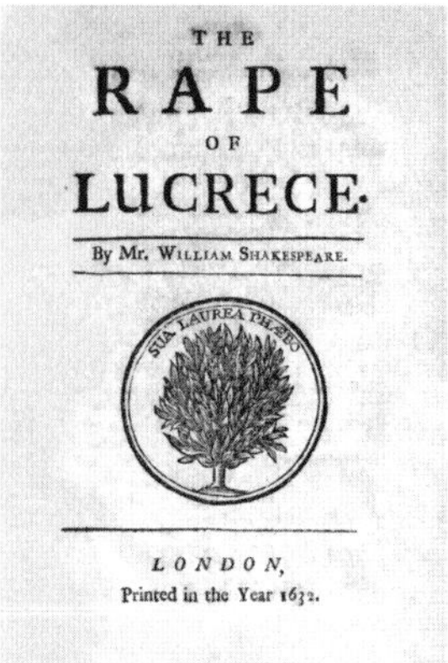

9 William Shakespeare, *The Rape of Lucrece* (1642), book cover.

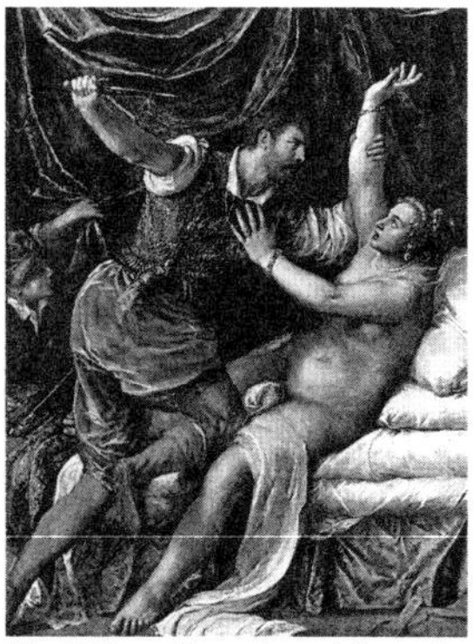

10 Titian, *Tarquin and Lucretia* (1571), painting, 188.9 × 145.1 cm.

11 On vision in literature, see Bal, *Figuraciones* (2021), with one chapter devoted to Shakespeare's Lucrece.

productive to distinguish vision from its most obvious vehicle, the *eye*. The issue is more complex than such media-essentialisms as the one privileging of the visual media might suggest. It is, in fact, twofold. First, vision does not automatically lead to 'authentic' witnessing. For, in addition to seeing, accounting for what is seen is required to achieve witnessing, and the problem may be situated in that mediation or transmission. This problem of transmission occurs strongly in the face of traumatic experiences, and as I will argue, it is not resolved unless language intervenes. Second, vision does not necessarily lead to *representation*. There are other modes of communicating vision, or not-being-able-to-communicate vision, in whatever medium. The artists I mentioned, among many others, are involved in searching for such alternative modes. In the context of the current chapter, which centres the question of Holocaust representation on visual art, I propose to first probe the importance and modalities of vision itself. That is to say, I will attempt to articulate what *vision* can mean, do, and achieve in the face of its most untenable confrontation, such as the one exemplified by Joan B.'s testimony. On the one hand, then, the visual imprint; on the other, the need to deal with it.

Visuality and Visual Incapacitation

Tadeusz Borowski's *This Way for the Gas, Ladies and Gentlemen*[12] acts out the dominant role of visual imprints in Holocaust 'memories' in an impressive way. In this chapter, I will take that book as a starting point to assess the place of visuality, seeing, and visual incapacitation in the commemoration of the Holocaust. The short stories included in this volume are inspired by Borowski's concentration camp

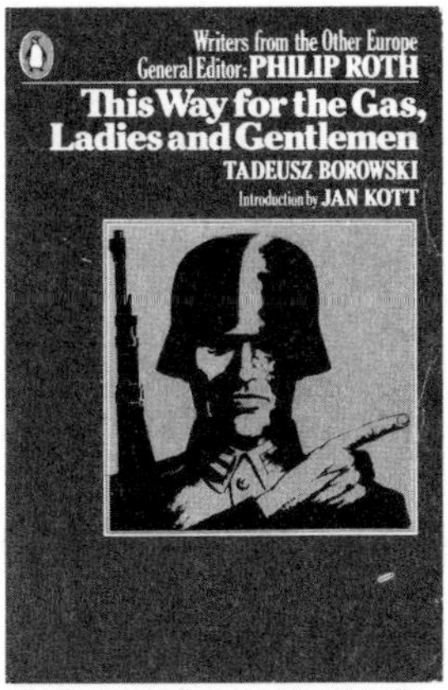

12 Tadeusz Borowski, *This Way for the Gas, Ladies and Gentlemen* (1976), book cover, transl. from Polish.

13 For an incisive analysis of the 'present tense' of looking, see Mitchell, 'Present Tense' (2021).

14 Borowski, *This Way for the Gas, Ladies and Gentlemen* (1976), 174.

experiences. But that background that informs them does not imply that they can be read as first-person testimonies in which the experiences of the narrator are central. Nor do they read that way. The first person in these stories identifies himself more like the reporter of a documentary: he recounts what happens around him. The order of the stories in the book is more or less chronological, although this order does not necessarily concern the chronological ordering of the life of the narrator. Rather, they are ordered according to the chronology of the generic event 'the camp'. Thus, the first story deals with arrivals in the camp, those which follow describe life in the camp, then we are told about the liberation. The three last stories, 'The January Offensive', 'A Visit', and 'The World of Stone', recount life after having survived the Holocaust.

Given the inevitable retroversive nature of such accounts, the moment of narration in a Holocaust testimony is by definition situated after the liberation. That is why in the case of *This Way for the Gas*, the last stories possess an essential relevance for the meaning of testimony as such. It is only in these stories that the narrated events are clearly distinguished from the narration of the events: the narration takes place after the liberation. In the stories set during life in the camp, in contrast, the often-used present tense, but also the typically narrative past tense, describe moments of narration that could, in a fictional mode, be contemporaneous with the events.[13]

'A Visit' begins as if it tells about life in the camp: 'I was walking through the night, the fifth in line. An orange flame from the burning bodies flickered in the center of the purple sky.'[14] The first-person narrator then discusses explicitly the impossibility of relating his feelings or self-experience. He presents himself as a kind of machine who could only record what he *saw*.

> In the soft darkness, I held my eyes open wide. And although the fever in my bleeding thigh was spreading throughout my entire body, becoming more and more painful with every step I took, I can remember nothing about that night except what I saw with my wide-open eyes.[15]

The *leitmotiv* of the visual act, of what the first-person narrator 'saw', emphatically structures most of the following text, thus qualifying the nature of that act itself.

> In the days that followed I saw men weep while working with the pickaxe, the spade, in the trucks. I saw them carry heavy rails, sacks of cement, slabs of concrete; I saw them carefully level the earth, dig dirt out of ditches, build barracks, watch-towers and crematoria. I saw them consumed by eczema, phlegmon, typhoid fever, and I saw them dying of hunger. And I saw others who amassed fortunes in diamonds, watches and gold and buried them safely in the ground. [...] And I have seen women who carried heavy logs, pushed carts and wheelbarrows and built dams across ponds [...] And I also saw a girl (who had once been mine) covered with running sores and with her head shaven.[16]

This narrative act of recounting what he has seen is first legitimized by the narrator as a kind of moral obligation to those who died in the Holocaust.

This is a recurrent *topos* in many Holocaust testimonies. It is also presented as a last act of *relating*—recounting as a way of establishing a relationship—that the dying requested, in their desperate attempt to stay related. For

> every one of the people who, because of eczema, phlegmon or typhoid fever, or simply because they were too

15 Borowski, *This Way for the Gas, Ladies and Gentlemen* (1976), 174.

16 Borowski, *This Way for the Gas, Ladies and Gentlemen* (1976), 175.

17 Borowski, *This Way for the Gas, Ladies and Gentlemen* (1976), 175.

18 Borowski, *This Way for the Gas, Ladies and Gentlemen* (1976), 176.

> emaciated, were taken to the gas chamber, begged the orderlies loading them into the crematorium trucks to remember what they saw. And to tell the truth about mankind to those who do not know it.[17]

But gradually it becomes clear that the narrator does not tell what he has seen out of moral obligation. *He simply cannot do anything else*. It is still the only thing he sees, long after, although historically the Holocaust belongs to the past.

It is only at the end of the story that it becomes clear that the story is told from the position of having survived the Holocaust.

> I sit in someone else's room, among books that are not mine, and, as I write about the sky, and the men and women I have seen, I am troubled by one persistent thought—that I have never been able to look also at myself.[18]

This impossibility implies that the narrator is not able to pay attention to what happened to himself in the camp, but not to his life in the present, after the Holocaust, either. The two incapacities are, of course, causally linked, but that causality cannot be perceived by the subject caught in its web. He can only see again what he has seen. The substance of narration is the visual version of a broken record. The record got stuck and the same images repeat themselves. The images from the past are more vivid and intense then what he sees in the present.

The impossibility to reintegrate himself in the present of post-Holocaust life is demonstrated in the last story, 'The World of Stone':

> In contrast to years gone by, when I observed the world with wide-open, astonished eyes, and walked along every street alert, like a young man on a parapet, I can

> now push through the liveliest crowd with total indifference and rub against hot female bodies without the slightest emotion [...].
>
> I climb unimpressed up the marble staircase, rescued from the fire and covered with a red carpet [...]. I pay no attention to the newly installed windows and the freshly painted walls of the restored building. I enter with a casual air the modest but cozy little rooms occupied by people of importance [...][19]

19 Borowski, *This Way for the Gas, Ladies and Gentlemen* (1976), 178–179.

The impossibility for the narrator to see the world around him after he survived the Holocaust, compels us to reconsider the indication of time in the story 'A Visit'. At first sight, time indications such as 'That night I saw ...' and 'In the days that followed I saw ...' seem to refer to specific moments during the life in the camp. But they now have become ambiguous. They can also refer to specific moments after the narrator survived, was liberated from the camp, moments in which he did not see anything else than these visual imprints from the past, more intense and immediate than the impressions in the present.

Kinds of Memory and Failed Memory

In order to further assess the role of visual imprints in Holocaust testimonies, the distinctions made by the French psychiatrist Pierre Janet between habit memory, narrative memory and traumatic memory can be helpful.[20] Janet, working at the beginning of the last century and who was of influence on the theories of Sigmund Freud with whom he worked when they were both interns at the Salpêtrière hospital in Paris, defines habit memory as the automatic integration of new information without much conscious attention to what is

20 See for a discussion of Janet's ideas: Kolk, van der & Van der Hart, in Caruth (ed.), *Trauma* (1995).

happening. This kind of automatic synthesis is a capacity that humans have in common with animals. Narrative memory, a uniquely human capacity, consists of mental constructs, which people use to make sense out of experience. Current and familiar experiences are automatically assimilated or integrated in existing mental structures. But some events resist integration:

> Frightening or novel experiences may not easily fit into existing cognitive schemes and either may be remembered with particular vividness or may totally resist integration.[21]

The memory of experiences that resist integration in existing meaning schemes, are stored differently and are not available for retrieval under ordinary conditions. It is only for convenience's sake that Janet has called these unintegratible experiences 'traumatic *memory*'. In fact, trauma is fundamentally (and not gradually) different from memory because 'it becomes dissociated from conscious awareness and voluntary control.'[22]

Trauma is failed experience, and this failure makes it impossible to *voluntarily* remember the event. This is why traumatic re-enactments take the form of drama, not narrative. Drama just presents itself, or so it seems; narrative as a mode implies some sort of mastery by the narrator, or the focalizer. This is a fundamental difference that will be shown to define the role of vision in memories of the Holocaust. Because of their fundamentally dramatic nature, traumatic re-enactments are dependent on the time frame of the 'parts' scripted in the drama. In the words of Mieke Bal:

> All the manipulations performed by a narrator, who can expand and reduce, summarize, highlight, underscore, or minimize elements of the story at will, are inaccessible to the 'actor' who is bound to enact a drama that, although

21 Kolk, van der & Van der Hart, in Caruth (ed.), *Trauma* (1995), 160.

22 Kolk, van der & Van der Hart, in Caruth (ed.), *Trauma* (1995), 160.

at some point in the past it happened to her, is not hers to master.[23]

23 Bal, in Bal, Crewe & Spitzer (eds.), *Acts of Memory* (1999a), ix.

Although from a formal perspective Borowski's stories are narrative, not dramatic, the narration is overruled by the compulsive need to relate the traumatic re-enactments of visual imprints. Or to put it differently: Borowski's narration loses control over what the narrator has recorded in the past. The logical coherence produced by narration fades away and we get a random sequence of descriptions of visual imprints. Within his narration Borowski demonstrates and enacts trauma.

Janet's clinical distinction between narrative and traumatic memory ultimately concerns a *difference* in distance towards the situation or event. A narrative memory is retroversive, it takes place after the event. A traumatic memory, or better, re-enactment, does not know that distance from the event. The person who experiences a traumatic re-enactment is still *inside* the event, present within it. This explains why these traumatic re-enactments impose themselves as visual imprints. The original traumatic event has not yet been transformed into a mediated, distanced account. It re-imposes itself in its visual and sensory directness.

Visual Imprints

The writings of French Holocaust survivor Charlotte Delbo[24] convey quite intensely this feeling that she is still inside the event which she relates.[25] She does not narrate her stories 'about' Auschwitz, but 'from' it. It is first of all the visual directness of the way she narrates which produces this effect. But from time to time she explicitly comments on the position

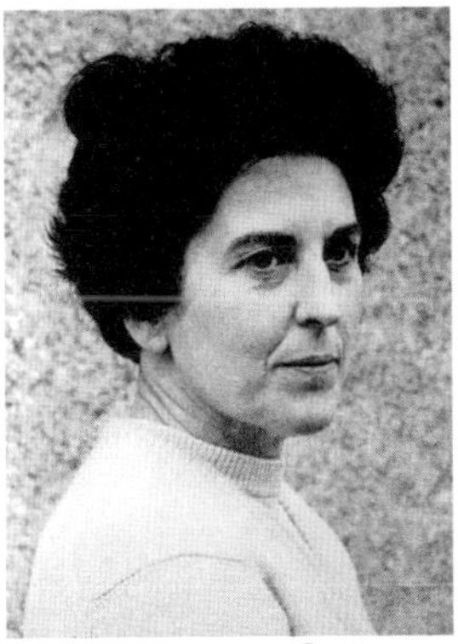

24 Charlotte Delbo © Photo Eric Schwab.

25 Delbo, *Auschwitz and After* (1995). This trilogy, translated from the French, consists of the following parts: *None of Us Will Return* (originally published in 1965); *Useless Knowledge* (1970); *The Measure of Our Days* (1985).

26 Delbo, *Auschwitz and After* (1995), 267.

from which she speaks. The words which she gives to her character Mado also account for her own writing:

> People believe memories grow vague, are erased by time, since nothing endures against the passage of time. That's the difference; time does not pass over me, over us. It doesn't undo it. I am not alive. I died in Auschwitz but no one knows it.[26]

'That's the difference': difference, as absolute as that between traumatic 'memory' and narrative memory in Janet's theory, defines the importance and specific function of vision in Holocaust memories. Delbo tersely indicates that traumatic re-enactments imply a different ordering of time. The traumatic event that happened in the past does not belong to a distanced past: it is still present in the present. In language, this would be the difference between the *pretérito* or *passé simple*, a narrative form that represents a punctual event that once happened and is now gone, and the imperfect whose effect continues in the present. In the rest of this chapter I will show how this ordering of time caused and implied by trauma brings with it a reliving of the traumatic event as intensely sensory and especially *visual*.

Delbo was born in 1913 not far from Paris. During the war she joined a resistance group in Paris. Her husband Georges Dudach was also a member of that group. In March 1942 she and her husband were caught by the French police in their apartment, where they were producing anti-German leaflets. The police turned them over to the Gestapo. Her husband was executed in May. She herself was sent to Auschwitz in January 1943 in a convoy of 230 French women, most of whom were not Jewish (nor was Delbo) but were involved in underground activities. Until January 1944 she stayed in Auschwitz and in the camp Rajsko, not far from

Auschwitz. Then, she was sent to Ravensbrück. Near the end of the war she was released to the Red Cross, who moved her to Sweden to recover from her malnutrition and ill health. Delbo has written many plays, essays, poems and stories, all of them based on her camp experiences. Her most famous work, however, is the trilogy *Auschwitz and After*. She wrote the first part of this trilogy, *None of Us Will Return*, already in 1946, but published it only in 1965. The second part, titled *Useless Knowledge*, also written immediately after the liberation, appeared in 1970, and the third part *The Measure of Our Days* shortly after that.

In her essays Delbo has made a distinction between 'common memory' and 'deep memory'. This distinction is comparable to Janet's distinction between narrative memory and traumatic memory. Common memory is capable of situating Auschwitz within a chronological ordering. If a survivor is able to remember Auschwitz as integrated in a chronological ordering, it implies in fact that survival has been at the same time a redemption from the horrible events. Auschwitz is now at a distance: it belongs to the past. 'Deep memory' on the contrary, does not succeed in situating the events in the past, at a distance. Auschwitz still does not belong to the past and it will not do so in the experience of those survivors who remember in the mode of 'deep memory'.

Delbo uses another distinction that acknowledges yet another crucial aspect of trauma: that between 'external memory' and 'sense memory'. External memory is articulated in the distancing act of narration. The person who has external memories knows that they remember. When Delbo narrates 'about' Auschwitz her words do not stem from deep memory, but from common, external memory. The emotional and physical memory of Auschwitz is, in contrast, only approached by means of sense (deep) memory. The memory

27 Delbo, *Auschwitz and After* (1995), 22.

28 For the distinction between punctual and durative events and other narratological concepts, see Bal, *Narratology* (2017).

29 Delbo, *Auschwitz and After* (1995), 22.

is not narrated but it makes itself felt. This kind of memory is symptomatic for Auschwitz: it is not a mediated account of it, but a leftover that makes its ongoing presence felt.

In her narrative texts Delbo succeeds again and again to let external memories of events in the past slip into sense memories which convey the events as taking place in the present. The text 'Roll Call' in *None of Us Will Return* is a good example of such a categorical slippage. The text starts out as a description of a unique event belonging to the past: 'SS in black capes have walked past. They made a count.'[27] The narrated event seems to concern an event which is circumscribed in time: It is not an arbitrary roll call, but a specific one. The two short sentences are, however, followed by a third one: 'We are waiting still.' The past tense has been exchanged for the present tense; the progressive form is the linguistic marker of this exchange. The event which is punctual, hence, delimited in time has been transformed into an event which is durative, that is, which is ongoing in time and cannot be situated within a chronology.[28]

After this sentence eleven paragraphs follow, each consisting out of single, short sentences.

> We are waiting.
> For days, the next day.
> Since the day before, the following day.
> Since the middle of the night, today
> We wait.
> Day is breaking.
> We await the day because one must wait for something.
> One does not live in expectation of death. One expects it.
> We have no expectations.
> We expect what happens. Night because it follows day.
> Day because it follows night.[29]

The transition from past to present tense and from punctual to durative event brings with it a transition in kinds of memory. The text beginning as a narration of a memory which can be situated in a chronological past, slips into the narration of a situation which continues into the present. This slippage into the present (tense and time) is accompanied by a change of the position of the narrating subject. The narrator of this eternal waiting is still 'inside' the visual and sensorial experience of waiting which she describes. In the most physical way the sensorial experiences caused by this eternal waiting crawls upon the narrator and upon us, readers. The memory of the infinity of waiting is not described 'at a distance', but is brought about sensorially and visually.

A similar effect is solicited in the story 'One Day', also in *None of Us Will Return*. It is again produced by a subtle use of grammatical tense. The title evokes the conventional beginning of a chronologically ordered account. First, we read three long paragraphs in the past tense. In these paragraphs the efforts of a totally exhausted woman to keep on her feet, that is, to stay alive, are described in great detail:

> She was clinging to the other side of the rope, her hands and feet grasping the snow-covered embankment. Her whole body was taut, her jaws tight, her neck with its dislocated cartilage straining, as were her muscles—what was left of them on her bones.
>
> Yet she strained in vain—the exertion of one pulling on an imaginary rope.[30]

The woman's struggle is focalized externally, from a distance. After some paragraphs the description suddenly continues in the present tense: 'she turns her head as if to measure the distance, looks upward. One can observe a growing bewilderment in her eyes, her hands, her convulsed face.'[31] As

30 Delbo, *Auschwitz and After* (1995), 24.

31 Delbo, *Auschwitz and After* (1995), 24.

32 Delbo, *Auschwitz and After* (1995), 24–25.

33 Delbo, *Auschwitz and After* (1995), 25.

unexpected as this change in grammatical tense is, another change takes place: external focalization is exchanged for character-bound focalization. The thoughts of the woman are directly quoted.

> Why are all these women looking at me like this? Why are they here, lined up in close ranks, standing immobile? They look at me yet do not seem to see me. They cannot possibly see me, or they wouldn't stand there gaping. They'd help me climb up. Why don't you help me, you standing so close? Help me. Pull me up. Lean in my direction. Stretch out your hand. Oh, they don't make a move.[32]

After this quotation of the thoughts of the woman, the narration falls back into past tense, third-person narration.

Then, following yet another paragraph, a first-person narrator takes the place of the external narrator. This time, however, the first person is not the struggling woman but one of the crowd of onlooking women. These onlookers are like Joan B., unable to relate what they see to themselves, hence, unable to relate to the lone woman they are getting imprinted on their retina:

> All of us were there, several thousand of us, standing in the snow since morning—this is what we call night. Since morning starts at three AM, dawn illuminated the snow which, until then, was the night's sole light—the cold grew bitter.[33]

We read another page of the third-person narration of the dying woman. Then, the first-person narrator/witness returns:

> I no longer look at her. I no longer wish to look. If only I could change my place in order not to see her. Not to

> see the dark holes of these eye sockets, these staring holes. What does she want to do? Reach the electrified barbed-wire fence? Why does she stare at us? Isn't she pointing at me? Imploring me? I turn away to look elsewhere. Elsewhere.[34]

Looking elsewhere first takes on a spatial meaning: she looks at another woman—a dancing female skeleton—in front of the gate of block 25. This object of the look is just a continuation of the sight of the dying woman which she could not bear any longer. But then the 'looking elsewhere' is transformed into a temporal displacement. The following paragraph consists of only one sentence:

Presently I am writing this story in a café—it is turning into a story.[35]

'Presently' (*maintenant*) marks a present, the moment at which the text is being narrated or written. The description of the woman's death struggle, however, also slips into the present: the past tense is again and again exchanged for the present tense. There seem to be two 'presents' which don't seem to exist after each other, but next to each other.

The narrator's remark that her words are turning into a story seem to imply a negative judgment on her narration. When her words are forming a story, the narrated events are situated at a distance, that is, in the past. Such a mode of narration does not do justice to her immediate and visual experience *in the present* of these events which consists of nothing else but 'onlooking'.

The text that follows introduces an alternative mode of narration. Without indicating the changes, the narrative situation keeps transforming, even within one single paragraph. First-person narrators change in identity: the 'I' who looks on and who witnesses transforms into an 'I' who narrates a

34 Delbo, *Auschwitz and After* (1995), 26.

35 Delbo, *Auschwitz and After* (1995), 26.

childhood experience; this 'I' becomes the first-person who turns out be the dying woman:

> She no longer looks at us. She is huddling in the snow. His backbone arched, Flac is going to die—the first creature I ever saw die. Mama, Flac is at the garden gate, all hunched up. He's trembling. André says he's going to die.
>
> I've got to get up on my feet to rise. I've got to walk. I've got to struggle still. Won't they help me? Why don't you help me all of you standing there with nothing to do.
>
> Mama, come quick, Flac is going to die.
>
> I don't understand why they won't help me. They're dead, dead. They look alive because they're standing up, leaning one against the other. They're dead. As for me, I don't want to die.

Voices and temporalities intermingle: it is almost impossible to distinguish them from one another, to become part of one present. This seems to be the narrative alternative for the onlooking women who cannot bear to see what they are watching. Although they are not able to relate to her (they are not in a situation to do that), they absorb her into their self-experience. They become one.

When the dog of the SS-er finally kills the woman by a bite of his fangs, a scream is being heard:

> And we do not stir, stuck in some kind of viscous substance which keeps us from making the slightest gesture—as in a dream. The woman lets out a cry. A wrenched-out scream. A single scream tearing through the immobility of the plain. We do not know if the scream has been uttered by her own or by us, whether it issued from her punctured throat, or from ours. I feel

> the dog's fangs in my throat. I scream. I howl. Not a sound comes out of me. The silence of a dream.[36]

The absolute distance which had defined the relation between the dying woman and the onlooking women so far, has ultimately disappeared. The external memory in the past tense of a dying woman in the camp changes gradually into the sensorial experience of someone who is dying herself. The text we have read is at the end no longer the witnessing account of a specific event in the past. It has transformed into a direct experience *in the flesh*. When, in Auschwitz, the act of seeing has been fundamentally disrupted and as a result, 'to see' no longer implies to relate to the object of the look so far—when seeing can still only mean onlooking—then, a narrative solution is introduced to heal the insufferable condition of onlooking. Instead of seeing the other (focalizing her), the narrator becomes her, by absorbing the woman's voice into hers.

The final paragraph of the story is a telling variation on the earlier reflection on the act of narrating this text. After a blank space the following sentence ends the story: 'And now I am sitting in a café, writing this story.'[37] This writing no longer consists of producing a testimony of what has happened in the past. In a painstaking process, Delbo's writing transforms *before our eyes* into a performance which gives voice to the object of her look: to the woman who died in the camp while she just looked on. The present in which this writing takes place emphatically does not situate the represented events in relation to it. It is not continuous with it; it rather is a second present juxtaposed to the present in which the text is being written. Whereas finally the end of the woman's death struggle is systematically written in the present tense, this other or second 'present' has to be explicitly

36 Delbo, *Auschwitz and After* (1995), 28–29.

37 Delbo, *Auschwitz and After* (1995), 29.

38 Delbo, *Auschwitz and After* (1995), 52/147.

marked in order not to merge with it: 'And *now* I am sitting in a café, writing this text.'

The title of the second part of Delbo's trilogy, *Useless Knowledge*, can be read as an outspoken statement to the effect that the visual and sensorial imprints left by life in the camps, should not be confused with the substance of memory. Especially the story 'The Stream' is a good example of this distinction. The Holocaust is ineffable, specifically, unnarratable because of the monotony of the days. There were barely any specific events. The text begins as follows:

> Strange, but I don't recall anything about that day. Nothing but the stream. Since all the days were the same, a monotony interrupted only by heavy penalties and roll calls, since the days were the same, we certainly had roll call, and, following roll call, work columns were formed, I must have been careful to stay in the same column as my group, and later, after a long wait, the column must have marched through the gate where the SS in the sentry box counted the ranks passing through. And after? Did the column go right or left? Right to the marshes, or left toward the demolition work, or the silos? How long did we walk? I have no idea. What work did we do? Neither do I recall that.[38]

While the narrator tries to recall a particular day—to represent it to her mind—she only remembers those things which recurred day after day. Nothing came to interrupt the repetition of the same.

The lack of markings in time can be sensed in the sentence that goes on and on. Just as the days were no longer separate units of time, Delbo's sentences espouse that sameness and continuity. Both are but a stream as formless as the stream in the marshes near which they were forced to do the digging. Now and then there is the slow-down marked by a comma, but no full stop to mark the end of the sentence. The narrator remembers only the stream. The memory of that stream has cast out all other impressions. But there were certain things that she can reconstitute: how many women of her convoy were still alive on a particular day. The day of which she remembers only the stream must have been in early April, for it was 67 days after their arrival in the camp. That day there were still seventy women of the group living. In the stream that is life in the camp the only marked, the only remarkable, fact is the presence of the other women with whom she was taken to Auschwitz.

But there is a second reason why life in the camp cannot be remembered in narratable moments. And, like the strong visuality we have seen at work so far, this reason belongs to the domain of the senses. The stench in the camp was unbearable. Constantly the stench of the crematorium, the stench of one's own body or that of others, so many smells numbed one's senses, so that no smell could be specifically smelled:

> What amazes me, now that I think of it, is that the air was light, clear, but that one didn't smell anything. It must have been quite far from the crematoria. Or perhaps the wind was blowing in the opposite direction on that day. At any rate, we no longer smelled the odor of the crematoria. Yes, and what also amazes me is that there wasn't the slightest smell of spring in the air. Yet there were buds, grass, water, and all this must have had a smell. No, no memory of any odor. It's true that I can't recall my own smell when I lifted my dress. Which proves that our nostrils were besmirched with our own stink and could no longer smell anything.[39]

After this testimony to the death of the sense of smell, the

39 Delbo, *Auschwitz and After* (1995), 57–58/149–150.

narrator describes in great detail the moment of that one day when the kapo allowed her to wash in the stream. Yet the text ends with the sentence: 'It must have happened like this, but I have no memory of it. I only recall the stream.'[40]

40 Delbo, *Auschwitz and After* (1995), 153.

This contradiction does not mean that the narrator invented what happened that one spring day. It means only that this day is part of her 'external memory' of Auschwitz. Her deep or sense memory only sees, feels, smells the monotonous stream. It is this stream that defines life in Auschwitz and the only possible memory of it. Washing *in* the stream, that one event that stands out, is, in the sense, the one moment that she could wash herself *of* the stream.

Kinds of Literature: Images or Imprints

The psychiatric distinction of Janet between narrative and traumatic memory shares with Delbo's distinction between 'ordinary' and 'deep' memory, as well as that between external and sense memory, that they all seem to be confirmed by the existence of two kinds of Holocaust literature. These two kinds of literature maintain a distinctive, defining relationship with visual images as either imprints or 'relatable'—capable of entering in a relationship, as well as narratable—images. Thus, we can conclude, visuality, the specific power of images, is definingly significant for the specific kind of memory that struggles to survive the Holocaust, remember it, and yet transform visual fixation that assaults into visual active remembrance that works through. Images confirm and further qualify a distinction made in an important article by Sidra DeKoven Ezrahi.[41]

41 DeKoven Ezrahi, 'Representing Auschwitz' (1996).

DeKoven Ezrahi distinguishes two different ways of representing the Holocaust which reflect, in fact, two different aesthetics. Both kinds of literature, which I wish to differentiate in their relationship to vision, share a common point of departure that is at the same time their point of arrival: Auschwitz is the ultimate point of reference. It is a spot or event with which imaginative representations do or fail to correspond. Both writer and reader are constantly positioned in relation to this epicentre, this point of no return. But Auschwitz as epicentre of the earthquake that the Holocaust was in human history, is both a literal and a metaphoric notion. Auschwitz has become the metaphor of the earthquake that destroyed not only people and buildings, but also the 'measure' through which destruction can be measured.[42]

42 DeKoven Ezrahi, 'Representing Auschwitz' (1996), 122.

This destruction of the measure to gauge destruction results in the fundamental ambiguity of Auschwitz as a historical site and event, as well as a symbol: forever caught in the ambiguity of its signifying force, Auschwitz can never be more than a symbol of what can no longer be symbolized. For we have lost the measure to decide of what Auschwitz is a symbol. In this sense, too, Auschwitz, and the Holocaust for which it synecdochally stands, cannot be represented, because the metaphorical principles of language have ceased to function. As a metaphor, /Auschwitz/ is overdetermined: 'it' is so rich in meaning that nothing can be metaphorically compared to it. On the other hand, /Auschwitz/ is underdetermined as a metaphor, because it has no precise, measurable meaning. As an 'empty' metaphor, it cannot illuminate new or unexpected aspects of human existence, as metaphors are called upon to do.

DeKoven Ezrahi then proceeds to distinguish between two possible attitudes toward this paradoxical status of Auschwitz as reference point of a metaphor that is both over- and underdetermined. One can adopt either a static or a dynamic attitude. The static or absolute attitude places the

43 DeKoven Ezrahi, 'Representing Auschwitz' (1996), 122.

subject in front of a historical reality that is unbending and from which we can never be liberated. The dynamic attitude approaches the representation of the memory of Auschwitz as a construction made up of strategies deployed in order to come to terms with this historical reality, over and over again.[43] This dynamic attitude implies, for example, that the unbudging reality of this past can sometimes be made livable by the deployment of certain conventions to represent the past. Such softening cannot be acceptable within the absolute attitude. For when a softening or even a curing emerges within the memory or representation of Auschwitz, the danger of a relativizing of the ultimate evil that happened there, would threaten Auschwitz's status as the decisive point of reference of that evil.

It is here that Delbo's use of visuality can be of help. As in the case of Janet's distinction between narrative and traumatic memory, the issue is the *distance* that can be taken toward Auschwitz. The absolute attitude esteems any distance ethically unacceptable, indeed, cognitively impossible. Auschwitz is a historical reality which continues in the present; in grammatical terms, it is the agent of a progressive form. The dynamic attitude is continuous with narrative memory whereas the absolute attitude appears to be the consequence of traumatic memory. DeKoven Ezrahi alleges, precisely, Borowski's use of the present tense as an example. Borowski writes that 'all of us walk around naked', implying that in post-Holocaust times we can only walk around naked. The ordering of temporality in his work is the temporality of trauma in which the past is like a second present, continuously determining the present.

According to DeKoven Ezrahi, Primo Levi writes about his experiences in Auschwitz from a totally different position. His writership consists of the mission to testify to the events which he experienced in the past. He communicates something which is over and belongs to the past. Thanks to that it can be narrated by means of conventional modes. It is thanks to this position that Levi writes in such a clear and accessible style. He does not have to struggle with a past which persist in the present in which he writes. For him Auschwitz is a delimited event in history. It is important to emphasize that DeKoven Ezrahi's claims about Borowski and Levi are not psychological conclusions about the feelings of these authors. Her conclusions concern the position in time from which they write in relation to the time they write about. They are conclusions about different kinds of narration. From this perspective she even goes as far as to make a distinction between Levi's and Borowski's suicide, but also Celan's suicide. According to her, Levi's suicide is not 'caused' by Auschwitz, because Auschwitz belonged for him to the past when he killed himself. It must have been something arbitrary which made him do it. The suicides of Borowski and Celan, however, are the direct consequence of Auschwitz. Although they survived, they still lived 'inside' the Holocaust after their liberation. Until their suicides they remained 'forever trapped within the electrified barbed wire'.[44]

44 DeKoven Ezrahi, 'Representing Auschwitz' (1996), 125.

DeKoven Ezrahi's analysis can be of help to characterize Delbo's writings as analyses of visuality as memory sense. Delbo's writings are exemplary for the aesthetic which DeKoven Ezrahi has called 'the static attitude towards the event'. This attitude makes itself felt by extreme visuality and directness of the Holocaust past: so visual and direct that this past is experienced as present. Mado's descriptions of her memories of the other inmates in the camp in *The Measure of Our Days*, do not show any distance in time. She *sees* the other inmates and joins them.

45 Delbo, *Auschwitz and After* (1995), 261.

46 Delbo, *Auschwitz and After* (1995), 267.

> I'm not alive. I'm imprisoned in memories and repetitions. I sleep badly but insomnia does not weigh on me. At night I have the right not to be alive. I have the right not to pretend. I join the others then. I am among them, one of them. Like me they're dumb and destitute. I don't believe in life after death, I don't believe they exist in a beyond where I join them at night. No. I see them again in their agony, as they were before dying, as they remained with me.[45]

In this passage, Delbo emphatically takes distance from the idea that her visions are dreams or hallucinations of a life beyond. Her visions are her memories. They are just as visual as dreams are.

But here, a tragic irony appears. Past and present change places. Whereas memories of the past appear to her as radically visual, her sensorial awareness of life after Auschwitz is veiled. There is something in-between the present and her access to it. She cannot really, clearly, see that present. She describes the different conditions of being in the present her husband and she live in, as two different kinds of sight:

> For him, I'm there, active, orderly, present. He's wrong. I'm lying to him. I'm not present. Had he been deported too it would have been easier, I think. He'd see the veil over the pupils of my eyes. Would we then have talked together like two sightless people, each possessing the inner knowledge of each other?[46]

Whereas her sight of the past is bright, her sight of the present is veiled. Life in the present is literally overshadowed by the persistence of the visual and sensorial directness of when the Holocaust events happened to her in the past. Thus, the most crucial perversion the Holocaust wrought consists of blinding and sharpening sight, but in inverse proportion to what makes life livable. Past horror occupies the eye, blinding it for a present that can, therefore, not redeem, not erase, not facilitate forgetting.

Truth and/in Imagination

In the tradition of Western science and art, visuality has been the domain of both truth—in a positivist epistemology of observation—and imagination—as in visual art that 'presents before our eyes' what is to be seen as meaning, beauty, or tragedy. This is paradoxical. The paradox is reinforced when we realize that a third domain invoked through thinking about vision is that of affect, both in sentimental and in, for example, pornographic terms. Affect will be extensively discussed in the second part of this book. With Delbo's probing of a vision that does not see, as an image of a memory that cannot relate, a past vision whose present makes the present invisible, we understand the different possibilities of vision better. If we wish to understand the modalities of memorizing the Holocaust, as we must if we wish to prevent the past from recurring by its hallucinating power over us, the point is to distinguish between different kinds of vision, different kinds of looking. It may be perverse, but then, it may be, for that reason, only too appropriate, to invoke verbal memories written down by those who were there, to understand how it is that specifically art, today, can work over, elaborate, work through and keep in visual touch with a past that no image can represent.

Neither 'Post-' nor Memory

Second Generation Testimony, Transmission of Trauma, and the Concept of Postmemory

But we've never had camp.[1]

The Generation After, and Discontinuity

In discussions of second and third generation Holocaust literature and testimony, it is an accepted idea that the trauma of Holocaust survivors is often transmitted from the first to the second and later generations. In this chapter, the 'problems' of the second generation are analyzed in order to see if their problems can be understood in terms of the trauma of the first generation. This will be done on the basis of Eva Hofmann's *After such Knowledge: Where Memory of the Holocaust Ends and History Begins* and Carl Friedman's *Nightfather.*

Since the 1980s the 'second generation' or sometimes even the 'third generation' has become an important notion in reflections about the remembrance and the legacy of the Holocaust. The expression refers first of all to the children, or grandchildren, of those who survived the Holocaust. But it is also used in a more general way, not implying a familial

1 Friedman, *Nightfather* (1994), 2.

relation, and then it refers to the generation-after at large. But when one starts thinking about the 'second generation' as an analytical concept with conceptual implications, the term suddenly becomes very puzzling. Of course, a second generation presupposes a first one. But the expression 'first generation' is also elliptic. It leaves implicit the complement of generation. The first generation refers to survivors of the Holocaust, but not to all survivors. The second defining feature is something like 'victim-ship', shared with those who perished in the Holocaust. The notion of 'first generation' concerns survivors or, but also in an important sense, *and,* victims. They were irreparably hurt.

As a result, when we start using the term second generation for the children of Holocaust survivors, it seems to imply that they are also in one way or another both victims and survivors of the Holocaust. The term does not imply that the second generation is a completely new generation, one that differs fundamentally from the generation of their parents. On the contrary, the phrase seems to suggest a fundamental continuity between first and second generation. One might expect the experiences and memories of Holocaust survivors and of their children to be fundamentally different, but the expression 'second generation' seems to bridge that divide and to introduce the idea of continuity between the generations. I wish to question the possibility and the nature of that continuity.

Of course, this use of the phrase 'second generation' in the context of the Holocaust—with its implied victimhood—is not an isolated phenomenon. Around it, an entire culture of attention to victims emerged, first of all in the United States but in its wake also in the rest of the Western world. The nineteen-eighties and -nineties are not only the decades in which Holocaust studies and the idea of a second generation have gained a forceful presence in academic as well as public life. Those were also the decades in which the public media have embraced victimhood and survivorship as such. Talk shows in which victims of whatever disaster or event can tell their story have become major television events.

Unexpected for a legal culture of presumed innocence, this discourse also has fundamental influence on the juridical system. Whereas trials have always focused on the defendant, innocent until proven guilty, the role of victims has increased dramatically. At the heart of this change is the activity of story-telling, seen as healing. Since the nineties, more and more countries see the right of victims to tell their stories as fundamental. It is assumed, doubtlessly rightly, that expressing their experiences to a caring, believing audience contributes to the healing process. But the undesired consequence of producing a supportive public arena for this self-expression is a naturalized rhetoric: the rhetoric of victimhood has become an effective way of proving someone else's guilt.

In this chapter I will not further explore this legal shift. My interest lies in the way the attention for survivors and victims in public culture and media has led to an erosion of the term *survivor*. Whereas until the 1980s the term survivor concerned mainly someone who had survived a life-threatening event, it is now also used for those who were sexually assaulted, robbed, or even those who went through a divorce. A survey of current psychological and popular literature revealed more than ten groups claiming survivor status, including psychiatric survivors, domestic violence survivors, divorce survivors, cancer survivors, survivors with learning disabilities, child abuse survivors, alcoholism survivors, sexual abuse/incest survivors, and ritual abuse survivors.[2]

It is clear that the erosion of the terms 'survivor' and 'victim' in general, in their co-dependence, is part of wider

2 Randle, 'Deaths, Disasters, and Traumas' (2004), 12.

political developments and changes. But the implied victimhood of the so-called second generation is and is not part of this larger political climate. It is, because the success and almost immediate applicability of the expression 'second generation' depends partly on the dominance of 'victim culture' and 'emotional pain culture' as such. At the same time, it is not, because the expression 'second generation' cannot be dismissed as just a case of rhetorical abuse or manipulation. Something real is clearly at stake with the second or later generations, of 'the generation after'. Simply put, according to many, the effects of the Holocaust on those who survived it have been transmitted to their children. They often suffer from clinical symptoms that can or should be understood in terms of their parents' Holocaust trauma. Far be it from me to deny that something of this order is the case. On the contrary, I wish to explore the most helpful way to address that 'something'.[3]

In order to do so productively, I will invoke that most subtle of discourses, literature. In particular, I will focus on a literary fictional testimony of a child of a Holocaust survivor, Carl Friedman's *Nightfather* (1994),[4] in Dutch *Tralievader* (1991);[5] and also, on Eva Hoffman's book *After Such Knowledge: Memory, History and the Legacy of the Holocaust* (2004). Although Hoffman's book does not belong to literature in the strict sense, its mixture of memoir, testimony, and essay is as subtle as literature can be. Both authors describe in great detail and with enormous evocative power the kind of relationship between parents and children that is at issue, a relationship determined in fundamental ways by the fact that the parents, or one of them, are survivors of the Holocaust. The question I will address to these texts is ultimately very simple. Without presuming anything suggested by current analytical discourses, I will explore what exactly

3 Peter Novick has expressed extreme wariness concerning the concept of trauma and its posttraumatic aftermath, particularly the transmission of posttraumatic symptoms to others through repetition, identification, or mimesis. Novick asserts that, except for Holocaust survivors themselves, 'the available evidence doesn't suggest that overall, American Jews (let alone American gentiles) were traumatized by the Holocaust, in any worthwhile sense of the term'. See Novick, *The Holocaust in American Life* (2000), 3. Novick also dismisses the relevance of what has been called postmemory and the intergenerational transmission of trauma. On this term, see below. For another critique on intergenerational transmission of trauma, see LaCapra, *History in Transit* (2004).

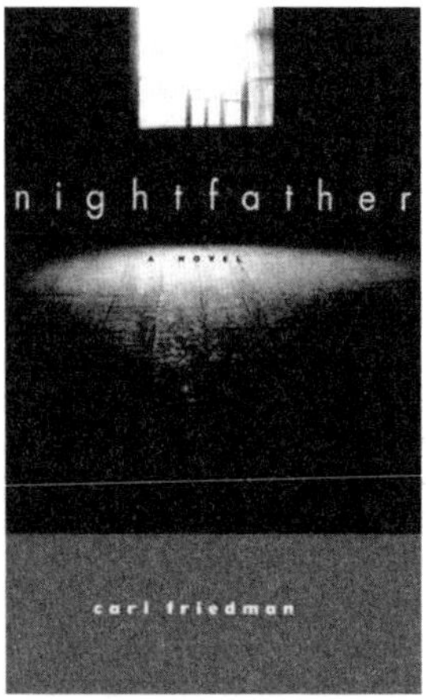

4 Carl Friedman, *Nightfather* (1994), book cover, transl. from Dutch.

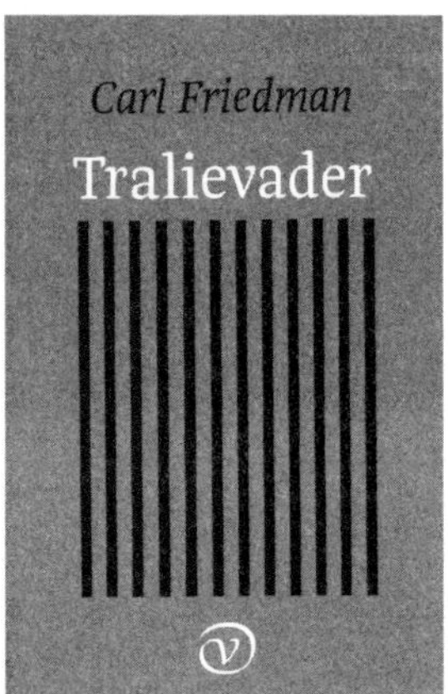

5 Carl Friedman, *Tralievader* (1991), book cover, original Dutch version.

happens in the parent-child interaction described there. On the basis of the answers these literary testimonies suggest, I will then ask if the frequently alleged phrase, 'the transmission of trauma', is appropriate and helpful in these cases. Or are there other processes at work within these relationships?

But before attending to these literary testimonies by children of survivors, let me first acknowledge two early scholarly texts on the subject; they already question the then still unspoken discourse of transmission of victimization. These texts that can be seen as founding texts to the extent that they have established this special attention for the 'generation after'. I am referring to Helen Epstein's *Children of the Holocaust: Conversations with Sons and Daughters of Survivors* (1979)[6] and Nadine Fresco's essay 'Remembering the Unknown' (1984). Both texts were published just before or right at the beginning of the surge of interest in victims and survivors as such. It is precisely for this reason that I find them helpful in shedding some of today's naturalized suppositions.

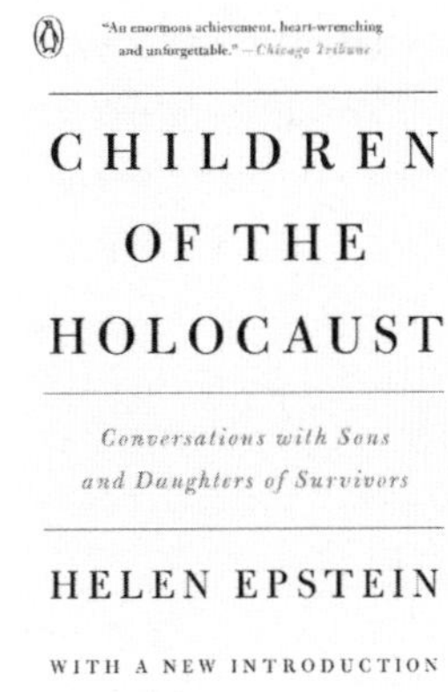

6 Helen Epstein, *Children of the Holocaust* (1979), book cover.

Significantly, in the subtitle of Epstein's book 'Conversations with Sons and Daughters of Survivors', the term 'generation' is not used. The relationship between parents and children is not qualified in terms of continuity. The parents are survivors but it is not suggested that their offspring are also by definition victimized by that legacy. Nor does Epstein use the expression 'second generation'. Instead she speaks of 'children of survivors'. She also comments on publications in which the children of survivors are dealt with as a group with special problems. In some of these publications, the relationship between survivors and their children is explicitly described in terms of continuity and the transmission of trauma. She thus quotes an Israeli psychiatrist who gave a talk in 1977 at Stanford Medical School:

7 Epstein, *Children of the Holocaust* (1979), 299–300.

8 Epstein, *Children of the Holocaust* (1979), 91.

> The trauma of the Nazi concentration camps is re-experienced in the lives of the children and even the grandchildren of camp survivors. [...] The effects of systematic dehumanization are being transmitted from one generation to the next through disturbances in the parent-child relationship.[7]

Although it is thanks to this talk that *The New York Times* became interested in Epstein's writings and that she was able to publish a long article there about the children of survivors, it seems that Epstein herself does not support the diagnosis of the transmission of trauma. Throughout her book she refrains from discussing the children of survivors in such terms.

Earlier in her book, she quotes a Dr. Henry Krystal from Detroit:

> We now see increasing numbers of children of survivors suffering problems of depression and inhibition of their own function. This is a clear example of social pathology being transmitted to the next generation.[8]

Although Epstein only claims to assess which specialists in the field have noticed the children of survivors, she immediately distances herself from Krystal's view:

> Other researchers were not so quick to call what had apparently happened 'social pathology'. Instead, they identified 'disturbances in the parent-child relationship' in the families of survivors. They were puzzled by numerous contradictions in survivor families. Many had become extremely successful in real estate, construction or manufacturing, building mammoth businesses. Others worked in the most menial positions, sweeping floors or cleaning other people's homes. Some were vibrant and optimistic; others listless and depressed.

> No psychiatrist undertook to study what survivors were like as parents, and little was known about family dynamics in survivor families.[9]

Precisely that which most psychiatrists did not undertake to study became Epstein's project. Without assuming that trauma is transmitted, or even resisting that suggestion, she interviewed children of survivors in order to learn about the dynamics in survivor families, her own family included:

> Like most survivors, neither imagined how, over the years, I had stored their remarks, their glances, their silences inside me, how I had deposited them in my iron box like pennies in a piggy bank. They were unconscious of how much a child gleans from the absence of explanation as much as from words, of how much I learned from the old photographs hanging on our apartment walls or secreted away in the old yellow envelope below my father's desk.[10]

Epstein describes the dynamics and communication between her and her parents as indirect, as consisting of silences and obliquities. Thus, the continuity between the two generations is not established smoothly. And to the degree it exists, it is more the result of the interpretative urge of the daughter than of any active role of the parents.

Nadine Fresco's essay 'Remembering the Unknown'[11] is the second early text that can serve to denaturalize the discourse of transmission. Fresco describes the problem of the children of survivors who, after their liberation, emigrated to France, as suffering from lack of memories and a lack of continuity after their families emigrated to France:

> Those Jews who have come late upon the scene, burdened by their posthumous life, infatuated by an

9 Epstein, *Children of the Holocaust* (1979), 91.

10 Epstein, *Children of the Holocaust* (1979), 297.

11 Fresco, 'Remembering the Unknown' (1984).

12 Fresco, 'Remembering the Unknown' (1984), 421.

> irreparable nostalgia for a world from which they were excluded on being born, feel a vertigo when confronted by the time 'before', the lost object of a nameless desire, in which suffering takes the place of inheritance.[12]

Like Epstein, Fresco uses expressions that avoid the idea of continuity between parents and children. Instead of second generation or generation after, for example, she uses in the rest of her essay the idiosyncratic expression 'latter-day Jews'. For her, these latter-day Jews are like people who have had a hand amputated that they never had. The suffering caused by this amputation is a phantom pain, in which amnesia takes the place of memory. The only memory there is, is that one remembers nothing. This paradox undermines the notion of memory, which is at stake, but only in its absence.

It is important to notice that these two 'founding' texts by Epstein and Fresco assess the dynamics between survivors of the Holocaust and their children as one which utterly *fails* to establish continuity between generations. According to them, it is precisely this failure that causes the intense desire for it on the side of the children. But Epstein and Fresco avoid consistently any suggestion of transmission of trauma or inheritance, or the idea of continuity between generations. Subsequent Holocaust studies, especially those focusing on the generation-after problematic, have taken a lot of its inspiration from these two works, but without seriously paying attention to how these authors characterize the dynamics between parents and children and resulting problems of those children. That is why at formulating what is at issue, I propose to return to their characterizations of these dynamics.

Obsessive Talking and Failing Address

With this in mind, let us turn to the writings of Carl Friedman[13] and Eva Hoffman[14], who provide a vivid image of the survivor/children dynamics. To begin with Friedman's novel *Tralievader* (*Nightfather*), this work challenges the conventional idea that trauma manifests itself in silence, the inability to tell or talk. In Friedman's novel, the young daughter of a concentration camp survivor tells about the efforts she and her two brothers make to try to bridge the gulf opened between themselves and their father—not by his silence on his camp experiences but, on the contrary, by his speech. Their father feels compelled to tell the details of his ordeal and cannot stop talking about it. Any daily event or situation in post-Holocaust life invariably evokes in him the urge to go back to the past and relate it to his children and to his wife. The father relates his Holocaust stories *all the time*. The question is, what *kind* of relationship with his children does this obsessive telling establish? Or to put it differently: what kind of problem does the father's obsessive telling *cause* in his children?[15]

Although the age of the three children is never specified, it is clear that they are all still very young: at the age when they still have to learn the exact meaning of words, the ontological status of stories, of fairy tales, of reality, and the difference between words and reality. Strikingly, at their age, having to listen to their father's Holocaust experiences creates above all, a *discursive* problem. Not that the knowledge of history, of the world and of humanity assumed by the father's stories is too enormous for them to grasp. Instead, they do not understand where those stories stop and their own world begins. This confusion is emblematically present in the father's use of the expression 'camp'. For, the father, as it is

13 Friedman, *Nightfather* (1994).

14 Hoffman, *After Such Knowledge* (2004).

15 The way Friedman's *Nightfather* is narrated can be compared to Henry James' *What Maisie Knew* (1897). A very young girl with a limited understanding of the world around her, is the main focalizer, through whom we readers get access to the described world.

16 Friedman, *Nightfather* (1994), 1–2.

17 Friedman, *Nightfather* (1994), 2.

once phrased in the novel, 'has camp'. The phrase sounds like an illness. The first of the forty short chapters is all about the way he uses the word 'camp' and how his children struggle with its meaning.

The father never mentions the camp by name. He talks as if there had been just one. He is outraged when he watches a film about 'the camp' that shows inmates frying eggs for breakfast. 'An egg!' he says shrilly. 'In the camp!' His daughter deducts the following conclusion from his outburst:

> So, camp is somewhere where no one fries eggs.
>
> Camp is not so much a place as a condition. 'I've had camp,' he says. That makes him different from us. We've had chicken pox and German measles. And after Simon fell out of a tree, he got a concussion and had to stay in bed for weeks.
>
> But we've never had camp.[16]

But the fact that she and her two brothers have never had camp does not imply that this condition uniquely applies to their father. When she and her two brothers visit the zoo, she starts to cry when looking at the wolf. Her older brother Max comes to her.

> 'Well?' he said in a bored voice when we were standing in front of the wolf's cage. 'What's the matter with him?'
>
> 'He has camp!' I sobbed. Max glanced through the bars.
>
> 'Impossible,' he said. 'Wolves don't get camp.'[17]

But at the moment that the scope of the word 'camp' seems to become limited to the past and the condition of her father, her vision of the world is confused again when Nellie, her school friend, uses the expression in an unfamiliar context. Nellie goes to the Girl Scouts, the 'Brownies', every Wednesday afternoon. The narrator asks her parents if she might also join the Brownies. But that is out of the question, because before and during the War, the Dutch scouts maintained very good relations with the Hitler Jugend. The next day the narrator informs Nellie that she is not allowed to join.

> 'Too bad,' she says. 'Then you're going to miss a whole lot of things, movies, tracking, things like that. And camp.'
> 'Camp?' I repeat, wide-eyed.[18]

She again has to reconsider the scope of the term. Wolves cannot have camp, but nor is camp restricted to the past and the condition of her father.

In this respect, the term differs from others, which she never encounters outside her father's stories:

> 'What a funny father you have,' Nellie says, giggling. She looks at me expectantly but I avoid her eyes. What can I say? She knows nothing about hunger or about the SS. Words like *barracks, latrine,* or *crematorium* mean nothing to her. She speaks a different language.
> Nellie's father doesn't have camp, he has a bicycle that he rides to the factory, with a lunch box strapped to the carrier.[19]

If the past and the condition of her father are fundamentally different from her own world and other people's condition, then his stories can perhaps be compared to fairy tales. And indeed, the father sometimes talks as if he were telling a fairy tale. When the children hear a camp story in which the father's pants suddenly begin to talk to him, this solution is seriously considered:

> 'What did they [the pants] say?' I ask.

18 Friedman, *Nightfather* (1994), 40.

19 Friedman, *Nightfather* (1994), 21.

20 Friedman, *Nightfather* (1994), 87.

21 Friedman, *Nightfather* (1994), 88.

> 'They spoke in German,' says my father. 'I don't feel like translating all of it right now, but one of the things they told me was that they answered to the name of Heinrich and that they had once belonged to Adolf Hitler. They'd been looking up Adolf's asshole for years and had learned the most confidential state secrets that way. Then, one day, they were arrested and sent to the camp because they knew too much.'
>
> 'Talking underpants? But that can't be true!' says Simon. My father raises his hands helplessly.[20]

When the three siblings go to bed, they evaluate this story:

> Simon still finds it hard to believe.
>
> 'Clothes can't talk,' he says while we're getting undressed. Max, who doesn't have to go to bed for a long time, leans against the closet.
>
> 'Why not?' he says. 'Crazier things happened in the camp, people were gassed there.' Simon shrugs his shoulders.
>
> 'Of course people were gassed there,' he says. 'That's what a camp is for, isn't it?'[21]

The siblings come to different conclusions. Simon, the youngest, feels too old for fairy tales. They are untrue, they contradict his frames of reference of reality and normality. The camp, however, is part of his frame of reference. He has heard so many stories about it. So, camps where people are gassed is a matter of normality; they are known.

At this point, let me assess the status of the discourse here. Although the father in Friedman's novel contradicts the common idea about traumatized people as silent and unable to talk about their experiences, this does not mean that he is able to relate to his family through his telling. He does tell stories, but to whom does he address them? He is often like the character Mado in Charlotte Delbo's *The Measure of Our Days*[22], who after the Holocaust is unable to communicate with her non-Holocaust-survivor husband, as I have discussed in the previous chapter. Mado is never really present when in his presence, but only superficially addresses him. She can only relate to the others with whom she was in the camp and with whom she shared the same experiences. In *Nightfather,* this problem of address becomes especially acute when the father sings:

> My father sings every evening. When we leave the table, one by one, after supper, he stays in his chair. He opens his mouth a little and rocks backward and forward, as if pumping his voice up from very deep down. It takes a little while for the sound to come out.
>
> We don't understand his songs. He learned them from fellow-sufferers drawn from every corner of Europe, people who shared barracks or bunks with him, or perhaps a piece of bread. They are dead, they can no longer speak, and they can't hear him. Yet it is for them that he sings. His long, drawn-out Slav vowels float over our heads, but they're not meant for us.[23]

The songs cannot be understood by the children for the very simple reason that they do not understand the languages in which they are sung. But there is more to it. The songs are not addressed to them either. Proper address seems to be another precondition for real understanding, for effective communication. It is in this respect that the singing of these incomprehensible songs is emblematic for the people to whom he tells his camp stories.

The father usually forgets to bridge the gap between his frame of reference and those of his children. Yet, it is only

22 Delbo, *Auschwitz and After* (1995).

23 Friedman, *Nightfather* (1994), 28–29.

24 Friedman, *Nightfather* (1994), 97.

when this gap is bridged that relating one's past can become an effective way of relating *to*, in the sense of establishing a relationship. From time to time, the inability of the father to address his children causes violent emotional conflicts, especially with the oldest son Max. During a moment of growing tension, when the father tries to reassure Max that he loves him, Max responds as follows:

> 'It's not true!' shouts Max. 'All you love is your SS! When we're at the dinner table, you go on about starvation. When we have a cold, you go on about typhus. Other fathers play soccer in the street with their kids, but when I bring a friend home just once, all you can do is talk about the camp. Why didn't you damn well stay there!'[24]

This outburst—so true, yet so unfair, but how can Max know?—brings me to a theoretical conclusion. *Nightfather* is more about children who are raised by traumatized survivor parents, than about the nightmares and trauma of the survivor. The two are related, yet, the problems those children have to struggle with are of a very different nature than those of the survivor parent. That is why I contend that it makes little sense to speak of the *transmission* of trauma. Children of survivors can be traumatized, but their trauma does not consist of the Holocaust experience, not even in indirect or mitigated form. Their trauma is caused by being raised by a traumatized Holocaust survivor.

In order to develop this argument, I will first elaborate on the concept of trauma involved. As I explained in my 1997 book *Caught by History*, and in the first chapter of this book, trauma is not caused by an event or situation as such. It is not the extremity of the event which causes trauma. An event or situation can become traumatic for someone when this person's symbolic order does not provide consistent frames of reference in terms of which that event or situation can be experienced. The difficulty many (but not all) survivors of the Holocaust have in expressing their experiences can be explained by the fact that the nature of the events that happened to them is in no way covered by the terms, positions and frames of reference that the symbolic order offers them. In short, the problem that causes trauma is not the *nature* of the event itself, or any intrinsic limitation of representation per se, but the split between the *living* of an event and the availability of forms of representation through which the event can be *experienced*.

This discursive notion of trauma enables us to assess the precise cause of the problems that the children in *Nightfather* have to struggle with. Whereas the trauma of survivors is caused by the discrepancy between the Holocaust events and the symbolic order with which these events can be experienced, the trauma of the children (if we want to use that term for their problems) originates in an even more basic phase of the process of experience. The symbolic order in which they enter in their childhood is fundamentally inconsistent or diffuse. They don't have clear frames of reference at their disposal with which they can easily make sense of the world. For them it is never really clear where stories of murder and humiliation stop and reality begins. On this issue, the study by Janneke Lam[25] is particularly illuminating.

Among the fundamental principles of the symbolic order is that it generates and produces meaning on the basis of differentiation. This principle does not function well in the case of these children. Differences remain puzzling for them, the ontological status of stories, fairy tales and reality remains diffuse. It is not that their symbolic order is just *different*—in its distinctions among ontological statuses—but that the world in which they grow up is not only the family situation with the

25 Lam, *Whose Pain?* (2002).

26 Friedman, *Nightfather* (1994), 98–99.

survivor parent, nor only that of school and friends. Those two worlds and their implications for the development of a symbolic order are in conflict. This does not lead to a different symbolic order, but to one which contains major diffuse areas.

When Max shouts to his father that he would have done better to have stayed in the camp, he clearly transgresses the distinction between what you are allowed to say and what is forbidden to say, what is supposed to be cruel talk and what is not. His inability to draw this boundary leads to situations that wound his father and wound himself. After the mother has overheard the conversation between father and son, she intervenes:

> 'Just leave those building blocks,' my mother says to us, 'we're going for a short walk.'
>
> As we walk down the hallway, we can hear Max howling in his bedroom. We can still hear him down in the street. Only when we have turned the corner does an icy silence descend.[26]

Turning the corner and the resulting silence are replete with symbolic meanings. They seem to stand for the failure to recognize the problems of the children of survivors, as problems that are not minor, and hence, weaker variants of the trauma of their parents, but are problems of a different nature. One cannot simply 'turn the corner', ignore what happens, because then an icy silence descends. But recognizing the problem does not in itself solve it.

Communication and Incoherence

Seemingly agreeing with Max, Eva Hoffman in *After Such Knowledge*[27] considers the possibility that the situation of the

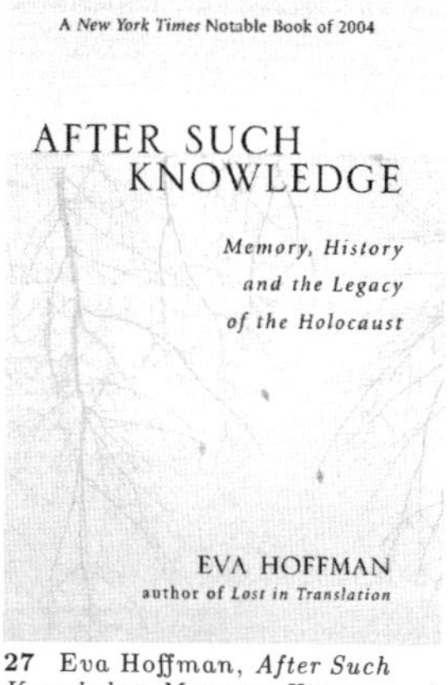

27 Eva Hoffman, *After Such Knowledge: Memory, History and the Legacy of the Holocaust* (2004), book cover.

children is in some respect even worse than that of the survivor parents. After having gone through so much, with all the terrible persecution behind them, the parents seem to be able to cope better with life than their children. In many cases they get less depressed, anxious or afraid. In an attempt to explain this, Hoffman conjectures that the survivor parents have in some way been more fortunate than those who came after, because they had lives before the Holocaust: 'The difference between coming into the world imbued with the Holocaust and having experienced a more normal world before turns out to be significant.'[28]

Hoffman argues subsequently that the term 'memory' is not at all applicable to how the children of survivors relate to the Holocaust. Like Friedman, she prefers to compare the condition of those children to fairy tales:

> The Holocaust, in my first, childish reception, was a deeply internalized but strangely unknown past. It has become routine to speak of the 'memory' of the Holocaust, and to adduce to this faculty a moral, even a spiritual value. But it is important to be precise: We who came after do not have memories of the Holocaust. Even from my most intimate proximity I could not form 'memories' of the Shoah or take my parents' memories as my own. Rather, I took in that first information as a sort of fairy tale deriving not so much from another world as from the center of the cosmos: an enigmatic but real fable.[29]

In contrast to the family situation in Friedman's *Nightfather*, however, Hoffman's parents are not compulsive narrators. They do not express memories but rather

> something both more potent and less lucid; something closer to enactment of experience, to emanations or

28 Hoffman, *After Such Knowledge* (2004), 182–183.

29 Hoffman, *After Such Knowledge* (2004), 6.

> sometimes nearly embodiments of psychic matter—of material too awful to be processed and assimilated into the stream of consciousness, or memory, or intelligible feeling.[30]

For the children, this different kind or order of expression does not lead to a coherent, intelligible symbolic order, either, because the parents' intensely emotional language was utterly chaotic:

> In our small apartment, it was a chaos of emotion that merged from their words, rather than any coherent narration. Or rather, the emotion, direct and tormented, was enacted through the words, the form of their utterances. The memories—no, not memories but emanations—of wartime experiences kept erupting in flashes of imaginary; in abrupt, fragmented phrases; in repetitious, broken refrains. They kept manifesting themselves with a frightening immediacy in that most private and potent of family languages—the language of the body.[31]

Hoffman stresses the incoherency of those first communications about the Holocaust. They involved broken speech, which was broken under the pressure of pain; just fragments or episodes, repeated but never elaborated upon. They remained compressed and packed. The fact that these communications could not be integrated into a coherent narrative, into the rest of their symbolic order, turned them into 'wondrous fairy tales'.[32] For, in fairy tales, too, the ontology cannot be integrated into those taken for realistic:

> [...] the mythology passed on in this way conveyed a universe of absolute forces and absolute unreason, a world in which ultimate things happened without cause or motive, where life was saved or lost routinely and

30 Hoffman, *After Such Knowledge* (2004), 7.

31 Hoffman, *After Such Knowledge* (2004), 9.

32 Hoffman, *After Such Knowledge* (2004), 6.

> through reflex movement, and where the border between life and death was dangerously permeable. Irrational as the world that my parents endured had been, I made of it something more utterly irrational still.[33]

Hoffman concludes that, in the case of the survivors as well as their children, the trajectory of response to the Holocaust events is the opposite of the trajectory of memory. According to her, the experiences of the survivors became narratable, became a coherent narrative, albeit only much later. They became narratable not because they processed their memories, connected pieces of memory into a coherent epic. The coherence, rather, came from outside, through literature and film, through memoirs and testimonies of others, which circulated more and more in public culture. So, 'official' and public accounts of the Holocaust enabled personal memories to become narratable. They provide the narrative framework in which memory fragments can be integrated. The coherence of these outside sources was achieved by survivors (and historians) who were less traumatized than most.

The trajectory of the generation after is in many ways the opposite of the process of memory of their parents:

> For while the adult world asks first 'what happened,' and from there follows its uncertain and sometimes resistant route towards the inward meaning of the facts, those who are born after calamity sense its most inward meanings first and have to work their way outwards toward the facts and the worldly shape of events.[34]

The normal trajectory of memory is fundamentally *indexical*. Memories, partial, idealized, fragmented or distorted as they can be, are traces of the events of which they are the memories. There is continuity between the event and its memory.

33 Hoffman, *After Such Knowledge* (2004), 12.

34 Hoffman, *After Such Knowledge* (2004), 16.

And this continuity has an unambiguous direction: the event is the beginning; the memory is the result. In the case of the generation of survivors, the continuity between event and memory is hampered. There has been an indexical relationship but the memory in which it results, is too unprocessed, that is, un-experienced. The memory is more like an unmediated return of the event than an indexical, hence mediated account of it in the form of memory. But, as Hoffman explains, it is thanks to the outside world, the world of addressees, or the world of public culture and the films, books, narratives that circulate in that culture, that the un-experienced return of the event can belatedly be 'worked through'. The coherence of narrative or of experienced events is, eventually, introduced, albeit from the outside. The hampered indexical relationship between past and present, between event and its memory is restored thanks to the help of others, or of culture as such.

In the case of the children of survivors, the indexical relationship that defines memory has never existed. Their relationship to the past events is based on fundamentally different semiotic principles. It is only confusing to speak of memory in this context, because memories are missing, by definition. That does not mean that the generation of the children has no knowledge of their family's past. That knowledge is, however, the result of a process of conveying, of combining historical knowledge and the memories of others. And importantly of constructing: it is the result of a strong identification with (the past of) the parents, of projecting historical, familial knowledge of a past one is disconnected from, onto one's own life history.

Postmemory as Wishful Thinking

This crucial disconnectedness makes it necessary to say a few words about the term 'postmemory,' as introduced by Marianne Hirsch.[35] In her explanation of this concept, Hirsch focuses on the prefix post-, while the term 'memory' seems to her more or less self-evident. The prefix post- does not imply for her that later generations are 'beyond memory' and thus, rather, in history. Postmemory is, instead, distinguished from memory by generational distance, and from history by deep personal connection.[36] 'Post-' indicates that the following noun concerns a very particular kind of memory, one that connects to its object not through recollection but through an imaginative investment and creation. The fact that postmemory is the result of an imaginative and creative act does not distinguish it *fundamentally* from memory, because, according to Hirsch, memory is also mediated—a view with which I fully agree. There is only a relative difference: memory is 'more directly connected to the past'.[37] The problem of distance created through mediation is altogether different from that of generational difference. The connection of memory to the past is basically an indexical one: the person whose memory it is has lived that past. In this respect, postmemory is not relatively but fundamentally different from memory. By calling the phenomenon post*memory*, Hirsch implicitly claims indexical connectedness for it. However, the 'deep personal connection' claimed by Hirsch for the generation of survivors' children, concerns first of all a connection with the parents. And only through the deep connection with the parents is a connection with the latter's past established, which results from a strong identification with the parents and does not have an indexical origin as such. If I may suggest an alternative: this deep connection with the past is a

35 Hirsch, *Family Frames* (1997).

36 Hirsch, *Family Frames* (1997), 22.

37 Hirsch, *Family Frames* (1997), 22.

38 Fresco, 'Remembering the Unknown' (1984).

39 Raczymow, in Astro (ed.), *Discourses of Jewish Identity in Twentieth Century France* (1994).

displacement of the connection with the parents. In claiming connection through displacement the notion of memory becomes, I think, more self-evident than is warranted, and thus the concept unwittingly comes to beg the question it raises.

Positing the mediated state of memory is not the same as *explaining* why postmemory is imaginative and creative, yet remains a case of memory. When memories are taken to be mediated, this implies that they are not transparent accounts of the past. The narrative discourse used for expressing the memories adds specific significations to the memories. This constructed or mediated aspect of memory does not imply, however, that memory is imaginative or the result of creative projection onto the past. In contrast, this quality is precisely what defines *post*memory. By arguing for a relative instead of a fundamental difference between memory and postmemory, Hirsch risks confusing the dependency on language and narrative conventions for the expression of memory, with discussions about the fictionality of certain genres. And that seems to me a dangerous fall into relativization—which I know to be the last thing Hirsch would want.

It is, however, especially the notion of 'memory', rather than the prefix post-, that needs legitimation in this context of the generation after. Hirsch contrasts her term to Nadine Fresco's notion of 'absent memory'[38] and affiliates it to Henri Raczymow's 'mémoire trouée' (memory shot through with holes).[39] But this indiscriminate use of the term memory leads to a potential contradiction: Hirsch wants to use the term memory because of the children's close personal *connection* with the parents, while at the same time speaking of a memory that is indirect and *dis*-connected. But then, I wonder if calling what happens 'memory' is the most adequate way to explain the process at stake. If indexicality defines memory, by the relation between memory and its object, one can speak of the memories children have of their parents telling about their Holocaust experiences. But using the term memory, post- or not, only confuses the intergenerational processes, which are, I would say, post- by definition, with the image the children have of their parents' past. The term 'postmemory' risks, I think, becoming unwittingly symptomatic of the *desire* of the generation of survivors' children to connect to the past of their parents, a desire that remains frustrated. This desire is so strong because of the radical *dis*-connection with that past, because of 'absent memory'. To describe this situation of disconnection by means of a term that implies connection, may ultimately not help to understand the specificity of the problems of children of survivors, and of the special dynamics between survivor parents and children.[40]

40 In a productive ongoing discussion, Hirsch responded to an earlier version of this chapter published in 2006. See Hirsch, 'The Generation of Postmemory' (2008), and Hirsch, *The Generation of Postmemory* (2012). For another critique on intergenerational transmission of trauma, see LaCapra, *History in Transit* (2004).

This brings me to my conclusion. The term postmemory shares with the idea of intergenerational transmission of trauma, the claim of a fundamental continuity between generations. As I have argued on the basis of the writings of, first, theorists Epstein and Fresco, then imaginative writers Friedman and Hoffman, the dynamics between children and survivor parents is rather defined by dis-connection, hence dis-continuity: disconnection not in an emotional, personal sense, but in terms of intelligibility. I would even say that the more children feel disconnected from the past of their survivor parents—the less they are able to know it or understand it—the deeper they feel personally connected to them or the more they need that connection. But to posit that connection as the basis of what happens is, it seems to me, close to a form of, literally, wishful thinking.

Legacies of Stalinism and the Gulag

Shame and Nostalgia

> Kolyma is a twin of Hitler's death camps. But it is also different.... The difference is that in Hitler's death camps, the victims knew they were killed.... Those who died in the Kolyma or other Soviet camps, died bewildered.[1]

> Something like that was not thinkable, something like that could not happen.[2]

Black Holes

Yevgenia Ginzburg, daughter of a Jewish family of pharmacists, studied social sciences and pedagogy. She married the mayor of Kazan and became a member of the communist party. In 1937 she and her husband were thrown out of the party because they were alleged to have contacts with the Trotskyists. In July of the same year she was arrested and sentenced to ten years of forced labour (her husband to 15 years). The two of them survived a long odyssey through

1 Mikhail Geller, quoted in Etkind, *Warped Mourning* (2013), 204.

2 Ginzburg, *Journey into the Whirlwind* (1995), 212.

3 Ginzburg, *Journey into the Whirlwind* (1995), 212.

4 Aksyonov, *Generations of Winter* (1994).

several prisons, work camps, and places of exile, including the women's camp Alzhir (*Akmolinskiy lager' zhen izmennikov Rodiny*) near Karaganda. Ginzburg was released in 1949, although she was not permitted to leave the Siberian Magadan zone. In 1950 she was arrested again and exiled to Kolyma. She was not allowed to return to Moscow until 1953, after Stalin's death, and it took another two years for her to be rehabilitated.

Back in Moscow Ginzburg wrote her memoirs *Journey into the Whirlwind* (*Krutoi marshrut*), first published in 1967, but only outside of Russia. Internationally, her memoirs became famous for so impressively describing the horrors of the Stalin era. 'The most absurd feelings have torn me', she writes, 'but the most important one was amazement. Something like that was not thinkable, something like that could not happen.'[3] One of Ginzburg's two sons, Vasily Aksyonov, also became a well-known writer. After being exiled to the United States, he wrote *Generations of Winter*[4] (*Moskovskaia Saga*), a panoramic novel describing Soviet life from 1925 to 1945. This work is regarded as the *War and Peace* of the twentieth-century. Although both mother and son depict Soviet life under Stalin in their works, the genres they use are strikingly different: the mother writes her memoirs, the son writes a novel which is fictional but anchored in the recent historical reality. The novel has nothing about it that suggests a testimony or memoir of the second generation, or that it stems from the child of a victim of Stalinism.

Aksyonov's style of writing is far from realistic; it has been characterized as headlong and ruminative as well as wildly surreal. In the narrative, animals, trees and birds interact with human beings. Although the horrors of Siberian exile are also represented at length, it is never clear if the testimonial stories of Aksyonov's mother play any role in this novel.

I am alleging this example of Ginzburg and Aksyonov, a mother and a son who are both writers, as an example of the dynamic discussed in the previous chapter, between the first generation of survivors, in this case of the Gulag, and the second or later generations, in other words the generation of the children or grandchildren of those survivors. In the context of another apocalyptic past, namely the Holocaust, a great deal of discussion has centered on the dynamic between the different generations arising out of the transmission of trauma, a process that is also referred to, problematically as I have argued, as 'post memory'.[5]

Predictably, in the case of Ginzburg and Aksyonov, it is unclear whether one can speak of a transmission of trauma. Although both writers deal with the past and specifically with Stalinist terror, it is not all obvious that Aksyonov's account is in any way determined by the traumatic personal history of his mother. It is as if he were writing as an exiled Russian citizen using his imagination and not as the son of a woman who suffered every possible terror of the Stalinist regime herself. Although Aksyonov's imaginative novels can be understood as the result of the desire to bridge the gap between himself and his mother's life in the Gulag, this desire is only ever expressed indirectly, never upfront.

So, let me move to another case. In his book *Messages from the Black Hole: Post-Soviet Literature in Search of a Russian Identity*, Boris Noordenbos concludes about Dmitry Bykov novel *Justification* (*Оправдание*) of 2001 that it contains conflicting visions: 'The empire as a traumatic historical experience, and the empire as venerable and restorable manifestation of Russia's mission and identity.'[6] These conflicting visions can be explained as the result of the two affects that are predominant in the second or younger generations, those of shame over and nostalgia for the Soviet past. This (short)

5 In a personal conversation Aleida Assmann proposed to replace the term postmemory with post memory, as two distinct words, which makes clear that later generations have no real memories and that the relation they establish with the past of the earlier generations goes 'beyond memory', or is a relation established after memories no longer exist. So in this chapter I will use the term 'post memory' where necessary for the sake of brevity.

6 Noordenbos, *Messages from the Black Hole* (2016), 177.

7 Noordenbos, *Messages from the Black Hole* (2016), 157.

8 Bykov, *Justification* (2001), 54.

chapter, then, is a transitional one: between the previous discussion of the (non-)connection between generations, and between trauma as re-enactment, and affect as transmission.

Justification, first published in 2001, tells the history of the Stalinist era in unexpected ways. An important role is reserved for the resurrection or 'return' of the victims of Stalinist terror. Their return is part of Russia's historical vision and of post-Soviet identity.[7] Another important role is played by 'a black lake'. This lake is accessible to someone called Kretov, an old neighbour of the much younger protagonist Rogov. As Kretov claims, the lake has no bottom. The black lake clearly symbolizes a collective post-Soviet historical oblivion and confusion about the past. This past seems to resist comprehension because it is lost and shattered. The protagonist Rogov is a young historian who is obsessed with the political oppression under Stalin, and more particularly with the fate of his grandfather, who was arrested in 1938 and disappeared. Rogov is really puzzled why Stalin exterminated so many Russians:

> I don't understand though, maybe for the purpose of keeping up the fear.... or crushing the opposition, the arrests were truly necessary, but just not quite so many of them? Not on this scale? [...] I don't see the principle. I cannot see the criteria he used to exterminate.[8]

At this moment still puzzled, he later comes up with the explanation:

> The repression acted as an immense filtering apparatus, and the few who bravely withstood torture, and did not confess to the (fabricated) crimes brought up during interrogation, were not shot or deported to the regular camps. They were medically treated, and after their

> wounds healed they were sent to special Siberian settlements, where they became members of a new elite, a 'golden squadron' of unbreakable people. Many of whom assisted in the defense of Stalingrad. Stalin's purges were a way of selecting the toughest people.[9]

The old man Kretov explains that this elaborate and cruel selection procedure was the only way to secure and preserve the Soviet empire.

The young Rogov initially does not believe Kretov's theory of Stalin's state terror as a filtering apparatus. But after having served two years in the army, he becomes more and more impressed by the qualities of obedience and strength. He rejects the loose morals of post-Soviet society, which is for him a world of moral decay. The Stalinist Empire, in contrast, is seen as the admired lost realm of discipline, wholeness, devotion, and brutal grandeur.[10] It is clear that his feelings towards past and present are a mixture of shame for the generation before him responsible for the post-Soviet state and nostalgia for the Stalinist Empire.

These two affects come about in different social frames. The affect—to allude to the second part of this book—of nostalgia is transmitted by the social frame of the present nation of Russia. Because of the many social and political problems of contemporary Russia, the empire of the Soviet Union is longed for 'as the venerable and restorable manifestation of Russia's mission and identity'. The second affect, of shame, is usually transmitted in a much smaller social framework, namely the family. What defines contemporary Russia is that the smaller social frame of the family is not peacefully embedded in the encompassing one of the Nation; there is intense tension between the two with the result that relations within the family are endangered: the younger generations do not

9 Bykov, *Justification* (2001), 159.

10 Bykov, *Justification* (2001), 160.

identify with the older generations, but they feel embarrassment and shame for them.

In this chapter I will deal with the dynamics between the first generation of survivors, in this case of the Gulag and Stalinism, and the second or later generations, in other words the generation of the children or grandchildren of those survivors. In the context of that other apocalyptic past, the Holocaust, on which I have dwelled so far, one speaks usually of a dynamic between the different generations that consists of transmission of trauma. In the case of the Gulag and Stalinism, it is, however, unclear whether one can speak of transmission of trauma or post memory. In order to better understand this dynamic between first and later generations, we first have to understand the differences between the Holocaust and the Gulag. Because it is not only the present social and political situation that determines the affective relations between generations, but also the differences between the Holocaust and the Gulag as historical, apocalyptic events.

Differences between the Gulag and the Holocaust

Alexander Etkind[11] has adequately pointed out the main differences between the Nazi regime and its most notorious practice, the Holocaust, and the Stalinist regime in Russia and the Gulag. First of all, the Stalinist regime in Russia lasted much longer than the Nazi regime in Germany. Whereas the Holocaust lasted five years, the terror of the Gulag lasted at least three decades. In addition, the Soviet regime lasted for seven decades, and Russia is less distant from the collapse of its Soviet state than Germany is from the collapse of its Nazi state.[12] According to Etkind this difference implies that the concept of generation is less useful in

11 Etkind, *Warped Mourning* (2013).

12 Etkind, *Warped Mourning* (2013), 203.

the case of Russia and the Gulag than in the studies of Holocaust survivors and their offspring.

A second important difference concerns the distinction between victims and executioners, the perpetrators. In the case of Nazism this distinction is clear and absolute. Who the victims were is clearly defined: first of all Jews, but also Romani, homosexuals and political enemies. The Soviet victims, however, were significantly more diverse than the Nazi victims; their descendants are more dispersed, and have competing interests, which creates multiple memory conflicts in the post-Soviet Union.[13] Not only are the victims more diverse, the distinction between executioner/perpetrator and victim was not stable. Someone who had been a executioner/perpetrator for a long time could suddenly become a victim him- or herself. These roles, or subject positions were to a certain extent flexible. And Stalinism made different kinds of victims. Not only those who were sent to the Gulag were victims of Stalinism; also those who were forced to migrate from Western Russia to the East can be considered as victims of Stalinism.

A third difference concerns the later generations. The descendants do not share or recognize the concepts that were used by the perpetrators to victimize their parents or grandparents. Notions like 'the Kulaks', 'saboteurs', 'bourgeoisie', 'social parasites', 'anti-Soviet elements', 'class enemies' have no meaning to them. These notions do not enable later generations to feel compassion or empathy with (the generation of) their parents. It is usually the opposite: they feel shame or are bewildered because of the strange accusations against their older relatives. It alienates them from them. In the case of the descendants of Holocaust victims or survivors, it is exactly the opposite. Even those who had not identified so far as Jewish, the past of their (grand)parents has made them

13 Etkind, *Warped Mourning* (2013), 203.

Jewish through identification with them. A fourth difference concerns the end of the Nazi regime and of the Soviet Union respectively. Germany's post-war transformation was forced upon it by military defeat and occupation. Russia's post-Soviet transformation, was, instead, a political choice. These four differences have great repercussions for the aftermath of Stalinism. In Russia there is nothing like a (full) list of victims or of the executioners. Nor are there adequate, authoritative memorials, museums, or monuments, which could stabilize the understanding of these events for generations to come.[14]

There is more to say about the identity of the victims of Nazism and Stalinism, however. As Etkind points out: 'the Nazi theory of racial purity was implemented with consistency, the application of the Soviet theory of class warfare was more arbitrary'. Although this is not true for the assimilated Jews from especially Germany itself, most of the Jews and Romani who died in the Nazi camps agreed with their jailers that they were Jews or Romani, though of course, they did not agree that this should be cause to kill them:

> In contrast, most of those kulaks, saboteurs, and enemies of the people who died in the soviet camps disagreed with their jailors that they were kulaks, saboteurs, and enemies of the people. Some of them hated 'enemies of the people' just as much as their jailors did. In the Stalinist camps, many political prisoners shared the principles of their perpetrators but clung to the belief that in their personal cases, they had been mistakenly identified.[15]

In the Nazi camps the victims objected to the reasons for their persecution, but not to their identification as Jew, Romani, political enemy, or homosexual. In what follows, we will see these differences between the two catastrophes at work in the cultural aftermath.

14 Etkind, *Warped Mourning* (2013), 10.

15 Etkind, *Warped Mourning* (2013), 204.

Has the Gulag Been Traumatic?

After having pointed out the differences between German Nazism and Stalinist Communism, and between the Holocaust and the Gulag, Etkind comes up with the following conclusion: '[…] one thing is clear: the very nature of the Soviet terror makes it difficult to comprehend, remember, and memorialize.'[16] Indeed, I share his conclusion. However, when he explains in his introduction the guiding concept for his whole book, namely mourning, he defines mourning and trauma in such an idiosyncratic way that the ramifications of the impossibility of comprehension, remembrance, and memorialization are getting blurred instead of disentangled. He distinguishes mourning from trauma, a concept that is according to him close to, but different from trauma.

> Trauma is a response to a condition that had been experienced by the self; mourning is a response to a condition of the other.[17]

In my understanding, trauma is a failed experience, an event or situation that could not be experienced by the self. It becomes a trauma when the symbolic order does not offer concepts in terms of which the event can be understood. And mourning is not a response to a condition of the other, but to a condition of the self. Mourning is the response to the loss of the other, but this loss happens to the self, it is the self that loses the other. It is with this different notion of trauma and mourning that I will revisit the issue that the Soviet terror made it difficult to comprehend, to remember, and to memorialize.

The amount of camp literature about the Gulag is extensive. Many survivors of the Gulag have written down what happened to them, how they ended up in the Gulag,

16 Etkind, *Warped Mourning* (2013), 11.

17 Etkind, *Warped Mourning* (2013), 14.

18 Oxford Russian Life History Archive, n.d.

how they survived it, and what life was like after they had returned. In this respect the Gulag seems not to be different from the Holocaust: both apocalyptic events have resulted in memoirs and testimonies of those events. The genres used to convey the experiences of the survivors are historical: memoir, autobiography, testimony. Although the number of testimonial texts about the Gulag as well as the Holocaust is extensive, within those texts the irrepresentability of what is, paradoxically, being represented is a returning issue. This is how we must understand Yevgenia Ginzburg's terse statement in her memoirs *Journey into the Whirlwind* quoted as epigraph to this chapter:

> Something like that was not thinkable, something like that could not happen.

Her bewildered assertion is emblematic for how trauma comes about. Events that happen to a subject cannot be understood, grasped, or experienced. As a consequence, the inexperienced events stay with the subject and are re-enacted in unmediated form, as trauma.

Still, there is an important difference between the many memoirs that came out of the Holocaust and those in which the Gulag resulted. As indicated in the *Oxford Russian Life History Archive* the history of the Russian Revolution was strictly controlled by the Party History committee:

> Personal history in the sense of autobiography has a strictly defined role: loyal citizens of the Soviet state were supposed to recite their lives. [...] Life histories were also collected in order to buttress the official aetiology of the Soviet State. [...] In later decades of Soviet history, much testimony relating to experience of the Second World War was also collected.[18]

However, this process of orchestrated collecting of testimony was highly selective. It marginalized testimonies 'that recovered practices, processes and "inner experiences", rather than events. Ordinary Soviet people learned to think of life writing or life narrating in certain constrained contexts.'[19]

In great contrast with the Holocaust, the emotion that is prevalent in memories and post memories of the Gulag is shame, not mourning (*pace* Etkind). But how should we understand this affect of shame? I will first try to understand shame from a psychological perspective before tracking its social ramifications. Shame is not the result of prohibition nor of repression; it is not the product of an internalized intra-psychic structure or mechanism. Instead, shame is the result of an inter-relational structure. It is a disruptive moment in a circuit of identity-constructing and identificatory communication with another person. Shame occurs when an expectation is not met and the communication fails. We can say that the Stalinist executioners of the Gulag did not meet the expectations of those who became prisoners of the Gulag. Communication between fellow communists failed. The Stalinist people in power refused to play their part in the continuation of mutual gazes. The fallen face with eyes down and head averted as main symptom of shame was the result.[20]

Shame is, however, not only produced in failed communication between the Stalinists and the so-called enemies of the people sent by them to the Gulag. The social isolation of the prisoners of the camps repeats itself after they had survived the Gulag and come home. Their children and other relatives are often not able or willing to 'mirror' themselves in the expressions of the first-generation survivors of the Gulag. Being embarrassed by their ordeal, the second generation is not able to play its part in the 'continuation of mutual gazes'. The second generation is not able to give the feedback

19 Oxford Russian Life History Archive, n.d.

20 For more on shame, see Alphen, van (ed.), *Shame! And Masculinity* (2020).

the first generation needs in order to re-construct their identity after survival. The second generation is not able to do so, because they cannot mirror themselves in the gaze of people who were accused of being enemies of the people. So, there is no easy continuation between first and second generation; that relation is undermined and broken up by multiple productions of shame. This relationship between first and second generation is radically affected by shame. This is almost the complete opposite of the relationship between first- and second-generation survivors of the Holocaust. Although the second generation experiences an absolute gap between their world and the (pre) Holocaust world of their parents, the desire to bridge that gap compels a strong identification with the parents, which succeeds in bridging that gap. In the case of the Gulag, shame on the side of second generation as well as first generation makes such identification and the bridged gap as a result, impossible. If the most important affect that determines the dynamic between first and second generations is shame instead of mourning, the notion of post memory cannot easily be used in order to assess that dynamic.

The Generation After, and Discontinuity

How does this assessment of the dynamic between first- and second-generation Holocaust survivors compare to the legacies of Stalinism and the dynamics between first- and second-generation survivors of the Gulag? My expertise in Russian literature and culture is limited, but still, the following is the impression I have. The literature of the first generation, the so-called camp literature, seems vast. And like the literature of the first-generation Holocaust literature, the majority of this literature is testimonial. Camp literature consists mainly of memoirs and autobiography. The expressions of the second generation are, however, rather different from the expressions of the Holocaust second generation. They are different because the affects that determine the second and later generations' relation to the past of the first generations are different and highly ambivalent. The affects that are most prominent are not mourning but suspicion, shame and nostalgia, and sometimes all three occur at the same time. Later generations are literally not able to face the past of the earlier generation, to look them into their eyes. Whereas shame and suspicion define the way the generation directly after the first one relates to the first generation, later generations are less defined by shame than by nostalgia to the period that victimized the first generation. Different as shame and nostalgia may be, they have in common that both affects avoid a direct 'facing' of the first generation.

But these affects are not expressed directly, by means of testimonial genres. They are often expressed by genres that belong to the fantastic, where ghosts and zombies figure as the indirect expressions of how later generations look back with anxiety as well as desire to the past of earlier generations still part of the Stalinist area. The past is not directly identified in the traumatic past of first-generation survivors, but returns indirectly in the shape of ghosts and zombies.

An example of a different order is Andrey Zvyagintsev's film *The Return*.[21] Through the rather simple narrative of two sons and the return of their father, this film represents allegorically the intergenerational dynamic between the first-generation survivors and executioners of the Gulag, and the second generation of their children, taken as a group or literally as their real children. The relation to Stalinism and the Gulag is never made explicit. On the level of the plot, of a crisis within a family. There are no connections established to

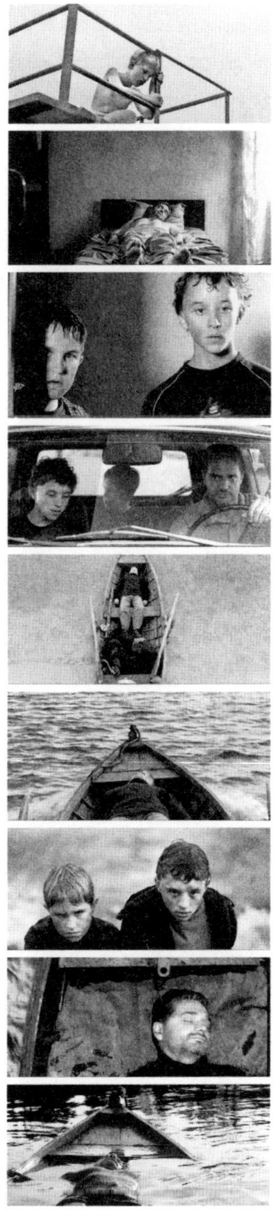

21 Andrey Zvyagintsev, *The Return* (2003), film stills.

22 Abraham, 'Andrei Zvyagenitsev's "Vozvrashcheniye" (The Return)' (2006), n.p.

this past of Russia. It is only on an allegorical level that this family narrative can be read as a narrative about the dynamic between generations after the Gulag.

This film has been praised for the many different levels on which it can be read. According to the most literal reading it is a chronicle of two children who, with the help of a log-book, record the events of a trip with their father who has returned after an absence of twelve years. This trip functions then as their transformation from childhood to manhood; in other words, as a rite de passage. At yet another level the film is read in religious terms. The father is then a kind of Christ coming to the world to help the world. The problem of such religious interpretations is that they only read isolated scenes or motifs but are not able to provide an encompassing reading of the film as a whole.

More interestingly, the film has also been read politically. The father figure represents then the strong Communist Soviet Union and the death of that state.

> The two sons can be interpreted as one representing the section that accepted subjugation by the state and the other that rebelled against the state and demanded free-dom and democracy. Today both kinds of former-USSR citizens yearn for the 'FATHERland' of the past for different reasons.[22]

I will elaborate this political reading by probing the psycho-logical dynamic between father and sons. Through such a reading of the psychological ramifications of a political read-ing, the dynamic between the first and second generation after Stalinism and the Gulag can be understood more clearly.

The film begins with an underwater scene. The wreck of an old wooden boat can be recognized on the bottom of the sea. In the next scene we see young boys jumping from a high structure into the sea. We assume that the boys jump into the water that we already saw from below. At the very end of the film we have to reconsider this reading. It is at the end that the dead father sinks to the bottom of the sea with the leaking boat on which he had been laid down by his two sons. This has significant implications. The film is not playing in an abstract, unidentified present tense; the film that follows the first under water scene is a long flashback. It is all set in a time long past.

In the beginning of the film two brothers, Andrej (the oldest) and Ivan, come home after they have been playing with some other boys. The mother says: 'Father is sleeping.' 'Who?', they ask. 'Father. Go and look for a second', responds the mother. The two boys are clearly flabbergasted, because it turns out that the father has returned after twelve years of absence. They peek into the bedroom and Ivan, the youngest, immediately leaves and goes looking for on old book with mythological/religious prints in which an old photograph of the whole family is hidden: the mother, the father, the two sons; but many years younger. Ivan cannot accept that this man is his father. He needs proof, because he mistrusts this man who has returned after such a long time. One of the major reasons for this suspicion is that nobody is able or willing to specify from what or where the father has returned. This suspicion of the youngest son is made explicit in the conversation the two boys have in bed later that evening.

> ANDREJ: Have you seen him. What a bear! He certainly practices a fight sport. Certainly.
> IVAN: But where does he come from?
> ANDREJ: Just like that, he has returned. Are you not happy?

IVAN: Oh yes. But Mama once said that he was a pilot. But he does not look like a pilot.
ANDREJ: Ah, he is on vacation, then he does not have to wear a uniform.

Ivan is not yet convinced. His answer is: 'Maybe'. In contrast with his older brother, Ivan is not able to identify with this man who claims to be his father. In all respects he keeps him at a distance. This becomes very outspoken the next day, after the three of them have left by car for a two-days fishing trip. Ivan, who sits in the back of the car, is addressed by his father by his name:

FATHER: Ivan?
IVAN: What?
FATHER: What, Papa.
IVAN: What?
FATHER: Why don't you say: What, Papa?
IVAN: What, Papa?
FATHER: Good, much better so. What is wrong? Are you ashamed to call your father, father?
IVAN: No.
FATHER: Do not lie.
IVAN: I do not lie.
FATHER: Call me then father, like any son does. Understood?
IVAN: Okay, Papa.
FATHER: Very good, my little son.

Although Ivan finally speaks with two words and addresses his father with the required word 'father', in the rest of the film he again refuses to do so. During this conversation between father and son, the father watches his son via the rear-view mirror, and vice versa. There is no direct exchange of looks. This scene makes clear that it is not only suspicion that makes it impossible for Ivan to address his father as father. Whereas the father uses all the time diminutives like little son, or little one, to express his affection towards his youngest son, Ivan is not able to return these signs of affection because he feels shame for his father. He refrains from facing his father directly; he looks away or looks at him via the rear-view mirror.

Although the suspicion and shame of Ivan does not seem to be shared by his brother Andrej, this oldest son also does not seem to be impressed by the occasionally very authoritarian behaviour of his father. When he is forced to leave the car in order to look for a place where they can have lunch, he stays away for three hours. Although he found a restaurant very quickly, he just wanted to look around. He is punished verbally for it by his father. Although he accepts the man as his father, he does not seem to have much respect for his authority. When the father has caught a young man, who had stolen his wallet, Andrej refuses to take revenge on this young man when the father demands him to do so. The authoritarian, homosocial system of competition, punishment and revenge is wasted on both sons.

The distance between the father and his two sons is most acutely felt by the youngest. He creates distance not only through his suspicion and shame, but also through heavy irony. When the father asks his sons to take the bus back home, because he has suddenly something else to do, Ivan is seriously resentful:

> IVAN: But you had promised us a trip!
> FATHER: Later.
> IVAN: Yes. Over twelve years.
> FATHER: What did you say?

IVAN: I said that you will take us to the waterfall another time: Over twelve years. Did I say something wrong? (he walks away from his father, not waiting for an answer)

After the two brothers have settled in the bus to take them home, the father reconsiders his plans and he takes them to a small deserted island before the coast. That night the two brothers have the following conversation after they had dinner with their father. During that dinner the father refuses to eat the fish the sons had caught with the argument that once, somewhere far away from here, he had eaten too much of it.

IVAN: What did he say about eating fish? Where can anything like that happen?
ANDREJ: I don't know. Perhaps high in the north.
IVAN: Did you notice that he did not say anything anymore when you asked him about it. Why would that be?
ANDREJ: God may know. Perhaps he wants to forget.
IVAN: But why?
ANDREJ: Why, Why! You do not know another song?
IVAN: What do I know? He is just lying!
ANDREJ: That is not true. How do you know where he has passed his time?
IVAN: Why are you laying it thick with him?
ANDREJ: Who is laying it thick?
IVAN: You are! Papa this, Papa that! As if he is the only one! You believe any of his words. But do you know who he is? Perhaps he is a gangster! It could well be that later somewhere in the woods he will cut our throats.
[...]
ANDREJ: You are an idiot, little one.
IVAN: Wait until he pulls his knife. You do not get it. We are here completely alone with him. Why would he

be our father? Idiot!
ANDREJ: Because that is what Mama has said. He is father. Okay?

This time Ivan, the little one, expresses his suspicion, mingled with shame and anger, to his older brother. The next day he has a confrontation with his father after the father has first left him in the middle of nowhere when Ivan complains about the fact that they have left an excellent fishing spot. When the father returns to pick him up after it has started to rain, the father begins the conversation with a remark filled with irony:

FATHER: Did they bite? (with irony) Put dry clothes on (with affection)
IVAN: Why have you come? (he begins to cry) Why? Why did you take us with you? Why is it that you care for us? It all went Okay without you! With Mama and Grandmother! Why have you come? Why did you take us with you? Do you really care for us? Give me an answer!
FATHER: Mother asked me so.
IVAN: Yes! Mama has asked you to do it! But you! You yourself?
FATHER: I also wanted it.
IVAN: Why? To bully us!
FATHER: Put dry clothes on. (with affection)

The past of the father is never disclosed. At a certain moment the father leaves the two boys on their own in order to look for something on the deserted island. In a ruined house he excavates an old chest. After opening the chest, there turns out to be a smaller box in it. He does not open this box but takes it with him and hides it in the boat. After he has died by falling from the watchtower, his two sons take his body to the boat to bring it home. After arrival at the main land, the boat, with father and his secret box, drives away and sinks to the bottom of the sea. The little box symbolizes the unknown past of the father. But the box is never opened and the two sons even do not know of its existence. The father takes it with him to the bottom of the sea.

At significant moments in the film it is suggested that Ivan suffers from fear of failure. In the beginning, just after the opening scene, he does not dare to jump of the elevated structure into the sea. Later, on the deserted island, he has to clean the plates in the sea but he lets his father's plate sink in the sea. When he tells his father, he proposes Ivan to teach him to make a new one of birch wood. Ivan's answer is: 'I won't succeed'. After the father's death, son Andrej adopts the authority of the father and orders his younger brother to pull the father to the beach. Ivan's answer is again: 'I won't succeed!'

The ultimate scene in the film is when, after another outburst, Ivan runs away to the watchtower. Earlier he did not dare to climb the watchtower because of vertigo. But now he climbs it, overcoming his vertigo. At the top, out of reach of his father after he has closed the hatch, it looks as if he is going to jump from the tower. Is he trying a second time to jump from a tower because he failed to do that at the beginning of the film with the other boys? Or is he trying to commit suicide? Or the one through the other? Is his death then at the same time his overcoming of his fear of failure? This ambiguity cannot be resolved, but it is suggested that his fear of failure is the result of not having a convincing father as a role model. The moment the father returns, Ivan refuses him as father, but nevertheless the return seems to have helped him to overcome his fear of failure. He would have jumped if the father would not have fallen from the tower and died.

Let's now come to a conclusion. With the examples of the novel *Justification* by Dmitry Bykov and Andrey Zvyagintsev's film *The Return,* I have tried to show how the dynamic between first- and second-generation survivors of the Gulag differs radically from the kind of dynamic at stake between survivors of the Holocaust and the generations after them. This dynamic is not determined by mourning and by identification of later generations with the first generation. The later generations relate rather with shame and suspicion to the first generation, and generations after the second one even look back with nostalgia to the Soviet Empire of which their earlier generations were the victims. This dynamic is much more complex than the generational dynamic after the Holocaust. It expresses itself indirectly, not through 'direct' historical genres like testimony or memoirs, but more indirectly through imaginative genres in which ghosts or zombies figure as the return of a past that has not been worked through. Although this conclusion is based on close-readings of a novel and a feature film, it is fully supported by Svetlana Alexievich's oral history *Second Hand Time: The Last of the Soviets.*[23]

23 Alexievich, *Second Hand Time* (2016).

Part 2

Transmissions of Affect

Explosions of Information, Implosions of Meaning

The Release of Affects

Talking about changes in the art world in the early 1990s, Cuban-American artist Félix González-Torres noticed that there has been a shift away from the 'sloganeering' art that appropriated the media, exemplified by the work of Barbara Kruger, toward a more personal voice. According to González-Torres a more personal voice is necessary because the recent historical situation requires new modes of contestation. His description of an artwork by American artist Roni Horn[1] is exemplary for this new kind of art and for the way it relates to the viewer:

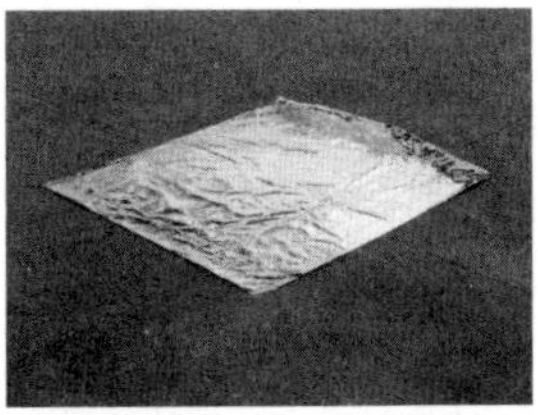

1 Roni Horn, *The Gold Field* (1980–1982), sculpture, 124.5 × 152.4 × 0.002 cm.

> The *Gold Field*. How can I deal with the *Gold Field*? I don't quite know. But the *Gold Field* was there. Ross and I entered the Museum of Contemporary Art, and without knowing the work of Roni Horn we were blown away by the heroic, gentle and horizontal presence of this gift. There it was, in a white room, all by itself, it didn't need company, it didn't need anything. Sitting on the floor, ever so lightly. A new landscape, a possible horizon, a place of rest and absolute beauty. Waiting for the

2 González-Torres, in Ault (ed.), *Félix González-Torres* (2006), 150.

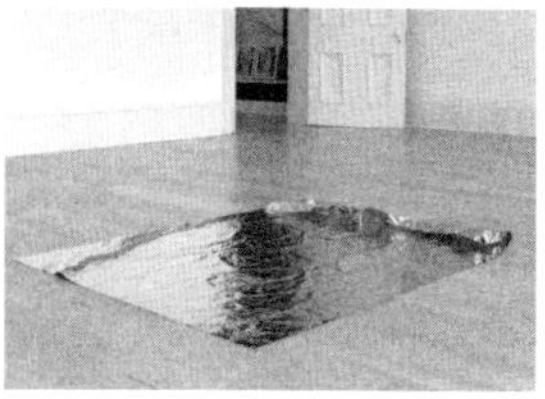

3 Roni Horn, *The Gold Field* (1980–1982), sculpture, 124.5 × 152.4 × 0.002 cm.

4 The expression 'shocked to thought' refers to the title of a book on expression and affect in the work of Deleuze and Guattari, in Massumi (ed.), *A Shock to Thought* (2002a).

5 Nickas, in Ault (ed.), *Félix González-Torres* (2006), 44.

> right viewer willing and needing to be moved to a place of the imagination. This piece is nothing more than a thin layer of gold. It is everything a good poem by Wallace Stevens is: precise with no baggage, nothing extra. A poem that feels secure and dares to unravel itself, to become naked, to be enjoyed in a tactile manner, but beyond that, in an intellectual way too. Ross and I were lifted. That gesture was all we needed to rest, to think about the possibility of change. This showed the innate ability of an artist proposing to make this place a better place. How truly revolutionary.... A place to dream, to regain energy, to dare. Ross and I always talked about this work, how much it affected us.[2]

González-Torres' description of the *Gold Field*[3] (which dates from 1980–1981) neither deals with signification, the meaning of the work, nor does it articulate the work within a discursive framework. What it describes, instead, is how this artwork affects him, the viewer. He and his partner enjoyed it initially in a tactile manner. It lifted them. Next, it made them think about the possibility of change, which is why they call it 'truly revolutionary'. 'Change' and 'revolution', however, were not the only thoughts they were stimulated to have. Change and revolution also characterize their response to the artwork. They are affected by it in such a way that they are 'shocked to thought'.[4]

In another text González-Torres dwells on the recent sociohistorical situation, which necessitated a 'more personal voice' for works of art. Characterizing this situation tersely, he writes that '[r]ight now we have an explosion of information, but an implosion of meaning.'[5] Here he refers to the situation in which people are bombarded by information that concerns them personally, but strangely, this information does not transform into meaning in their daily lives. One of his examples is the lack of health care in the United States. People are informed about this, they know it, but, according to González-Torres, it does not mean much. For example, it does not lead to political positioning, nor does it lead to a specific voting behaviour.

In the 1970s and 1980s increasing the accessibility of information and by doing so intensifying the production of meaning were important cultural pursuits and political goals. Information was seen as a precondition for meaning production.[6] But if we agree with Félix González-Torres' assessment of the 1990s, this cultural and political project has failed because it has turned against itself. The explosion of information has not led to more meaning and better understanding, but rather to an implosion of meaning as such. He suggests that this implosion of meaning has heightened the sensitivity for affect and its transmission. Later in this chapter I will elaborate on why the mentioned explosions and implosions have this kind of consequence.

Cultural analyst and psychoanalyst Teresa Brennan also notices an increase of affects at the end of the twentieth century. Her explanation and historical understanding of this increase is, however, rather different from that of González-Torres. She argues that, whereas the idea of the transmission of affect was well accepted until the seventeenth century, it faded away after that century because of the rise of individualism since the Enlightenment. Without making a clear distinction between affects and emotions, she assesses that when the notion of the individual gained strength, 'it was assumed more and more that emotions and energies are naturally contained, going no further than the skin.'[7] Individualism has made it unthinkable that our emotions are not altogether our own, that some of our emotions have been transmitted to us

6 Of course, the dissemination of information as a precondition for meaning production is not just an outdated ambition that is no longer relevant for present concerns. Especially in countries that are in transition to democracy, lots of funding still goes into increasing the amount of information to its population via media initiatives. This is seen as fostering democracy. But at the same time the limits of this ambition are also recognized because the production of meaning has not been necessarily the result of the increase of information.

7 Brennan, *The Transmission of Affect* (2004), 2.

8 Massumi, 'Everyone You Want to Be' (1993), 3–37.

9 Brennan, *The Transmission of Affect* (2004), 15.

and that they come from an external source. In his essay on 'fear' Brian Massumi also argues that any mode of cultural, political, or social analysis has a problem with understanding affective mechanisms to the extent that it continues to treat the self as a bounded space, even if that boundary is conceived as porous.[8] The belief that emotions are our own and come from within could be sustained because unwanted affects can always be projected onto somebody else. Brennan distinguishes two different ways of processing transmitted affects. The first is to resist the affect and to project it outward without consciously acknowledging that we are doing so. The second one she calls 'discernment' and consists of consciously examining the affect. What has changed in the course of the 1990s is that the unconscious projection of unwanted affects on others is not as easy anymore as it was in the past: Have boundaries come to matter because self-definition by projection is less available than it was during the last few sexist and colonial centuries— there are now too few willing receptacles—or because of an accumulation of environmental inflicted affects? Either way, boundaries may matter now because there is too much affective stuff to dispose of, too much that is directed away from the self with no place to go.[9]

This concern with boundaries and the increasing failure to maintain these boundaries by means of projection has led in the 1990s to the fact that, for example, depression was the most rapidly growing disorder in Europe and the United States. According to Brennan this increase is not coincidental but is instead historically produced, or what she calls 'environmentally inflicted'. Boundaries, like identities, were not an issue when the transmission of affect had more currency historically. Boundaries especially become an issue in periods when the transmission of affect is denied. In the 1990s boundaries and identities have become contested issues, not only as the result of political and intellectual debates but also because boundaries and identities are in themselves more and more experienced as uncertain and porous. This contested status brought with it the results that transmissions of affects increased and that those affects have to be dealt with in one way or another, productively or unproductively (depression). Brennan's assessment of the 1990s and of the increasing role of affects in those decades focuses on contested identities and the difficulty of drawing boundaries and constructing or maintaining identities. Identity politics as a result of feminism and of global, postcolonial changes are seen as the defining historical actors. González-Torres' assessment of the same decade differs in the sense that for him it is especially the growing role of media and the explosive growth of the distribution of information that is responsible for fundamental changes in the 1990s.[10]

More than forty years ago Susan Sontag, in her programmatic essay 'Against Interpretation', pleaded passionately for more serious attention to what I will call the affective operations of art and literature. She declared that the prevalent idea that a work of art is its content, or that a work of art says something, is 'today mainly a hindrance, a nuisance, a subtle or not so subtle philistinism'.[11] According to Sontag the transformation of texts or works of art into meanings is a revenge of the intellect upon the world. 'To interpret is to impoverish, to deplete the world—in order to set up a shadow world of "meanings".'[12] To counter this tendency she pleads for a more immediate experience of the object or text itself. What is important now is to recover our senses. We must learn to see more, to hear more, to feel more. And she ends her essay with the famous words that 'in place of a hermeneutics of art we need an erotics of art'.[13]

10 Also in the field of economics and political economy, the increasing significance of affect in the 1990s has been argued. The claim is that the process of modernization is over and that the global economy is today undergoing a process of postmodernization toward an informational economy. In this informational economy the role of 'affective labour' is crucial. It is directly productive of capital but also functions at the very pinnacle of the hierarchy of labouring forms. In the informational economy production has become communicative, affective, deinstrumentalized, and elevated to the level of human relations—but at a level of human relations entirely dominated by and internal to capital. Although affective labour is immaterial, it is now directly productive of capital, and it has been generalized through wide sectors of the economy. As a component of immaterial labour, affective labour has achieved a dominant position of the highest value in the contemporary informational economy. See Hardt, 'Affective Labor' (1999).

11 Sontag, 'Against Interpretation' (1967), 5.

12 Sontag, 'Against Interpretation' (1967), 7.

13 Sontag, 'Against Interpretation' (1967), 15.

14 Sontag, 'Against Interpretation' (1967), 13.

What is remarkable about her essay is that she too motivates her plea for an erotics of art by a historical urgency. Like González-Torres and Brennan, Sontag claims that a fundamental historical change necessitates other artistic practices and processing of them. Although she is talking about the 1960s and not about the 1990s, her assessment of those years necessitates this eroticism. Hermeneutics is not bad in itself, but it has become a harmful, or better yet powerless, mode of reading at this particular historical moment:

> Interpretation takes the sensory experience of the work of art for granted, and proceeds from there. This cannot be taken for granted, now. Think of the sheer multiplication of works of art available to every one of us, superadded to the conflicting tastes and odors and sights of the urban environment that bombard our sense. Ours is a culture based on excess, on overproduction; this result is a steady loss of sharpness in our sensory experience. All the conditions of modern life—its material plenitude, its sheer crowdedness—conjoin to dull our sensory faculties.[14]

Sontag's proposal for more serious attention to the affective operations of art and literature is motivated by another historical condition than the one discussed so far. The 1960s are not the same as the 1990s. But what these decades have in common is radical changes in how subjects relate to their social environment. Whereas its explosion of commodity culture can define the 1960s, an increasing explosion of information culture can characterize the 1990s. In both periods the subject is exposed to an abundance, an abundance that is ultimately sensorial and that brings with it the need for an increased sensitivity for affects.

Another difference is that in Sontag's account the diagnosis does not consist of an implosion of meaning but of a loss of sharpness in our sensory experience. The need for an increased sensitivity of affects is motivated by the fact that our sensory faculties are dulled by the explosion of commodity culture. In her argument against interpretation, an implosion of meaning could, one could argue, even be a solution for realizing this increased sensitivity. Whereas in the 1960s Sontag contests meaning and interpretation, in the 1990s meaning is no longer contested because, according to González-Torres, an implosion of it has taken place.

Sontag thinks that the development of another mode of reading and looking will be able to bring our sensory faculties to life again. What is needed is another critical attitude. But as I already pointed out at the beginning of this chapter, according to Félix González-Torres it is not only a different engagement with texts and art objects that the changing historical conditions ask for, but also different modes of artistic and cultural contestation. I would like to argue that both are needed and that a more sensorial or affective response to artworks is also, at least partly, conditioned by characteristics of artworks and texts.

Understanding Affect: Why?

The diagnoses of culture since the 1990s by Félix González-Torres and Teresa Brennan, different as they are, both imply the urgency to understand better what affect is and how it works. It is clear that several disciplines in the humanities are trying to do precisely that. But what often happens is that when a concept or term becomes fashionable, it loses its meaning. The term is used more and more without any critical ramifications. It is often used in such a way that it means something general like 'personal' or 'subjective'. But, as I will

15 Massumi, in Patton (ed.), *Deleuze* (1996), 220.

argue, affect is the opposite of personal: it is social.

The cultural and social effect of these emerging forms is itself often a function of their capacity to generate and transmit affect or to engage a viewer in a particular, transformative way. Thus the politics of art and literature since the 1990s can no longer be understood simply in terms of its programmatic meaning or message. The new modes of contestation require an 'affective approach' in order to understand how recent culturally and politically engaged work 'works'. The implosion of meaning, which González-Torres notices in the larger sociopolitical domain, is, I contend, also at stake in the artistic and literary domain. But this does not imply that recent art and literature have lost cultural and political impact. Their impact is, instead, established by means of powerful transactions of affect.

But in general, one may claim that much could be gained by thinking through the affective operations of art in cultural theory. As Massumi has claimed, our cultural-theoretical-political vocabulary offers few possibilities to deal with affect. Our entire vocabulary has derived from theories of signification. These theories and approaches

> are incomplete if they operate only on the semantic or semiotic level, however that level is defined (linguistically, logically, narratologically, ideologically, or all of these in combination) as a symbolic. What they lose, precisely, is the expression event—in favor of structure.[15]

In her book on trauma and art, Jill Bennett argues something similar. Not all art is representational, and even if art is representational many aspects of that art are not, and operate instead on the basis of nonrepresentational strategies. Ultimately art is ill served by a theoretical framework 'that privileges meaning (i.e., the object of representation, outside art) over form (the inherent qualities or modus operandi of art)'.[16]

This plea for more attention to the affective operations of art does not at all imply, however, a privileging of a more formalistic approach to art. On the contrary, as already pointed out in the example of González-Torres responding to the *Gold Field*, the transmission of affect 'shocks him to thought'. This expression, 'shock to thought', is Deleuzian, and Deleuze has another expression that indicates this intimate relationship between affect and thought, namely 'the encountered sign'. He introduced the term in his book *Proust and Signs*. The encountered sign is a sign that is felt rather than recognized, or perceived through cognition, or through familiarity with the 'code'. But the sensation of the encountered sign is not an end in itself. For Deleuze this sensation is a catalyst for critical inquiry or thought. For him an affect is a more effective trigger for profound thought than rational inquiry because of the way in which it grasps us, forcing us to engage involuntarily: 'More important than thought there is "what leads to thought"... impressions which force us to look, encounters which force us to interpret, expressions which force us to think'.[17]

Deleuze quotes Proust himself to illustrate the nature of the encountered sign:

> The truths which intelligence grasps directly in the open light of day have something less profound, less *necessary* about them than those which life has communicated to us *in spite of ourselves* in an impression, a material impression because it has reached us through our senses.[18]

As Bennett explains, in this Proustian and Deleuzian view, art and literature are seen as the embodiment of sensation that

16 Bennett, *Empathic Vision* (2005), 4.

17 Deleuze, *Proust and Signs* (1964), 161.

18 Deleuze, *Proust and Signs* (1964), 161.

19 Bennett, *Empathic Vision* (2005), 8.

20 Bennett, *Empathic Vision* (2005), 37.

21 Deleuze, *Proust and Signs* (1964), 160 (emphasis in original).

22 Deleuze, *Proust and Signs* (1964), 162.

stimulates thought.[19] Art does not illustrate or embody a proposition, but it produces sensations or affects that stimulate thought. It is the affective encounter through which thought proceeds and moves toward deeper truth. By means of this affective view of art and literature Deleuze deconstructs the conventional opposition between philosophy and art, or between thought and sensation. For him both are modes of thinking. But whereas philosophers think in concepts, artists think by means of sensation.

> Sensation is generated through the artist's engagement with the medium, through colour and line in the case of the painter, so that it is not the residue of self-expression, or a property of some prior self, but emerges in the present, as it attaches to figures in the image.[20]

As modes of thinking, art and literature vie with philosophy. Deleuze seems to agree with Proust's critique of philosophy. The truths formulated by or within a philosophical discourse remain arbitrary and abstract, so long as they are based on the goodwill of thinking. It is based on the conventional. Philosophy is

> ignorant of the dark regions in which are elaborated the effective forces which act on thought, the determinations which *force* us to think.... Minds communicate to each other only the conventional; the mind engenders only the possible. The truths of philosophy are lacking in necessity, and the mark of necessity.[21]

Deleuze quotes Proust again to explain the shortcomings of philosophy: 'The ideas formed by pure intelligence have only a logical truth, a possible truth, their choice is arbitrary.'[22] In his book on the painter Francis Bacon, Deleuze explains how sensations are the means of the artist's way of thinking:

> Sensation is what is being painted; what is being painted on the canvas is the body. Not insofar as it is represented as an object, but insofar as it is experienced as sustaining this sensation.[23]

It is this sustaining of sensation that thrusts viewers into thinking and into an encountered or embodied mode of critical inquiry. The thought activated by the encountered, sensuous sign is truly critical and creative (instead of conventional or arbitrary) for, Deleuze argues,

> it does us violence: it mobilizes the memory, it sets the soul in motion; but the soul in its turn excites thought, transmits to it the constraint of the sensibility, forces it to conceive essence, as the only thing which must be conceived.[24]

What Is Affect and How Does It Operate?

In order to understand better the affective operations of art and literature, I will first take a momentary step backward and try to assess more thoroughly what affect is, how it works, and how it relates to notions with which it is so often confused, like feeling and emotion. And where do affects originate, just in human beings or also in objects, like artworks or texts?[25]

The term 'affect' comes from the Latin *affectus*, which means passion or emotion. Affects have an energetic dimension; they are, in Deleuze's words, 'intensities'. According to Deleuze affect is an intensity embodied in autonomic reactions on the surface of the body as it interacts with other entities. It precedes its expression in words and operates independently. According to psychologist Silvan S. Tomkins, one

23 Deleuze, quoted in Bennett, *Empathic Vision* (2005), 37.

24 Deleuze, *Proust and Signs* (1964), 166.

25 For this discussion I rely on the work of Silvan S. Tomkins, Brennan, *The Transmission of Affect* (2004), and Bennett, *Empathic Vision* (2005).

26 Tomkins & Demos (eds.), *Exploring Affect* (1995), 355–356.

27 Brennan, *The Transmission of Affect* (2004), 3.

28 Brennan, *The Transmission of Affect* (2004), 5.

of the most important theoreticians of affect, affect extends beyond individuals, and it does not pursue the same goals as either drives or cognitive systems. Yet affect is the essential amplifier of other drives 'because without its amplification nothing else matters and with its amplification anything else can matter.'[26]

The transmission of such 'intensities' has a physiological impact. Affects can arise within a person but they also come from without. They can be transmitted by the presence of another person, but also by an artwork, or a (literary) text. They come from an interaction with objects, an environment, or other people. Because of its origin in interaction one can say that the transmission of affect is social in origin, but biological and physical in effect.[27] The experience of affect is usually seen as a kind of judgment. The person who receives the affect has to do something with it. It will be projected outward or it will be introjected. The projection or introjection of a judgment is the moment when the transmission takes place. As argued before, the notion of affect has had such an uncomfortable place in Western, seventeenth-century Enlightenment culture because the Enlightenment's individualism is peculiarly resistant to the idea that our affects are not altogether our own. Affects are not necessarily our own because they may have been transmitted by somebody else or by an object or environment. We are then 'possessed' by emotions that have their origin elsewhere or in somebody else.

Affects are judgments or evaluations in the sense that they are the physiological shifts accompanying a judgment (or evaluation). The physiological shift takes place as a result of the evaluative, positive or negative, orientation toward an object or other person.[28] This notion of affect as physiological shift implies that affects are not the same as feelings. Feelings include something more than a physiological shift or sensory stimulation. They suppose a unified interpretation of that shift or stimulation. For that reason Brennan defines feelings as 'sensations that have found the right match in words'.[29] Similarly, Jill Bennett defines feeling as 'the moment of awareness of affect through which the self is experienced—experienced as deformation of itself.'[30] This distinction between affects and feelings implies that affects as such have no particular content or meaning. In themselves they are just energetic intensities.

There are other psychological notions that are often conflated with affect: emotion, for instance. Yet affects and emotions follow a different logic and pertain to different orders. Emotions are more or less synonymous with feeling although in some theories emotions consist of a more complex organization of affect than feeling. In the words of Massumi (who, in the wake of Deleuze, uses intensity as exchangeable with affect),

> [a]n emotion is a subjective content, the socio-linguistic fixing of the quality of an experience which is from that point onward defined as personal. Emotion is qualified intensity, the conventional, consensual point of insertion of intensity into semantically and semiotically formed progressions, into narrativizable action-reaction circuits, into function and meaning. It is intensity owned and recognized.[31]

In the affect theory of Silvan S. Tomkins, the crucial notion is not 'intensity' but the more scientific sounding notion of 'density of neural firing'. He distinguishes a diverse range of basic affects on the basis of three variants of density of neural firing:

29 Brennan, *The Transmission of Affect* (2004), 5.

30 Bennett, in Van Alphen et al. (eds.), *The Rhetoric of Sincerity* (2009).

31 Massumi, in Patton (ed.), *Deleuze* (1996).

32 Tomkins & Demos, *Exploring Affect* (1995), 317.

> I would account for the difference in affect activation by three variants of a single principle—the density of neural firing. By density I mean the frequency of neural firing per unit of time. My theory posits three discrete classes of activators of affect, each of which further amplifies the sources which activate them. These are stimulation increase, stimulation level, and stimulation decrease.
>
> Thus any stimulus with a relatively sudden onset and a steep increase in the rate of neural firing will innately activate a startle response.... [I]f the rate of neural firing increases less rapidly, fear is activated, and if still less rapidly, then interest is innately activated. In contrast, any sustained increase in the level of neural firing, as with a continued loud noise, would innately activate the anger response. Finally, any sudden decrease in stimulation that reduced the rate of neural firing, as in the sudden redaction of excessive noise, would innately activate the rewarding smile of enjoyment.[32]

What the Deleuzian affect theorists have in common with Tomkins is a notion of affect in terms of an energetic 'stream', although they call it 'intensity' and Tomkins calls it 'neural firing'. A difference is, however, that in the Deleuzian notion affect as such has no content or meaning, although it produces feelings, emotions, thoughts. Tomkins, in contrast, develops a taxonomy of affects. Depending on density and temporal length of the neural firing, it results in, for example, startle, fear, interest, anger, distress, shame.

This brings us back to the issue of meaning in relation to affect. When the person to whom the affect is transmitted does not 'project' the affect outward, but 'discerns' it, at that moment the affect is given content. The affect then feels like depression, anger, or anxiety. But the way a transmitted affect is signified differs from person to person. The same affect can be given a completely different content by another person. Although affects are social, that is, they are the result of an interactive process from without, the linguistic or visual contents or thoughts attached to that affect belong to the person to whom the affect is transmitted.

Since the same affect can evoke very different feelings or thoughts in different people, the thoughts, feelings, or images evoked by affects are not necessarily tied to the affects they appear to evoke. A transmission of affect between two persons can result in the two people becoming alike; for example, someone's depression is transmitted to someone else who will then feel depressed as a result. This form of transmission is usually called *entrainment,*[33] or 'affective resonance' in Tomkins' work. But it can also happen that as a result of such a transmission people take up opposing or different positions in relation to a common affective thread. This is the case when, for example, somebody's depression gives rise to feelings of anger in the person to whom the affect was transmitted, or when somebody's hyperactivity makes another person feel depressed.

These examples of transmitted affects all concern transmissions between human subjects. Although these transmissions also imply that our emotions are not necessarily our own, this is even more difficult to acknowledge when the transmitting agent is not a human subject, but a text, a film, or a painting. I am not referring now to media that especially function as intermediary of the transmission of affect that migrates from body to body. It is obvious that especially film and television have this intermediary role of bodily transmission. For the moment I am now more interested in objects that are not limited to the role of intermediary, but that are,

33 Brennan, *The Transmission of Affect* (2004), 9.

34 Brennan, *The Transmission of Affect* (2004), 93.

35 To acknowledge matter and objects as possibly active does not, however, imply an animist worldview. The agency that is assigned to matter and objects as a result of affective transmissions is ultimately relational. The intensity of affect arises between an object, let's say an artwork, and a viewer. Animism, however, is not relational: it attributes the existence of souls or spiritual beings to natural objects.

for instance, abstract, like the Roni Horn's *The Gold Field*, which affected González-Torrez in such a significant way. In our current time it has become difficult to see such objects as active agents because humanism has led to the idea that everything outside human subjectivity is passive, unconscious, and material.

> [S]ubjective activity takes the definition of itself as the center of all definition and defines all 'activity' as having its own character. It labels 'passive' everything that is not active in its own way and which it is able to *bend its will*, passive if it does not assert itself against the subject. The objects making up the environment are seen as passive because they do not carry out intentions of their own. To be active is to carry out an individual intention.... The passive/active dichotomy, as consciousness understands it, is thus a product of the sense of self that divides itself from the rest of the world on the grounds of its difference. Its understanding of activity is synonymous with the idea of individual intentionality.[34]

Yet the so-called passivity of objects and of matter does not lie in a lack of action, but in a lack of free will or intentional agency. Active matter is passive in that it is not individual. But if we reject individual intentionality as the criterion for activity (that is, if we recognize the ideological nature of that criterion), then there is no reason not to acknowledge matter and objects as possibly active.[35] The transmission of affects by texts, films, or paintings is then no longer an imprecise, metaphorical way of speaking of our admiration for, or dislike of, these cultural objects. On the contrary, it is an adequate way of describing what cultural objects can do to us, and of how they are active agents in the cultural and social world. It is precisely because of the activity of matter and objects that literature and art can be affective, and that we can speak of the affective operations of art.

Affect and the Image

The explosion of information, the implosion of meaning, and the release of affectivity happen most of all through the dissemination of images. Although modern media such as film and television and new media such as the Internet and cell phones are not exclusively visual, it is their visuality that usually dominates our senses most. In the remainder of this chapter I will address the affectivity of the image and the increase of that affectivity since the 1990s. The visual medium that will be my example is that of the webcam, the small camera, which sends images to a computer connected to the Internet. After this new medium was introduced in the mid-1990s, it has become a standard apparatus in many studios, households, and bedrooms.

When I take the webcam as exemplary for fundamental changes in the role of affectivity of the image, I do not want to suggest that this medium has any essential function or specificity. Its medium specificity is only partly defined by its technical features and possibilities. It is also determined by how it is used, that is, by historical and cultural practices.[36] And, as I will argue, it is especially the ways webcams are used that are responsible for new, intense transmissions of affect. New media uses and practices usually cause changes in the media landscape at large. A new medial practice can cause shifts in the functions and practices of other media. For example, the introduction of photography into the media landscape of the mid-nineteenth century has deprived painting of, or perhaps we should say liberated it from, some of its

36 For a discussion of medium specificity, see Krauss, 'A Voyage on the North Sea' (1999).

functions. The same can be said of the webcam. The webcam has fulfilled some ideals that were earlier pursued by the video camera and longer ago by the film camera. The dream concerning one medium is realized in another, more recent medium. For many webcam users the ambition of a comprehensive representation of the world, spatially as well as temporally, is finally fulfilled: 'The webcam makes possible the endless, unedited film, the eternal film.'[37]

The ways and contexts in which webcams are being used are diverse. Its first use is extremely simple as well as exemplary for most of its later uses. The very first webcam was used in 1991 in the Department of Computer Science at the Cambridge University for surveilling a coffeepot.[38] In order not to walk in vain to the room where one could get coffee, the so-called 'Trojan room', and find there an empty pot, students installed this new apparatus on the pot and connected it to their computers so that they could check from their desk if there was any coffee left. Two years later they connected these images to the World Wide Web and shared the information with millions of people. The fact that so many people watched these images was not motivated by what the images showed, but by what they promised: a comprehensive representation of the world. Soon after, in 1996, Jennifer Ringley, a student from Pennsylvania, materialized part of the promise by showing on the Web images of her life at home in real time that were taken by a camera connected to her computer. Internet users could see everything she was doing: playing with her animals, sleeping, combing her hair, making love with her boyfriend, and so on. The stream of images was live, unedited, and it was in real time. The webcam is used as lifecam.[39]

As I stated before, the ideal materialized by Ringley's webcam as such is not new at all. There are films and videos

37 Stigter, 'Staren naar een stuk kaas' (2008), 4.

38 This history of the webcam is based on Stigter, 'Staren naar een stuk kaas' (2008).

39 The fact that the webcam is used as lifecam is even proven by fictional examples. The example of 'lonely girl15', who kept a video diary on YouTube, is telling in this respect. It turned out that lonelygirl15 was an actress who was playing this girl. She was, in fact, fictionalizing the real and authentic. This was possible because dominant use of webcams constitutes the webcam as lifecam.

in which a similar practice is demonstrated. Andy Warhol's films *Sleep* (1964) and *Empire* (1965) and more recently Bruce Nauman's video-installation *Mapping the Studio—All Action Edit (Fat Chance John Cage)* (2002) are probably the most famous examples. *Sleep* shows the poet John Giorno, Warhol's lover in those days, sleeping. He is filmed from a number of different angles and some shots are repeated. Although this film is not really or not completely in real time, it creates the impression of it. In that respect *Empire* is more radical. It consists of eight hours and six minutes of continuous real-time black and white film of the Empire State Building, from early evening until nearly 3 AM the next day. In his video-installation *Mapping the Studio,* Bruce Nauman records the nocturnal activity in the artist's studio of his cat and an infestation of mice during the summer of 2000. With seven projections and multiple audio tracks of ambient sounds, Nauman used this traffic as a way of mapping the leftover parts and work areas of the last several years of other completed, unfinished, or discarded projects.

Within their media—film and video—these examples are unique, not representative for a medium's specificity but for its exceptional dreams. Ringley's use of the medium of the webcam is not singular but demonstrates in an exemplary way a fundamental change in the 1990s caused by a new media landscape. It has given rise to a great diversity of practical uses of the webcam. Webcams are now focused on mountains, so that you can see if there is enough snow on the ski run; on young children, so that the parents can see if they are still asleep; on roads, so that drivers know if there are traffic jams; on the person behind a computer, so that the person s/he is chatting with knows what s/he looks like.

The latter example demonstrates a fundamental change in visual technologies. The possibility of showing your interlocutor at the chat box what you look like is first of all used by friends and family members in order to enhance the connection and its intimacy. The speaking or writing of words is completed by showing the face that speaks them. This possibility is fully exploited in the sex industry. Thanks to the webcam the client can not just chat with the girl or boy who is supposed to fulfil sexual desires, but the girl or boy also shows her/himself, or better his face and body while talking with the client. This use of the webcam is so extraordinary because voyeurism, a crucial aspect of more traditional visual technologies, is now overshadowed by its complementary other: exhibitionism. This exhibitionism is not only exploited in the sex industry. Most webcam images shown on the Internet are utterly boring. The first example on the Internet of the coffeepot in the Trojan room is again exemplary in that sense. Showing these images seems to be more important than seeing them. The transformation caused by the webcam is that for the first time people who want to be looked at have now a medium at their disposal which enables that.

This change is not only exploited by the sex industry, it also seems to be its demise. There are more and more websites specialized in amateur porn. Professionally made porn film with professional porn actors is now only one option for viewers next to amateur porn. More and more people who watch porn movies prefer now to watch amateur porn films shown on websites exclusively devoted to these webcam films. The fact that these films are clumsily made and that they usually do not show particularly attractive bodies appears not to be experienced as negative. The point is not *what* viewers are *seeing*, but *that* amateur actors are *showing*. It is the identification with these amateurs showing themselves that makes watching them into an erotic experience, an experience that is more exciting than watching voyeuristically attractive bodies performing sexual acts. The boredom caused by so many webcam images shown on the Web, pornographic or not, shows retrospectively also the boring nature of pornographic film as such. It is only in the fulfilment of the dream of pornography in webcam images that we become aware of how boring pornographic images always have been. Its excitement is not to be located in what can be seen in these images, but in the fact that they are shown.[40]

As already argued, this difference is fundamental, because it displaces the nature of our relationship to these images from voyeuristic to exhibitionistic. Something similar seems to be at stake in the visual landscape, as Patricia Spyer discusses in her contribution to the book *Images That Move* (2013).[41] In the wake of murderous conflicts with the Muslim population, the Christian population suddenly fills the public space of Ambon City with images of Christ. These images do not impel the voyeuristic desire to see what can be seen in those images. They are rather motivated by the exhibitionistic desire of the Christian population to become more visible.

The attraction of pornographic and other webcam images is foremost produced by their strong reality effect. Their reality effect is stronger than that produced by film images because, paradoxically, they are unedited and clumsily made. That we are aware of the fact that these images were made, and by whom, and where, from which position, makes the reality effect only stronger, for the production of these images stems from real life instead of from professional studios, where the production process can be made invisible.

In pre-new media times, intimacy with people you did not know could only be experienced in art and in literature. In other words, we needed art and literature in order to be intimate with strangers. And when I use the term 'intimacy'

40 For a critical reading of pornography, see Williams, *Hard Core* (1989).

41 Spyer, in Spyer & Steedly (eds.), *Images That Move* (2013).

I am not necessarily referring to sexual intimacy. I am using it to indicate a kind of relationship or contact in which we become aware of the most personal desires and anxieties of other people. By identifying with characters and situations in literature or art, we could share desires or anxieties of people we did not know. But this possibility offered by literature and art is conditioned by its fictionality. The webcam has taken over this possibility so far exclusively realized by art and literature. But the way the webcam enables intimacy with people we do not know differs ontologically from the way art and literature do it. Strong as the reality effects of art and literature can be, they are ultimately framed by their fictionality. The intimacy we can have with strangers via webcams is not with fictional persons. They are real (even if they are role playing); they exist, although we do not know them. This increases the reality effect of the intimate 'encounters' with them.[42]

The success of the webcam since its invention in the mid-1990s is in a double sense co-responsible for the explosion of information that defines that decade. First of all because webcams are now everywhere, built into computers or attached to computers, they distribute filmed information over the World Wide Web. But this quantitative explosion of information also has a qualitative dimension: the kind of information spread by webcams is potentially complete and comprehensive.[43] But comprehensive and complete as the webcam information may be, most of it is irrelevant, boring, and ignored by the viewer. That is why the webcam is not only exemplary for the 1990s explosion of information but also for the implosion of meaning. As I argued before, the webcam marks the first time that there are more people who want to be looked at than people who want to look. It is precisely in this displacement from voyeurism to exhibitionism

42 For an analysis of how webcams affect the relationship between private and public, self and Other, see Van Dijck, *Mediated Memories* (2007).

43 The information provided by webcams is, of course, not really complete and comprehensive. Usually it is so only in a temporal sense, when it visually controls a specific space twenty-four hours a day. But the view of a space is usually limited, only showing what comes inside the frame of the camera's lens. Only when several cameras are used from different perspectives can webcams provide complete and comprehensive information in a spatial sense.

that the intensities of affective mechanisms are released. This does not imply that voyeurism does not rely on affective mechanisms. But unlike exhibitionism it depends on a fascinating visual object, on its meaning, that is, whereas in the visual relationship of exhibitionism the visual object is much more irrelevant, because it is the act instead of the object of exhibitionism that fascinates. When using now the terms 'voyeurism' and 'exhibitionism', I am no longer applying them in the more limited erotic sense, as I did in my example of amateur pornography. Rather I use them in a more general sense, indicating a distinction between a passive consumerist attitude and a more active attitude of self-positioning. This can be erotic, but not necessarily so.

For the viewer of these images is not looking for their meaning, but gets access to them by means of identification with the exhibitionistic impulse behind them. Watching them is less a matter of signifying transactions than of an event that one experiences directly or bodily. The affective process of identification leads—in the case of webcam images—to feelings like excitement or anxiety. This counters the affect of boredom produced on the level of signification. The fact that many people continue to look at webcam images (besides in very practical situations of surveillance) should be understood in terms of the affects they produce and enable, not in the shadows of meaning that they nevertheless offer.

Francis Bacon and the Work of Sensation

Formal and Structural Dimensions

How Can We See Affects?

As we have seen in the previous chapter, in the turn to affect that has taken place the last ten years, the work of French philosopher Gilles Deleuze and American psychologist Silvan S. Tomkins are the sources of inspiration for an understanding of how texts and images work beyond—or before, or below—signification. In many respects, this has been a paradigmatic revolution, because with structuralism and post-structuralism, all attention was focused on the production of meaning by texts and images. But in her book *The Forms of the Affects*[1] film theorist Eugenie Brinkema criticizes the kind of criticism in which the affective turn has resulted. Instead, she proposes and elaborates a more productive notion of affect, responding to the question: how can we notice, see affects? What is it, in the forms of the text, that triggers affective responses? She critiques affect criticism, specifically in cinema studies, for disregarding textuality and close reading altogether, and for privileging the affected subject—meaning the affected critic or theorist: 'The net result, though, was that

1 Brinkema, *The Forms of the Affects* (2014).

in rejecting screen theory in favor of immediate seductive feeling, these theorists severed discussions of affect from any considerations of textuality.'[2]

The affective turn, Brinkema claims, has not resulted in attention for affects themselves, but for the production and generation of 'something' in the theorist. The affective turn has become a way of re-establishing the interiority of the theorist, an interiority that had become penalized, after the new critics William K. Wimsatt and Monroe Beardsley had condemned it for bringing about an *affective fallacy*. According to Brinkema, affect is wrongly seen as personal, as intensity without form or meaning. She criticizes the notion of affect as intentional, as a device for the generation of intensities in the theorist. When the theorist establishes her- or himself as a subject who is being affected, new readings and questions cannot arise. If affect theory re-establishes the interiority of a subject, such subjects can only talk about what they already know. Only by speaking of what is not yet known, about what is not yet interiorized, can new thought be generated.

Brinkema situates the force of affect in form, and she contends that it is the act of reading that releases or activates the affect, which is triggered by form:

> *it is only because one must read for it that affect has any force at all.* The intensity of that force derives from the textual specificity and particularity made available uniquely through reading, the vitality of all that is not known in advance of close reading, the surprising enchantments of the new that are not uncovered by interpretation but produced and brought into being as its activity.[3]

Brinkema thus redirects the affective turn, diverted under the name of radical formalism. For her, affects *can* have form. Affects should not be understood in terms of expressivity or

2 Brinkema, *The Forms of the Affects* (2014), 30.

3 Brinkema, *The Forms of the Affects* (2014), 38, emphasis in original.

interiority; rather, they consist of formal dimensions, such as, in the case of cinema, lines, colours, light and motion. Affects should not be placed and studied inside the subject; they can be studied as forms because 'forms are auto-affectively charged, and ... affects take shape in forms and temporal structures'.[4] By focusing on the forms of affect, Brinkema restores agency to form.

In the remainder of this chapter I would like to explore the possibility and productivity of the idea that formal or structural elements of texts and images trigger or activate affects, and that cultural analysts can read these 'forms of affects'. By doing so, I will go beyond the idea that affect is merely an energetic intensity effecting a reaction in a reader or viewer. Although affect can be, and will be, considered as intensity, attention will be displaced to what it is that *triggers* these intensities. Hence the subtitle of the volume I co-edited with Tomáš Jirsa.[5] When these formal and structural elements can be read, the question imposes itself how these legible forms can be distinguished from legible signs. Although signs have form, forms do not always result in conventional signs. The issue is, rather, how we process potentially signifying forms (signifiers): as conventional signs or as affective signs? Forms are 'striking' especially when they are not conventional. Deleuze scholar Brian Massumi has an appropriate term, cited in the previous chapter, for what these striking forms do, and for how affective intensities manifest themselves: they 'shock to thought'. The thoughts into which these shocks result are new, creative, productive, in the sense that they are unconventional, not established in what people or culture has accepted as shared, conventional ideas.[6]

Deleuze himself has another expression that indicates the intimate relationship between affect and thought or meaning, namely 'the encountered sign'. Using the concept of 'the

4 Brinkema, *The Forms of the Affects* (2014), 37.

5 Alphen, van & Jirsa (eds.), *How to Do Things with Affects: Affective Triggers in Aesthetic Forms and Cultural Practices* (2019).

6 Massumi used the term as title for his edited volume *A Shock to Thought* (2002a).

encountered sign' as an alternative for affect is at first sight highly paradoxical, if we consider affect to go beyond signification and the production of meaning. As mentioned, Deleuze introduced the term in his book *Proust and Signs*, defining it as a sign that is felt rather than recognized, perceived through cognition or through familiarity with the 'code'. But the sensation of the encountered sign is not an end in itself. For Deleuze, this sensation is a catalyst for critical inquiry or thought. For him, an affect is a more effective trigger for profound thought than rational inquiry or conventional productions of meaning, because of the way in which it grasps us, forcing us to engage involuntarily: 'More important than thought there is "what leads to thought"... impressions which force us to look, encounters which force us to interpret, expressions which force us to think.'[7]

For Deleuze, then, art and literature should not be approached as conventional sign systems, as iconographic for example, but as the enactment or embodiment of sensation that stimulates thought. Art does not illustrate or embody a proposition, but produces sensations or affects that inspire thought. It is the affective encounter through which thought proceeds and moves towards deeper truth. By means of this affective view of art and literature, Deleuze deconstructs the conventional opposition between philosophy and art, or between thought and sensation. For him, both are modes of thinking. But whereas philosophers think in concepts, artists think by means of sensation.

> Sensation is generated through the artist's engagement with the medium, through color and line in the case of the painter, so that it is not the residue of self-expression, or a property of some prior self, but emerges in the present, as it attaches to figures in the image.[8]

7 Deleuze, *Francis Bacon* (2002).

8 Bennett, *Empathic Vision* (2005), 37.

This understanding of sensation by Australian art historian Jill Bennett provides a beautiful guideline for my reading of the work of Francis Bacon, about which Deleuze as well as I myself have written extensively. In my own earlier book *Francis Bacon and the Loss of Self*,[9] I did not deal with affect explicitly. In the readings of Bacon's paintings that follow here, I will make the work of affect in Bacon explicit by engaging a conversation between Deleuze on Bacon and my own earlier work on Bacon. In this reading I will negotiate conventional significations with unconventional forms, encountered as sensations that shock to thought.

9 Alphen, van, *Francis Bacon and the Loss of Self* (1992).

Making Sense of Affect

The work of Francis Bacon has an impact that viewers cannot evade. That explains why their response is usually extreme: they love his work or they hate it; there is little in-between, because it never leaves them indifferent. Due to this strong impact, Bacon's work asks for a critical approach that is able to acknowledge and take into consideration the affects produced by it. As a starting point for such an 'affective approach' one could take the many interviews with Bacon, not only the most famous ones with David Sylvester, but also those, for example, with Michel Archimbaud. The questions they pose often demonstrate the impact Bacon's images have had on them. A reading of Bacon's work that more explicitly reflects on the affective impact of Bacon's images is offered by Deleuze in his *Logique de la sensation* (*The Logic of Sensation*), first published in 1981. It does not only comprise a general aesthetic theory, comparable to what Deleuze earlier formulated in his book with Félix Guattari about the texts of Franz Kafka, but provides at the same time a powerful assessment of Bacon's paintings. This assessment concerns not what they mean but how they work. Thus, Deleuze abducts the meaning of the phrase 'making sense' from the domain of semantics to that of the senses. According to Deleuze, a painting, and especially one by Bacon, should not be approached as a product but as *work* of art in the most literal sense: it is a union of forces, or a dynamic that has materialized onto a canvas.

By considering painting as a union of forces, Deleuze takes distance from the aesthetic notion according to which painting is a practice of *mimesis*. This conception of art goes back to the Greek legend in which it is told that the painter Zeuxis was able to paint grapes so realistically that his painting attracted doves. The birds assumed that they could be eaten. His rival Parrhasius wanted to outperform him, and painted a curtain so realistic that even the famous Zeuxis thought that he could open the curtain when he saw it. The legend exemplifies the idea that the power of art should be explained in terms of *mimesis*: the ability to represent, or imitate, the empirical world. Although for many centuries *mimesis* has been an almost self-evident aesthetic pursuit, in the twentieth century the situation has changed radically. The lack of recognizable forms in modern art has become completely accepted. This relatively recent tendency to leave behind *mimesis* as an aesthetic principle has resulted in the tension between two poles: the tendency toward abstraction and the tendency toward figurative narrativity. According to Deleuze, in recent history not many artists have succeeded in making great art by exploiting this tension between abstraction and narrativity. Instead, they escape either into complete abstraction (Pollock, Rothko, among others) or into figurative narrativity.

Francis Bacon, however, has resisted both tendencies that proved so attractive to twentieth-century painters. With a tone of contempt, he repeatedly distanced himself from abstract expressionist painters who made their careers in the same period as he did. And his remark about narrative painting in the interviews with David Sylvester is deadly, and expresses an equally strong contempt: 'And the moment the story is elaborated, the boredom sets in; the story talks louder than the paint.'[10] His dismissal of narrative painting is based on the fact that such painting only stimulates the viewer to identify or recognize the story. It is the story that either fascinates or not; the painting itself has no function besides that of illustrating or representing the story (mimesis). Such a practice of painting denies the specificity of art.

10 Sylvester, *The Brutality of Fact* (1987), 22.

Deleuze explains the specificity of art by contrasting it with the specificity of his own profession. Whereas the philosopher works with concepts and is supposed to create new concepts, the artist works with *affects* and *percepts*. Affects are the non-personal emotions or affections, which belong to the essence of art. When affects are non-personal they are not affections because they are disconnected from lived, human experience. Similarly, percepts are not the same as perceptions. They have not been processed by human experience (as phenomenology assumes), but they are part of the concrete matter of the painting. This aesthetic notion of the specificity of art implies also that a painting is not spiritual but bodily. It situates itself on the surface of perception without any active intervention of our consciousness. The paintings of Francis Bacon exemplify this aesthetic theory perfectly. Bacon's viewers are touched directly and almost violently by the material presence of his paintings. It is as if our skin is penetrated by affects generated by the presence of what we see: not a mediated story, but the material reality of the painting.

11 Archimbaud, *Francis Bacon in Conversation with Michel Archimbaud* (1993), 81.

12 Davies & Yard, *Francis Bacon* (1986), 110.

The fact that Deleuze (like Bacon) counters the recognition of stories or recognizable forms does not imply that he favours abstract art. On the contrary. According to the philosopher, artists always start a work with 'clichés', the so-called available images, forms and figures of our daily perception. They never begin to paint on an empty canvas as a creation *ex nihilo*. These available images and forms can be recognized. But an artist will struggle with these clichés; he will transform and re-contextualize them. This transformation of clichés disconnects the painted image from common experience and perception and enables the creation of really new figurations and experiences. Bacon himself describes this creative process as follows:

> I had put a whole heap of reference marks on the canvas, then suddenly the forms that you see on the canvas began to appear; they imposed themselves on me. It wasn't what I set out to do. Far from it. It just happened like that and I was quite surprised by what appeared. In that case, I think that instinct produced those forms. But that's not the same as inspiration.[11]

In another interview Bacon formulated this creative procedure similarly, but with less emphasis on the accidental and more emphasis on the input of the artist:

> Great art is always a way of concentrating, reinventing what is called fact, what we know of our existence—a reconcentration.[12]

To paint, then, means to make something visible that otherwise remains invisible. The 'reference marks' or 'what we know of our existence' are transformed into something new and which can only be described by what you see on the canvas. This invisible reality that has been made visible should, however, not be understood as meanings, ideas or truths, which were hidden under the surface of the painting. Instead, the viewer is touched by affects, that is, by the surface layers, which are senseless as such, but which are put into motion by the painter in such a way that they touch us.

This creation of new figurations and experiences is performed on the basis of what Deleuze calls affects and percepts. These affects and percepts activate and stimulate the viewer's senses. It results in the viewer in what in another of his works he has called 'abstract thought' or 'abstract experience'. This use of the term 'abstract' has, however, little in common with the way the term abstraction is used in art discourse. Abstraction in Deleuze's sense has nothing to do with a purification of forms or figures. Instead it is a form of becoming. Abstraction consists of forces that, in the words of John Rajchman, 'push art forms beyond and beside themselves, causing their very languages, as though possessed with the force of other things, to start stuttering "and...and... and...".'[13] This stuttering abstraction concerns a strange anorganic vitality, which enables viewers or readers to see in cliché figurations other, new ways of proceeding. With 'stuttering' Deleuze refers to the moment at which language is not yet language. The disintegration of language, or the inadequacy of it, is not an effect in retrospect but one that points to a language not yet possible, but may come about in the future.

In *The Logic of Sensation* Deleuze also discusses the films of Jean-Luc Godard as examples of abstract art. Godard's films are abstract in Deleuze's view, not because the context ceases to be narrative in the conventional sense and is, instead, largely self-referential. They are abstract because they are comprised of a wide range of elements, a variety of discourses, past and present, and because these are combined in such a way that a non-narrative continuity is created. The

13 Rajchman, 'Another view of Abstraction' (1995), 17–18.

14 Rajchman, 'Another view of Abstraction' (1995), 19.

15 Sylvester, *The Brutality of Fact* (1987), 30.

16 Davies & Yard, *Francis Bacon* (1986), 44.

abstraction is therefore not the result of a renunciation of narrative, but that of the attempt 'to attain an "outside" of other odd connections through a free abstract AND, which takes over the movement of the film'.[14]

Francis Bacon himself has described this process of creative becoming as distortion: 'What I want to do is to distort the thing far beyond the appearance, but in the distortion to bring it back to a recording of the appearance.'[15] And in another interview: 'You must distort to transform what is called appearance into image.'[16] The deformation and distortion described by Bacon results first of all in representations of movement, transformation, and animation. His figures seem to be 'in movement', 'in transformation' or in turmoil. But these acts of distortion should also be understood as acts of violence or as wounding interventions. The wounding violence is then, however, not only directed to the represented figures, but also to the viewers of his paintings. The viewers are touched by affects produced by the figures in movement. That is why one could say that Bacon's paintings do what they are about—to recall the words in which John Austin formulated his concept of the performative. They show 'wounded' figures in transformation and by doing that, they bring about in the viewer an affective transformation that can also be understood in terms of a 'wounding'.

Francis Bacon's transformation of clichés, or what Deleuze in other contexts would also call his abstraction or stuttering, makes the representational space we get to see into something unpredictable, grim and threatening. This 'touching', uninviting reality is in many respects inhuman; inhuman because unknown to human experience. This reality can be understood as a zone in which so-far unknown experiences come about. Michel Leiris has described this so-far unknown reality adequately as follows:

> These pictures [...] being spaces filled with pure living presences indicative of nothing other than themselves, and therefore stamped with an absence of sense—with, in other words, *nonsense*—seem, in the dazzling nakedness of the very moment [...], to be images in keeping the inanity of our situation in the world as ephemeral beings, more capable than other living creatures of brilliant and pointless ecstasies.[17]

17 Leiris, *Francis Bacon* (1983), 45.

Such a characterization of processes activated by Bacon's work concerns first of all the viewer and how she or he is affected by his images. But Bacon's images do not only 'work' on the viewer, as I argued above; they also show the kind of aesthetics that they activate. In other words, they demonstrate what they represent. In that sense, Bacon's images are also allegories of this notion of aesthetics. Bacon's aesthetics does not only comprise a theory of the creative process. It is at the same time a theory of aesthetic reception. The creative process is doubled or mirrored in the way the viewer processes his images; in the way the viewer is touched by affects that 'deform' and 'wound' her or him.

The allegorical dimension of Bacon's work is realized by his consistent use of highly specific motifs. In *The Logic of Sensation* Deleuze discussed three of those motifs, namely isolation, deformation, and coupling. The figures he represents are again and again defined by one of these three processes or activities, or a combination of them. I would like to add a fourth motif that can be recognized frequently in Bacon's images and that enables me to see his work as an allegory of the affective processes his work brings about. It is the motif of 'tools of vision', or more specifically, 'the mirror and the lamp'. I have explained this in my 1992 book, more extensively than I can do here.

At first sight these tools of vision are common, even banal elements. We notice them in a great number of Bacon's images. But because they are so banal, critics usually do not pay serious attention to them. The lamps in his works are just bare light bulbs hanging from a cord. These bulbs are often combined with light switches attached to the wall; in some cases, there is only a light switch, the light bulb is not even represented. Throughout the history of Western aesthetics, the motifs of the mirror and the lamp have, however, been loaded with meaning. An elucidation of the meanings of these motifs may provide an illuminating insight into Bacon's art and its specific aesthetic. For, in Bacon's work the significance of the mirror and the lamp differs radically from the special value these have held in Western aesthetics, where they have acted as metaphors for the revealing role of visuality and the human eye. In his influential book, *The Mirror and the Lamp: Romantic Theory and the Critical Tradition* from 1953, M.H. Abrams takes the mirror and the lamp as metaphors for two antithetical conceptions of the creative mind. In the image of the mirror the mind is compared to a reflector of external objects. In the lamp metaphor, the mind is compared to a radical projector that makes a creative contribution to the object it perceives. In the history of aesthetics, the mirror metaphor characterizes much of the thinking in terms of *mimesis* from Plato until the eighteenth century, while the lamp metaphor typifies the prevailing motif during the Romantic period.

Although at first sight Bacon appears to place himself within the Western tradition by taking the human body as his favourite subject matter, he distances himself from that tradition by subverting the role of the motifs of the mirror and the lamp. Whereas mirrors, lamps, and light switches are recurrent elements of his images, his mirrors do not reflect or reproduce adequately, nor do his lamps project or highlight satisfactorily. The bodies of his figures are not reflected or elucidated by these visual devices; instead they are dissolved by them. The figures lose their forms and boundaries as if this were caused by these visual tools. What we are confronted with is not the 'reflected body' or the 'illuminated body', but the 'body unbound'.

The Body Unbound

The motif of the mirror marks vision as thematic. The visible (the object of looking) as well as the visual (the act and experience of looking) are both framed by the mirror's reflection. According to the principles of the conventional mirror, the image we see in the mirror reflects our act of looking. Only the sense of sight is susceptible to the mirror effect. Although distorting mirrors exist, we expect perfect mimesis of a mirror. Hence, if the viewer who looks into a mirror does not see what is in front of it, a phenomenon has occurred that is at odds with the act of looking as mimetic. In varying degrees some of Bacon's works that contain representations of mirrors are instances of mimetic mirror reflections.

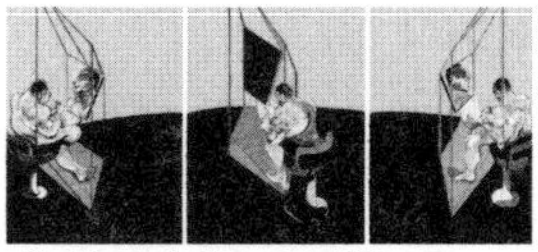

18 Francis Bacon, *Three Studies of the Male Back* (1970), painting, 198 × 147.5 cm.

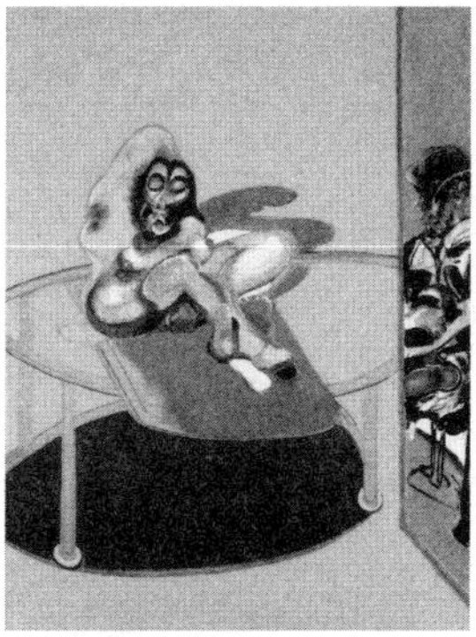

19 Francis Bacon, *Study of Nude with Figure in a Mirror* (1969), painting, 198 × 147.5 cm.

In Bacon's *Three Studies of the Male Back* (1970)[18] we see in the left- and right-hand panels a man shaving himself in front of a mirror. In the central panel the man is reading a paper. Although he is sitting in front of a mirror as in the other panels, we do not see his reflection. The reflections in the other panels appear as 'normal', suggesting mimesis. The central panel, however, does not function according to the conventional laws of the mirror. The mirror image is black.

A significant painting in this respect is *Study of Nude with Figure in a Mirror* (1969).[19] We see a female nude

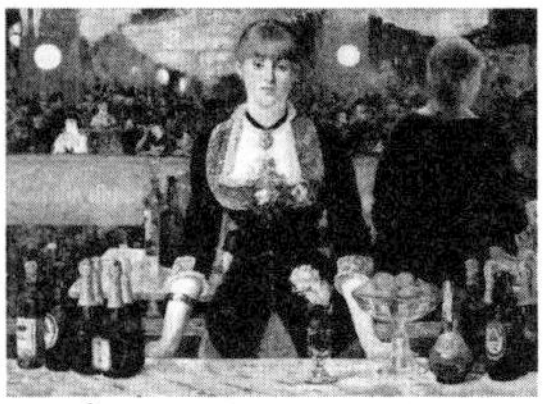

20 Édouard Manet, *Un Bar aux Folies Bergère* (1882), painting, 96 × 130 cm.

exposed to the viewer as in traditional painting. The mirror is not turned toward the woman, but toward the viewer who is in front of the painting. In the mirror we see a dressed man on a bar stool apparently watching the naked woman. It may be illuminating to read the painting as a commentary of Manet's *Un Bar aux Folies Bergère* (1882), in the collection of the Courtauld Institute in London.[20]

Bacon's painting seems to challenge the convention according to which the object of Western representation is traditionally female, and the subject is a male voyeur. Manet's painting, however, can hardly be accused of unambiguously accepting this ideology of vision. Indeed, it presents the mirror as a distorting element, bringing about an uneasy identification between the voyeur on the right and the viewer in front, both of whom are addressed by the woman. Yet the directness of the woman's gaze in the Manet painting only just begins to undermine the power of the louche voyeur, a bourgeois gentleman who seems to be out of place in the bar, but who is nevertheless still, along with the viewer, the master of this looking situation. The self-confident pose of the gangster-like man in the Bacon painting embodies a double critique of this situation. First, the objecthood of the observed woman is not softened by a smile or a complying or subordinate look as is normal in the tradition of the female nude. The man's look turns the woman into an animal. Her objecthood is sharpened by animal-like features (mouth and hair). Second, the woman's body is distorted; her legs replicate the posture of the man's legs. This similarity of pose suggests that the voyeur shares the animal features of the woman. And by analogy, so does the viewer, whose function is represented by this man. Thus, the onlooker is contaminated, his looking 'touches' his body as it touches her.

Conventional mirror images are seen as confirmations of the identity of the mirrored person. This is the case in mirror images in the literal sense, but also in mimetic representations that consider the mirror as a metaphor of what they pursue. Hence, in Bacon's work it is not only the mirror that figures as visual motif, but also paintings, photographs, cameras, shadows, or reflections figure as self-reflexive motifs of what representation is or does. What strikes the viewer immediately is that the conventional distinctions between ontological dimensions are not clear at all. The space of representation is an ambiguous zone, because represented space cannot clearly be distinguished from primary space. This entanglement of ontological dimensions is apparent in *Three Studies of Isabel Rawsthorne* (1967).[21] We see a female figure inside and outside a room; we see her as a shadow on the white door, and in a painting or drawing nailed on the wall. This image on the wall encapsulates the tensions produced by the painting of which it is a part. As in many other Bacon paintings, it is as if the represented figure is coming out of the image; or the other way around: the figure is sucked into the image. The figure is both inside and outside the image on the wall.

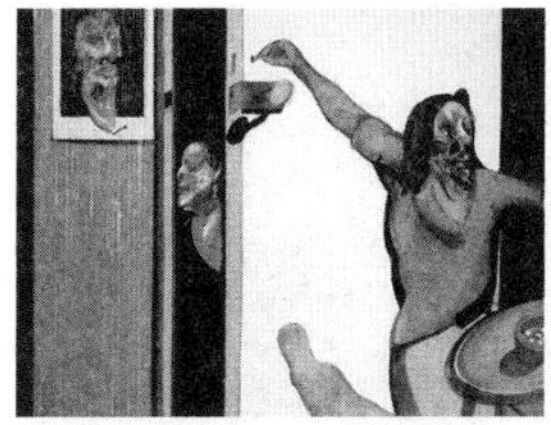

21 Francis Bacon, *Three Studies of Isabel Rawsthorne* (1967), painting, 124.2 × 157.1 cm.

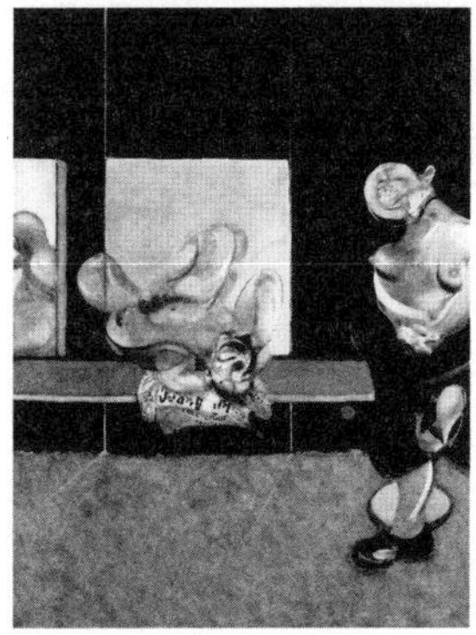

22 Francis Bacon, *Studies from the Human Body* (1975), painting, 198.1 × 147.3 cm.

Studies from the Human Body[22] contains a comparable situation. On the right side we see a female figure walking in the primary space. In the centre there is a male figure laying on his back, half inside half outside the flat surface of an image—or is it a window? On the left side a figure is totally encompassed by the dimension of representation. The direction in which the female figure walks, and in which the male figure looks, suggests that these figures are being sucked into the level of representation. If we read the direction of the movement in the painting in this way, it is also possible to read the framing of the female figure's face by a circle as the beginning of this process of transformation. The circle has

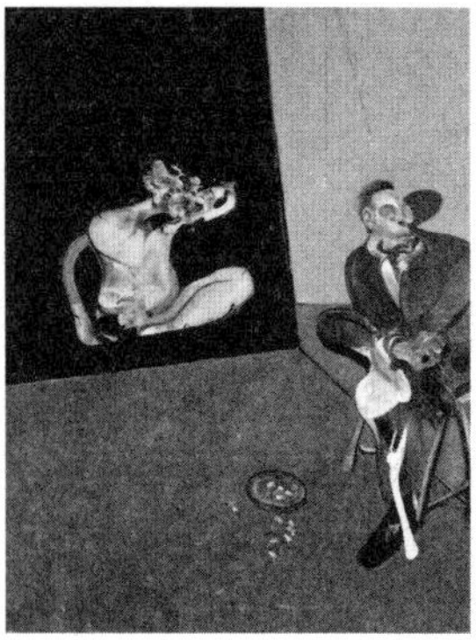

23 Francis Bacon, *Two Studies for a Portrait of George Dyer* (1988), painting, 198 × 147.5 cm.

the same light-blue colour as the two surfaces of the levels of representation.

The image in *Studies of Isabel Rawsthorne* (1967) is nailed onto the wall. This nailing of images is a recurrent motif in Bacon's work. Other examples are *Three Figures and a Portrait* (1975), in which we see a portrait of Leiris nailed to the back wall, and *Three Portraits: Posthumous Portrait of George Dyer, Self Portrait, Portrait of Lucian Freud* (1973) shows images of Bacon and Dyer nailed to the wall in the side panels. All these examples suggest that representations are attempts to *nail the body down*. The most detailed version of this literal statement can be seen in *Two Studies for a Portrait of George Dyer.*[23] The scene is clearly one of mimetic, iconic representation in so far as we recognize the represented George Dyer also in the represented image in the painting. Whereas Dyer is obviously sitting for the portraitist—his pose is a pose, again literally—according to the title he is already merely a portrait, and has been sacrificed to representation. And this sacrificial nature of portraiture is hinted at by the nails that penetrate his body in the painted portrait, his mirror, linking it to Bacon's *Crucifixion* paintings and his slaughtered oxen (see *Figure with Meat,* 1954). The two light bulbs, one for each portrait, provide the sitting George Dyer with substantial shadow and body extension, and the (doubly) painted Dyer with clear-cut black-and-whiteness: black background, white body. The embedded portrait is both emphatically iconic—it replicates Dyer's pose—and absurdly different; naked, nailed down, pinned up.

The mirror motif does not only return in Bacon's depiction of photographs, drawings and paintings in his images, but also in the motif of the double. Many of his works show *doppelgänger*. In the well-known *Triptych Inspired by T.S.*

Eliot's Poem 'Sweeny Agonistes' we see two resting women on the left panel and two wrestling men on the right panel who look like doubles. In *Crucifixion, 1965* we see two 'gangsters', and the central panel of *Triptych—Two Figures Lying on a Bed with Attendants* also has a pair of men who look like doubles of each other. Also, the figures in *Two Men Working in a Field* are represented in such a way that the identical identity of doubles is emphasised. Together, the motifs of the mirror, the doubles, and the represented pictures suggest identity as a problematic issue or conflict. Whereas the doubles have too much identity in the sense that they are identical, the identity of the mirrored and represented figures is not established in the mirror image or other kinds of images. Rather, the figures' identities are unbound or lost in these representations.

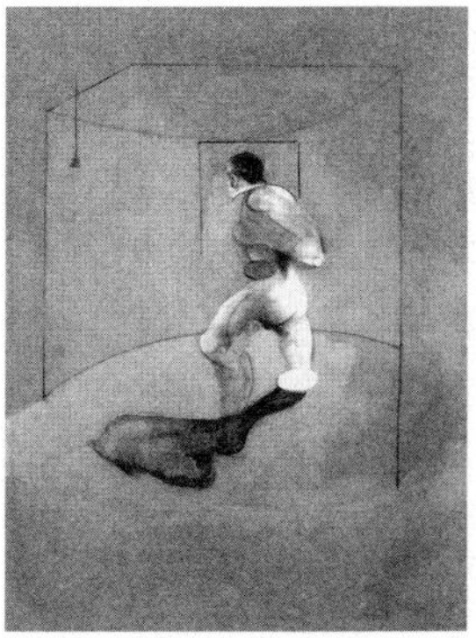

24 Francis Bacon, *Studies from the Human Body after Muybridge* (1988), painting, 198 × 147.5 cm.

The representational motif related to that of the mirror is the lamp. Sources of light in the form of bare bulbs hanging at the end of a cord also recur in Bacon's work. These centres of light never create a division between light and dark areas as they do in the painterly tradition of *chiaroscuro*, most famously practised by Caravaggio and Rembrandt. Bacon's light bulbs never illuminate some area of the represented space. All they do instead is creating shadows. But the shadows are not clear-cut, realistic projections of the figures; they never function as a mirror-image or repetition of the figure's profile, reconfirming his identity. The shadows are overly substantial, like bodily fluids streaming out of the figure's body; or the opposite: they are air-like as if the figure dissolves into a ghost. This ghost-like shadow appears, for instance, in *Self-portrait* (1973), whereas over-substantial shadows occur in *Study from the Human Body after Muybridge* (1988),[24] and *Lying Figure* (1969). There is a long tradition concerning the symbolic meaning of the shadow.

Shadows have been seen in relation to identity. They are supposed to confirm the identity of the subject; having a shadow substantiates subjectivity. Having a shadow has been, in fact, synonymous to being alive; whereas being a shadow means being dead, and not having a shadow means being fictional.

This symbolism of the shadow receives yet other meanings in Bacon's paintings. Reproducing light is represented as destructive in his work. It does not reconfirm identity, nor does it illuminate. The relationship between light and shadow lies elsewhere—in another insistent reflection on representation. The representation *of* the body coincides with perception *by* the body: they both unmake the body. Representation and perception are ultimately conflated. This statement requires a reconsideration of the narrativity of Bacon's images. Although no consistent narratives can be postulated from his paintings, this does not imply that narrativity plays no role at all. Even if it is not possible to recognize a story of which a painting is an illustration, narrativity is nevertheless intensely experienced by viewers. Something is going on. The illusion of narrative his work arouses, does not, however, concern the representation of a perceived sequence of events, but the representation of perceiving as a sequence of events. Sequentiality does not concern the object but the subject of perception. The narrative is not the content of perception, but defines the structure of perception itself.

Sensational!

Understanding perception as a sequence of events also illuminates the implications of certain key expressions used by Bacon in his interviews, such as 'orders of sensation', 'levels of sensation', 'domains of sensation', and 'moving sequences'.[25]

Deleuze has read these expressions as referring to the idea that sensation is a cumulative sum of responses by the several sense organs. A colour, taste, a touch, a smell, a sound, or a weight, constitute together the different levels of sensation. This would imply that Bacon attempts to give visibility to a unity of the senses: 'He is putting a multi-sensible figure into the visual range of the eye.'[26]

Such a reading of 'levels of sensation' acknowledges the fact that in Bacon's oeuvre the body is so central. For, the body in Bacon's paintings becomes one integrated sense organ. It is the space to which the sense stimuli are directed, and the place where the sense responses are made tangible. Bacon expresses the bodily tangibility of the responses of the senses in an extreme way as deformations of the body. It is as if the body is tortured by its abundance of sense organs and sense experiences. This deformation of the body can then be read as the bodily response of the senses, of the bodily experiences of the outside world via the senses. With this in mind it makes sense that in many of Bacon's paintings the heads of the figures are even more deformed than the rest of their bodies. Most of the senses are concentrated in the head: sight, smell, hearing, and taste. The head is exemplary for the body as a sense organ.

The body as a sense organ is not only a pertinent term for the body in Bacon's work, but also for the effect his paintings have on the viewer. Bacon himself, at least, aims for such an effect. In interviews he has declared several times that he does not want to address the viewer via her or his brains but via the nervous system, by means of affects. He rejects illustrative, narrative, as well as abstract art, because they work upon the brain and not upon the nervous system. These

25 Deleuze, *Francis Bacon* (2002), 31–39.

26 Deleuze, 'What Is a Minor Literature?' (1983), 16.

remarks about how he wants to affect the viewer imply that the figures in Bacon's paintings can be seen as representing viewers: the bodies in the paintings exhibit the kind of responses that the viewer is also intended to have. His figures are *hit* by sense perception in the same way as the viewers of Bacon's paintings are. Their sense experiences are depicted as body deformations. Responses of the senses do not represent stimuli proportionally; they are not controlled, automatic, and singular. Rather they work like chain reactions. The response of one sense works like a stimulus for the other senses. This causes the senses to run wild because the several sense organs are not independent of one another, but integrated into one big organ, the body.

Not only the figures in his paintings, but also the viewers of his paintings are touched, wounded, yes deformed, by the affects released in the perception of representation turned into the representation of perception. This explains why Bacon's aesthetic comprises a theory of the creative process as well of aesthetic reception: the figures in his work can be seen as allegories for how the viewer is affected. The dynamics materialized on the canvas demonstrate perception not as a process thanks to which the subject controls his world, but as a process in which the body disintegrates. His painting does what it is about and what it shows. It gives the phrase 'making sense' an unheard-of, new meaning.

Legible Affects

The Melodramatic Imagination in Painting

Reconsidering the Affective Turn

I am not yet finished with my reflections on affect. In this chapter, I continue those reflections through an artwork that is almost too emphatically affect-compelling. For this I return to Sontag. In spite of her strong indictment of interpretation, as I have presented it above, Susan Sontag is not in principle opposed to hermeneutics. For her, hermeneutics is not bad in itself, but has become a harmful, or better yet, powerless, mode of reading at a particular historical moment:

> Interpretation takes the sensory experience of the work of art for granted, and proceeds from there. This cannot be taken for granted, now. Think of the sheer multiplication of works of art available to every one of us, superadded to the conflicting tastes and odors and sights of the urban environment that bombard our sense. Ours is a culture based on excess, on overproduction; the result is a steady loss of sharpness in our sensory experience. All the conditions of modern life—its material plenitude,

1 Sontag, 'Against Interpretation' (1967), 13.

2 Massumi, in Patton (ed.), *Deleuze* (1996), 220.

> its sheer crowdedness—conjoin to dull our sensory faculties.[1]

Sontag's plea for an erotic, affective approach to art is historically motivated. It is the conditions of modern life that dull our sensory faculties, that require more attention for affect. But there are also theoretical reasons for the affective approach. As Brian Massumi has claimed, our cultural-theoretical-political vocabulary offers few possibilities to deal with affect. Our entire vocabulary is derived from theories of signification. These theories and approaches

> are incomplete if they operate only on the semantic or semiotic level, however that level is defined (linguistically, logically, narratologically, ideologically, or all of these in combination, as a Symbolic). What they lose, precisely, is the expression *event*—in favor of structure.[2]

Altogether, it seems that these historical as well as theoretical motivations to pay more attention to affect have resulted in an 'affective turn'. But this affective turn has recently provoked some important resistance, as we have also seen above, notably in the book by Brinkema. Heeding Brinkema's call for close-reading affects for their form, in this chapter I will further explore the legibility of affects, this time with an artwork that couldn't be more different from Bacon's work.

Christina's World

By searching for legible forms of affects, I will go beyond the idea that affect is an energetic intensity effecting a reaction in a reader or viewer. Instead, I will be analyzing the forms of affect in Andrew Wyeth's iconic 1948 painting *Christina's*

World.[3] After my close reading of this painting, I will return to affect theory. My concluding consideration will be the question of how my formal affective reading of this painting relates to close readings in terms of signification.

When I read that the female figure in *Christina's World* is modeled after a handicapped woman, I was astonished. It had never occurred to me. I am clearly not the only one who did not see a disabled person in this figure. Wyeth himself talks about the responses to his most iconic work as follows:

> It's very interesting that *Christina's World* has such a wide appeal. People seem to put themselves into it. I get literally hundreds of letters a year from people saying that it is a portrait of themselves. And then they describe their own life. And they rarely mention the crippled quality. They don't see that.[4]

To signify this figure by the woman who was its model is reductive for another reason as well. The figure was not only based on the destitute Anna Christina Olson, who was fifty-five years old when Wyeth made the painting. It was also modeled after Wyeth's twenty-six-year-old wife. According to Griffin, this 'accounts for the figure's attractive, well-defined derriere.'[5] In addition, Christina's hair was inspired by Wyeth's aunt Elizabeth. Only the pink dress and the arms and hands are modeled after Anna Christina Olson. Once I have acquired this information, I can indeed read it into the image. The arms are very thin, which can possibly mean that the figure has a handicap. But the thinness of the arms can at the same time mean many other things.

The power of an image relies not on the reality after which it is modeled. The meaning, the appeal, the effects are produced by the image itself, by what is present in the image. This obliges me to start my reading of *Christina's World* with

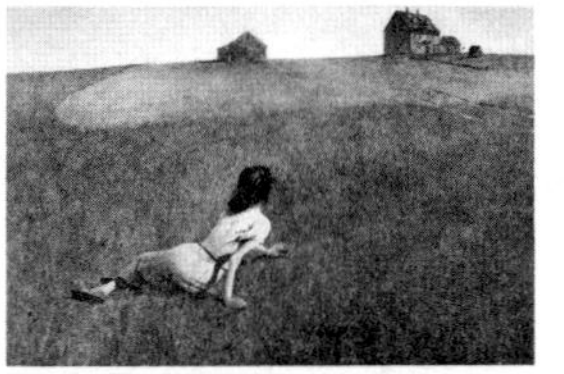

3 Andrew Wyeth, *Christina's World* (1948), painting, 81.9 × 121.3 cm.

4 Quoted in Griffin, in Cateforis (ed.), *Rethinking Andrew Wyeth* (2014), 113.

5 Griffin, in Cateforis (ed.), *Rethinking Andrew Wyeth* (2014), 119.

what I see in this painting, which is the following. The painting is abundantly narrative, for it includes many narrative possibilities. But, being a still image, we see only one moment from these many possible narratives. The narrative is condensed into a single moment; the narrative sequence of events is not elaborated. Although it is an enigmatic narrative because we get to see only one moment of it, the power of the image lies in its narrative seduction. Its narrative power depends, of course, first of all, on the female figure, looking intently toward the house, probably a farm, at some distance from her. Her act of focused looking expresses an urgency, whatever its cause. This urgency is also evoked by her hands; they are compressed, expressing tension. The woman, who is lying on the ground, is in the middle of the act of getting up and directing herself, her body, to the house on which her eyes are focused, as well. Her hair is slightly in disorder. This can be because of the movement her body is making, but can also be caused by the wind. Whatever the narrative cause is, it makes the figure erotically charged. This effect is enlarged by the dark shadow cast by her arm on her body, which suggests that the sun is standing low. It is either late in the day or very early.

Because the center of this painting consists of the enigmatic interrelation between the female figure and the farm she is looking at, I will deal with the spatial elements of this painting as characters. For these spatial elements are more than just a backdrop for the female figure. Together, they form the constellation through which the action of the painting is articulated. The spatial characters are the farm at some distance from the woman and the barn, separated from the farm by another distance in a different direction. With the woman, these two 'characters' form a triangle. The farm and the barn constitute, however, a kind of unity due to the grassland on which they are located, which has a different, slightly lighter colour, as if it has been recently mowed. The woman is isolated from the space where farm and barn are located, because the grassland she is lying on is darker; supposedly, it has not been mowed. She is positioned in the longer, untrimmed grass.

It is very appealing to speculate about possible narratives on the basis of the narrative elements I have so far identified. But I won't. What I will do instead is read the described constellation as *melodramatic*. At first sight this is a surprising project, because melodrama is a viable notion in literary studies and in cinema studies, but not in art history. In literature, melodramatic elements are especially visible in plots. These plots revolve around family relationships, star-crossed lovers and forced marriages, which figure prominently in secularized conflicts of good and evil, salvation and damnation. These emplotments are melodramatic, not only because of the nature of the conflicts around which they center, but also because the surface of the world in which the plot evolves (the surface of manners and gestures) consists of indices pointing to hidden forces and truths, latent signifieds. Gestures recorded in melodramatic novels must be metaphoric of something else.[6] Peter Brooks' 1976 *The Melodramatic Imagination: Balzac, Henry James, Melodrama, and the Mode of Excess* is the classic study analyzing such melodramatic emplotments in nineteenth-century literature. The approach of the melodramatic through plot explains why melodrama is not a viable notion in the analysis of artworks. Although many artworks are narrative, their narrativity is implied by one single image representing or condensing the whole plot. The narrative dimension of such images can be recognized, but the sequence of events of which the plot consists is reduced to a single moment. In other words,

6 Brooks, *The Melodramatic Imagination* (1995), 199.

narrativity defines the image's representation, but most of the plot is only implied, not represented in detail. *Christina's World* is a good example of such an image; it is highly narrative, but at the same time its narrative dimension is not spelled out. This makes it difficult to understand this image in terms of melodramatic emplotment.

Painting from the Melodramatic Imagination

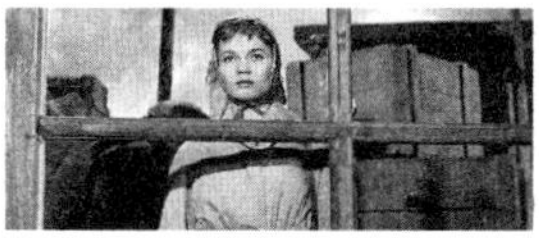

7 Douglas Sirk, *A Time to Love and a Time to Die* (1958), film still.

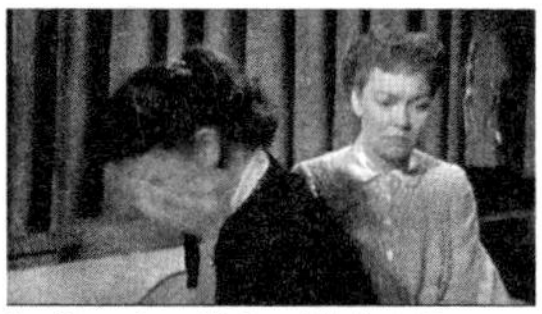

8 Douglas Sirk, *All that Heaven Allows* (1955), film still.

Thomas Elsaesser's article 'Tales of Sound and Fury: Observations on the Family Melodrama', originally published in 1972, seems a more promising starting point, because, focused on cinema, it is closer to the visual domain. In it, Elsaesser describes the development of melodrama from the eighteenth until the twentieth century. Starting with the eighteenth-century sentimental novel, he moves to the post-revolution, restoration melodramas of the nineteenth century in France, and the social, urban melodramas of Dickens in nineteenth-century England. His main interest is, however, the American manifestation of melodrama in, especially, Hollywood cinema. Elsaesser focuses on Hollywood family melodrama between 1940 and 1963, especially the films by Douglas Sirk,[7, 8] but also those of Alfred Hitchcock. He understands the melodramatic not so much as 'emotional shock-tactics and the blatant playing on the audience's known sympathies and antipathies', but rather as a 'non-psychological conception of the *dramatis personae*'.[9] In melodrama, the characters 'function less as autonomous individuals than to transmit the action and link the various locales within a total constellation.'[10] The characters in melodrama are not real autonomous individuals and they lack serious psychological motivation for their actions, because ultimately, they are the

9 Elsaesser, in Landy (ed.), *Imitation of Life* (1991), 69.

10 Elsaesser, in Landy (ed.), *Imitation of Life* (1991), 69.

result of the interiorization and personalization of ideological conflicts. For instance, reading Balzac's melodramatic plots, Elsaesser recognizes a Schopenhauerian struggle of the will:

> The ruthlessness of industrial entrepreneurs and bankers, the spectacle of an uprooted, 'decadent' aristocracy still holding tremendous political power, the sudden twists of fortune with no-good parasites becoming millionaires overnight (or vice versa) through speculation and the stock exchange, the antics of hangers-on, parvenus and cynical artist-intellectuals, the demonic, spellbinding potency of money and capital, the contrasts between abysmal poverty and unheard-of affluence and waste which characterized the 'anarchic' phase of industrialization and high finance, were experienced by Balzac as both vital and melodramatic. His work reflects this more in style than through direct comment.[11]

In order to understand the American manifestation of melodrama in the form of Hollywood cinema, Elsaesser returns to the dictionary definition of melodrama. According to common definitions, it is a 'dramatic narrative in which musical accompaniment marks the emotional effects.'[12] *Melos* in Greek means 'music'. This is for Elsaesser a useful definition, because it allows melodramatic elements 'to be seen as constituting a system of punctuation, giving expressive colour and chromatic contrast to the storyline, by orchestrating the emotional ups and down of the intrigue.'[13] This approach formulates the problems of melodrama not as issues of emplotment, but as issues of style and articulation.

In early cinema, the addition of music enabled directors to formulate certain moods such as sorrow, dread, suspense or happiness. Later technical innovations such as colour, wide screen and deep focus lenses, crane and dolly made it

11 Elsaesser, in Landy (ed.), *Imitation of Life* (1991), 73.

12 Elsaesser, in Landy (ed.), *Imitation of Life* (1991), 74.

13 Elsaesser, in Landy (ed.), *Imitation of Life* (1991), 74.

14 Elsaesser, in Landy (ed.), *Imitation of Life* (1991), 76.

15 Elsaesser, in Landy (ed.), *Imitation of Life* (1991), 76.

16 Elsaesser, in Landy (ed.), *Imitation of Life* (1991), 78.

possible to make the forms of melodrama more sophisticated. This cinematic form of melodrama is less defined as specific emplotment and more as an expressive code:

> [...] melodrama might therefore be described as a particular form of dramatic *mise-en-scène*, characterized by a dynamic use of spatial and musical categories, as opposed to intellectual or literary ones. Dramatic situations are given an orchestration which will allow for complex aesthetic patterns.[14]

When the melodramatic is given form through *mise-en-scène* instead of emplotment, it leads to very purposefully elliptical narratives or, in other words, to the feeling that there is always more to tell than can be said. The character's motivation is not explicitly told or made manifest through her actions, but is condensed in sequences of visual images that do not seem to advance the plot.[15] Impressionistic images of interiors or of a small-town setting are metaphoric condensations: they in fact tell and foretell the whole trajectory of the life of the main character, or of the relation between characters. In this melodramatic mode, scenes that have no plot significance whatsoever have an extremely strong emotional resonance. In the words of Elsaesser,

> this type of cinema depends on the ways 'melos' is given to 'drama' by means of lightning, montage, visual rhythm, décor, style of acting, and music—that is, on the ways the *mise-en-scène* translates character into action (not unlike the pre-Jamesian novel) and action into gesture and dynamic space (comparable to 19th-century opera and ballet).[16]

Melodramatic cinema uses an intensified symbolization of everyday actions, the heightening of the ordinary gesture, and setting and décor to reflect the characters' fetishist fixations.[17] This intensification of visual elements is not just a matter of style; it is, rather, a conscious use of style-as-meaning. This is why, in looking at Wyeth's painting, I distinguished between the grass around the buildings and that on which the figure of Christina is crawling as a differentiation that must have meaning.

According to Elsaesser, in the American context the *mise-en-scène* of melodrama can be recognized by its own iconography:

> Melodrama is iconographically fixed by the claustrophobic atmosphere of the bourgeois home and/or the small-town setting, its emotional pattern is that of panic and latent hysteria, reinforced stylistically by a complex handling of space in interiors to the point where the world seems totally predetermined and pervaded by 'meaning' and interpretable signs.[18]

I will revert to this in my conclusion, because the question is if such a fixed conventional iconography really exists. Nevertheless, for Elsaesser, the bourgeois home or the small-town setting are images of an inner self. When we see the protagonist (usually female) looking at this décor, she discovers that this world has become uninhabitable because it is both frighteningly suffocating and intolerably lonely. This drama is often played out against the vertical axis of a staircase. We see women waiting at home, standing by the window, 'caught in a world of objects into which they are expected to invest their feelings.'[19] This kind of imagery characterizes not only Hollywood melodrama, but also the paintings of Edward Hopper and Andrew Wyeth. *Christina's World* is a striking example of an American small-town setting condensed into a single house, some barns next to it,

17 Elsaesser, in Landy (ed.), *Imitation of Life* (1991), 79.

18 Elsaesser, in Landy (ed.), *Imitation of Life* (1991), 85.

19 Elsaesser, in Landy (ed.), *Imitation of Life* (1991), 84.

20 Elsaesser, in Landy (ed.), *Imitation of Life* (1991), 86.

21 Elsaesser, in Landy (ed.), *Imitation of Life* (1991), 89.

and another one further to the left.

One of the characteristics of melodramas in general is that they concentrate on the point of view of the victim. As Elsaesser argues, the critique—the questions of evil, of responsibility—is firmly placed on a social and existential level, away from the arbitrary and finally obtuse logic of private motives and individualized psychology. But in the American context this victimhood has a very specific shape:

> The linear trajectory of self-fulfillment so potent in American ideology is twisted into the downward spiral of a self-destructive urge seemingly possessing a whole social class.[20]

And a bit further Elsaesser continues:

> In the Hollywood melodramas characters made for operettas play out the tragedies of humankind, which is how they experience the contradictions of American civilization. … What strikes one as the true pathos is the very mediocrity of the human beings involved, putting such high demands upon themselves, trying to live up to an exalted vision of man, but instead living out the impossible contradictions that have turned the American dream into its proverbial nightmare.[21]

It is this cinematic form of melodrama that can also be recognized in Wyeth's painting *Christina's World*. The represented scene does not show a clear, unambiguous plot. But the *mise-en-scène* of this enigmatic emplotment produces an extremely strong emotional resonance. Following Elsaesser's reading of Hollywood melodrama in terms of the contradictions of American civilization, I suggest to read this emotional pattern in terms of self-fulfillment and the American dream.

Being positioned lower than the farm and the barn, the female figure is trying to move upwards. In the composition of the image her position is emphasized by the fact that the figure is crawling on the ground and moving in the direction of the house she is reaching for. The gestures of her two hands, one in front of her, the other to the right of her body, express the energy invested in her upward movement. The intensity with which she tries to reach the house can be read from the gestures of her two contorted hands, but also from her head, which suggest an intense gaze also directed at the house. This invisible but implied gaze signifies an intense longing or desire. The exact object of that desire, of course, is not known. In the elliptic narrative scene, the object of her longing could be the house itself, or someone or something inside the house.

The divide that separates the female figure form the house is emphasized by the separation in the grass (one part mowed, the other part not) and by a fenced area in front of the house. The mowed grass looks like an in-between area that first has to be crossed. But this divide is not absolute: the separation is crossed by a trail at the right side of the image, which connects the untrimmed grass with the mowed grass area where the farm and barns are also located. This trail is highly symbolic because it suggests that the house is not by definition out of reach, but can be reached if enough effort is put in. At the same time, the fact that the female figure is crawling instead of walking or running suggests that the pursuit of her desire is rather hopeless—that the object of her desire will remain out of reach.

So far, I have referred to the woman in the image as the female figure. However, the title of the painting gives this figure a name: Christina. This proper name contributes greatly to the emotional resonance of the painting. We are not looking at an unidentified woman who could be anyone. Whoever this Christina is, she is an individual person with her own name. This individualization enables the viewer to identify more easily with the figure. Such identification is, of course, already stimulated by the composition of the painting. The viewer enters the painting by looking at the female figure and, next, looking with her at the farm at a distance from her. The composition leads the viewer to Christina and her position within this constellation. Since the object of her desire is indeed out of reach, the viewer identifies with someone who is in the position of a victim, as is common in the melodramatic imagination.

The other element of the painting's title is the 'world' the female figure is looking at or is part of. If this is Christina's world, the painting indicates the smallness of it, suggesting that there is nothing to it outside of what is presented to the viewer. The small-town setting *is* America. It is the confinement in this small world that makes living in it suffocating. The smallness of Christina's world is symbolically represented by the lack of open sky above the horizon. Neither the house or farm nor the barn on the left are integrated into the landscape. Above the roof of the barn on the left, black birds flock as if portending a bad omen. House and barn balance on the edge of the horizon. The house does not open up to the sky above its roof either. There is no open sky above it. The house for which the female figure reaches is imprisoned between the horizon and the frame of the painting. The ladder standing against the house, as another attempt to reach upward, emphasizes the lack of space above the roof. If the house is the object of the Christina's desire, this object will not give her freedom but imprisonment. Thus, the emotional pattern evoked by the constellation of *Christina's World* is one of unfulfilled desire, frustration, panic and confinement.

These emotions are not explicitly represented as narrative elements, but evoked and reinforced stylistically by the *mise-en-scène* of an ambiguous emplotment. The intricate handling of spatial and compositional elements in the *mise-en-scène* is, to use the words of Elsaesser once more, 'totally predetermined and pervaded by meaning and interpretable signs.'[22]

So far, I have described the constellation of *Christina's World* as consisting of three major elements: the female figure, the house she is looking at and the barn to its left, and the separation in the grass. But what if the intense reaching for the house by the female figure is motivated by someone who is chasing her and whom we should imagine just outside the frame of the image? There is nothing in the painting indicating or symbolically representing a person chasing the woman. Nevertheless, such a narrative framing of the constellation is possible, even plausible, because it would explain and motivate the fact that the female figure is on the ground and crawling. While being chased, she has fallen. This framing produces emotional resonances slightly different from those described above, resembling more the melodramatic thrillers of Hitchcock. Elsaesser analyzed the melodramatic element of Hitchcock's films as follows:

> Hitchcock infused his film [*Rebecca*], and several others, with a unique intimation of female frigidity producing strange fantasies of persecution, rape and death—masochistic reveries and nightmares, which cast the husband into the role of the sadistic murderer.[23]

But there are no direct clues or signs in Wyeth's painting indicating the existence of a chasing husband or lover. There is only some circumstantial evidence: the fact that the woman is on the ground and crawling could mean that she is being chased by someone. However, speculating about a narrative

22 Elsaesser, in Landy (ed.), *Imitation of Life* (1991), 85.

23 Elsaesser, in Landy (ed.), *Imitation of Life* (1991), 81.

24 Berlant, *Cruel Optimism* (2011), 2.

in which Christina is part of a Hitchcock-like employment is not necessary, for the *mise-en-scène* of the elements present in the painting has enough meaning and interpretable signs to engage the viewer emotionally.

I prefer to understand this painting in terms of the failure of self-fulfillment, of unsuccessful longing in the context of the American dream. This does not result in a narrative, in a sequence of events, but only in the framework of a narrative delineating a desire focusing on an unobtainable object. This desire comes about in, is shaped by, an enclosed field of pressure, the American small-town setting. In this enclosed field of pressure, the mechanisms of displacement and transfer open up a highly dynamic feeling of non-fulfilment. Saying that the painting is about the failure of self-fulfillment does not imply that this failure is represented narratively. Rather, it is signified by strong emotions produced by a meaningful constellation of elements, by the *mise-en-scène* of spatial elements that are insignificant from a narrative point of view.

This reading of the painting evokes Lauren Berlant's notion of 'cruel optimism', which is also cast as an affective structure, related to the kind of desire capitalism fosters, e.g., 'good life', narratives. This includes fantasies of upward mobility, which are evoked in this painting, too, yet, which it fails to realize (especially, though not exclusively, in contemporary conditions of precarity). Optimism becomes cruel, for Berlant, 'when the object/scene that ignites a sense of possibility actually makes it impossible to attain the expansive transformation for which a person or a people risks striving.'[24] Fantasies, for example, of upward mobility have become more and more phantasmatic, not corresponding to how most people actually live. Yet, people remain stubbornly attached to these good-life narratives. This painting—and especially,

Christina's handicap—very strongly triggers this affective structure of cruel capitalism.

I began my reading of Andrew Wyeth's painting with the remark that melodrama is not a viable notion in art history or art criticism. Nevertheless, it has enabled me to read his painting productively by focusing on the articulation and punctuation of spatial and compositional elements. The resulting constellation could only be considered as 'constituted of meaningful signs' when considered as a melodramatic *mise-en-scène*. Does my use of this cinematic notion mean that Wyeth was directly influenced by melodramatic Hollywood film? Wyeth created his paintings in exactly the same period in which Sirk and Hitchcock were making their films.[25, 26] Should we therefore understand his work as typically cinematic?

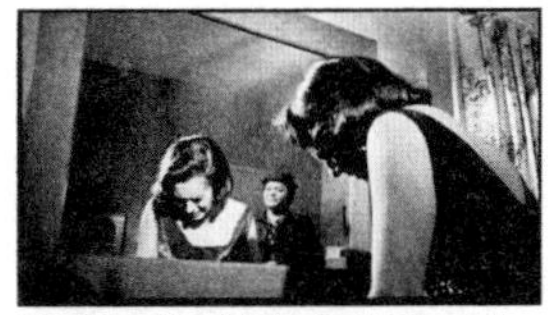

25 Douglas Sirk, *Imitation of Life* (1959), film still.

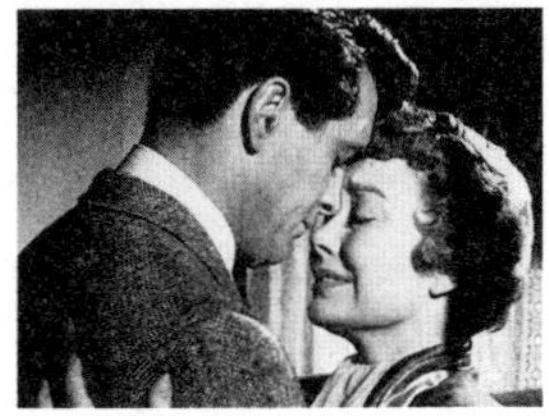

26 Douglas Sirk, *Magnificent Obsession* (1954), film still.

Not necessarily. Although melodrama has been described as a particular form of dramatic *mise-en-scène*, characterized by a dynamic use of spatial and musical elements, the special exploration of spatial categories in Hollywood cinema can also be seen as typically painterly. This is a plausible reading, since figurative painting has a long tradition of using space as more than a backdrop of a scene. It is rather common to consider spatial elements in painting as pervaded with meaning and interpretable signs. The main reason that the notion of melodrama has not been used much in art criticism is because of the sad tendency in some art criticism to understand representation and signification in terms of what the painting was modeled 'after'. Representation and signification, however, take place 'in' painting, in exactly the same way as articulation and punctuation in melodrama do.

Do Affects Have Forms?

In my reading of *Christina's World* I have focused on *mise-en-scène*, as if the *mise-en-scène* of the figure in this painting consists of spatial elements pervaded with meaning and readable signs. Although the reading was all about emotion and feeling, I have not really used the concept of affect or the vocabulary of affect theory. My formulations seem to have relied on the discourse of signification and the production of meaning. What role did affect play in my reading? And can my reading be reconciled with Brinkema's notion of the 'forms of affects'?

Although I have closely read spatial forms and assigned meaning to those forms, the significations did not follow the conventional semiotic path. A semiotic production of meaning is by definition conventional, it takes place on the basis of culturally shared conventions. In art history, it is first of all iconography that enables a semiotic reading of culturally shared codes. And, indeed, Elsaesser assumes that American melodrama has its own fixed iconography of the claustrophobic atmosphere of the bourgeois home and small-town setting. I would like to doubt the fixity of this iconography by not endorsing an opposition between conventional signs and unconventional, dynamic affects. The issue is rather how we process signifying forms (signifiers): as conventional signs or, with a somewhat contradictory term, as affective signs? The kind of significations of forms I have pointed out as striking, possibly significant, were rather unconventional, although also exploited in the genre of melodrama in intriguing ways without establishing a fixed convention. It was forms that 'shocked me to thought'.

As we have seen above, this expression, 'shock to thought', is Deleuzian, and Deleuze has another expression that indicates this intimate relationship between affect and thought or meaning, namely 'the encountered sign', developed through Proust. Using 'the encountered sign' as an alternative for affect is at first sight highly paradoxical, if we consider affect to go beyond signification and the production of meaning. As I have mentioned, Deleuze introduced the term in his book *Proust and Signs*, defining it as a sign that is felt rather than recognized, perceived through cognition or through familiarity with the 'code'. But the sensation of the encountered sign is not an end in itself. For Deleuze, this sensation is a catalyst for critical inquiry or thought. For him, an affect is a more effective trigger for profound thought than rational inquiry or conventional productions of meaning, because of the way in which it grasps us, forcing us to engage involuntarily: 'More important than thought there is "what leads to thought" . . . impressions which force us to look, encounters which force us to interpret, expressions which force us to think.'[27]

27 Deleuze, *Proust and Signs* (1964), 161.

For Deleuze, then, art and literature should not be approached as conventional sign systems, as iconographic for example, but as the embodiment of sensation that stimulates thought. Art does not illustrate or embody a proposition, but produces sensations or affects that stimulate thought. It is the affective encounter through which thought proceeds and moves towards deeper truth. By means of this affective view of art and literature, Deleuze deconstructs the conventional opposition between philosophy and art, or between thought and sensation. For him, both are modes of thinking. But whereas philosophers think in concepts, artists think by means of sensation.

> Sensation is generated through the artist's engagement with the medium, through color and line in the case of

28 Bennett, *Empathic Vision* (2005), 37.

> the painter, so that it is not the residue of self-expression, or a property of some prior self, but emerges in the present, as it attaches to figures in the image.[28]

This understanding of sensation of Jill Bennett provides a beautiful characterization of my affective reading of Andrew Wyeth's *Christina's World*, which was not based on conventional significations, but on unconventional forms encountered as sensations that shocked to thought.

Playing the Holocaust

Playacting and Toys

In an interview from 1994, French artist Christian Boltanski declares that all of his work is 'more or less about the Holocaust'.[1] This remark is not particularly revealing for the work that he has been making since 1984. His installations generically titled *Shadows, Candles, Monuments, Canada, Reserve,* evoke the Holocaust compellingly. But the statement is not as obvious when applied to his earlier work. Just how do the *Model Images* (1975) or the *Comic Sketches* (1974) relate to the Holocaust? This question opens the inquiry to which the current chapter is devoted. *Model Images* shows ordinary snapshots from the 1970s, ones that are common in photo albums of almost anyone who lived in Western Europe, Canada or the United States at the time. Their normality is the opposite of the apocalyptic horror of the Holocaust. The theme of the Holocaust is also hard to notice, at least at first sight, in the series of staged photographs titled *Comic Sketches*. In these works, Boltanski himself humouristically playacts scenes from ordinary childhood.

In 'The Shameful Kiss' for instance, he plays a young boy who meets a young girl at the beach. He wants to kiss

1 Marsh, in 'Christian, Carrion, Clown and Jew' (1990), n.p.

2 The series *Comic Sketches* consists of the following 'short stories': 'Le mariage des parents', 'La maladie du grand-père', 'Les souvenirs du grand-père', 'La toilette du matin', 'La mort du grand-père', 'La grossesse de la mère', 'Le baiser caché', 'Le grand-père a la pêche', 'Les bonnes notes', 'L'horrible découverte', 'La toilette de la mère', 'Le récit du père', 'L'anniversaire', 'La naissance de Christian', 'Le baiser honteux', 'La tâche d'encre', 'La dureté du père', 'La première communion', 'La visite du docteur', 'Le père à la chasse', 'La grimace punie.'

her, but he is too shy. In 'The First Communion' we see Boltanski playing a young boy who receives a host from a priest. In 'The Doctor's Visit' we see him as a young boy who is ill. His mother is worried and calls for the doctor, who comes and says that although the little one is very ill, it is not serious. This is a great relief to the mother. In short, the *Comic Sketches* show scenes that can be recognized by practically everyone. They are the most ordinary and archetypal childhood scenes imaginable.[2]

There is, however, a remarkable difference between the *Model Images* and the *Comic Sketches*. In the *Model Images*, Boltanski used found snapshots. Moreover, the images we see are 'serious', not comical. The scenes in the *Comic Sketches*, in contrast, are playacted. Importantly, all the roles are played by Boltanski wearing the same dark suit. By adding something simple to this outfit he can become another character—with glasses, a doctor; with a hat and flower, a mother. This minimalist play of distinguishing characters, together with the facial expressions, make the scenes comical. It is this aspect of *play* that interests me for this chapter. In *Comic Sketches* Boltanski, the child of a Jewish father who survived the Holocaust through hiding, foreshadows a younger generation of artists whose work deals with the Holocaust 'playfully'. These artists are second- or third-generation descendants of survivors or bystanders, and they use play or toys to represent the Holocaust or Nazi Germany.

I would like to single out three of these artists. The first is American artist David Levinthal, who photographed scenes from Auschwitz in his *Mein Kampf* series (1993–1994), staged by means of little dolls or figurines. The figurines remind us of the little tin soldiers, for decades a popular toy for young boys and a collectors' item for adult men. In a work that he made with Garry Trudeau titled *Hitler Moves East* (1977), Levinthal represented, in the same way, Operation Barbarossa, Hitler's invasion of the Soviet Union in 1941. The second is Israeli/Dutch artist Ram Katzir, who made a series of installations in which the audience was invited to colour the images of a colouring book or to make additions to it. The images of the colouring book were based on Nazi photographs or documentary Holocaust images. The third, Polish artist Zbigniew Libera, made *LEGO Concentration Camp Set*. This set consists of seven boxes in different sizes from which a miniature concentration camp can be built.

These artists represent a group, and their work a particular genre. This genre has a specific epistemic-artistic thrust. These artworks raise the following question: what is the function of *play* in Holocaust representation? Since Holocaust art centers on the question of remembrance, I rephrase this question more provocatively: Is there a place for 'playing' the Holocaust in Holocaust remembrance? The issue of generation is important. For it is striking that until these artists came along, representing the Holocaust playfully had been a strict taboo. Now it seems that a new generation of artists can relate to the Holocaust only in the mode of play. Why does the toy as memory occur now? In other words, what does it mean and how can we evaluate this phenomenon in terms of remembrance?

I broach this issue through the question of Boltanski's playful *Comic Sketches*. Taking seriously the artist's statement 'all my work is more or less about the Holocaust', I am interested in speculating in what way these pictures relate to the Holocaust. Again, the exaggerated poses of his characters and the rather silly events they enact evoke collective, ordinary notions of childhood and parenthood. They don't represent the specificity of Boltanski's autobiographical childhood,

3 Boltanski, *Christian Boltanski* (1994).

nor the situation of children in the Holocaust. I contend that their generic and ordinary plots are precisely the point.

Their point is replacement. Through their normality, these comic sketches actively and playfully replace the abnormality we expect from 'Holocaust Sketches' with sketches of ordinary childhood and parenthood. In an interview with Paul Bradley, Charles Esche and Nicole White, Boltanski says the following about his work:

> CB When I am doing art, I am a liar and I am mostly an awful professional artist, disgusting, it is my job … it is true that I really wanted to forget my childhood. I have spoken a lot about a childhood, but it was not my childhood. It was a normal childhood. I never spoke about something that was true, and in my art at the beginning it seemed biographical but nothing was true, and I was never speaking about the fact that I was Jewish or that it was impossible for my mother to move because she had polio. I never spoke about that and I never spoke about my weird grandmother. When I spoke about my childhood, it was this normal childhood and when I decided to make a photo album, I chose the photo album of my friend called Durant because Durant is just Smith in England, Durant is nobody, just a normal French man.
>
> NW Is this a way to re-create a better childhood?
>
> CB To erase and forget my own childhood. You know it was so tough, it was so awful, I mean all our parents are awful, but my father was so awful, my mother was so awful.
>
> NW But it is not just to forget, but to make something better.
>
> CB Yes, just normal.[3]

In this interview Boltanski refuses to say anything specific about his childhood, only that his father was awful and his mother was awful. That's it. In doing so, he suggests that all parents are awful, your own always a bit worse than those of others. What he makes clear is that, for him, art is a mode of telling lies. Art does not represent reality, autobiographical or not. Instead, it is a mode of transforming an insufferable reality into something normal—something sufferable, bearable. In this conception, art is not mimetic, but performative instead. This makes it easier to understand how the *Comic Sketches* are works of art 'about the Holocaust'. In post-Holocaust culture they act upon an intense desire for normality. This pertains to the domain of affect.

Boltanski's remarks also clarify that within his oeuvre the *Comic Sketches* are not at all unique. They are not divergent because of their playfulness. On the contrary, they are emblematic of all of his work, including the work he made in the late eighties and nineties. In another interview he explains how this is possible:

> At the time of the *Saynetes Comiques* (Comic Sketches) I was asking myself questions about the nature of representation and the double meaning of the verb 'to play' [...] In a small book of 1974, *Quelques interprétations par Christian Boltanski* I ask myself what differentiates the act of someone who drinks a glass of water and an actor's interpretation of someone drinking a glass of water. I realized that art consisted of making something with the intention of demonstrating the reality of these two situations.[4]

The *Comic Sketches* emphasize an aspect of art that, for Boltanski, defines art as such. Art is 'play' and 'play' is the reality of it. The reality of play is fundamentally different

4 The French expression 'interprétation' means interpretation in the sense of explanation but also 'performance', as in playacting. The quotation comes from Delphine Renard, 'Entretien avec Christian Boltanski', in Boltanski, *Boltanski* (1984), 85.

5 Katzir, *Your Coloring Book* (1996–1998).

6 A transcript of this emotional discussion can be found in Libera, 'Discussion' (1998).

from the reality to which art mimetically refers. This early work, then, has an artistic manifesto inscribed in its silly childishness.

In Boltanski's work, the notion of art as play has never been controversial. When this aspect of art becomes its theme, as happens in the *Comic Sketches*, the reference to the Holocaust is invisible or at most implicit. But that thematic restraint differs with a younger generation of artists that include Levinthal, Katzir and Libera. These artists enact the Holocaust playfully, with emphatic explicitness, using toys. Rightly or wrongly, toys stand for the lightheartedness of children, for the opposite of serious adult behaviour. In this respect, we cannot ignore the 'serious' dark suit that Boltanski wears beneath his children's attributes. In the context of modern art, toys are often considered bizarre or of marginal interest, but in the context of Holocaust representation they are provocative, even scandalous.

The work of Katzir and Libera has led to great controversies, especially because of the places where the art has been shown. When Katzir showed his installation *Your Coloring Book* in 1997 at the Israel Museum in Jerusalem, questions were even asked in the Knesset about how the installation might shock and hurt. Some people urged that it be closed down.[5] And when Libera showed and discussed his work in 1997 in Brussels at a conference on contemporary art and the Holocaust, organized by the Fondation Auschwitz, many were scandalized. Holocaust survivors in the audience became so emotional that they had to leave the room. Throughout the conference, people could not stop discussing the controversial nature of Libera's work.[6]

It seems safe to assume that artworks on the theme of the Holocaust using toys are controversial by definition, because of the special function automatically attributed to Holocaust art. Unlike other art that can claim autonomy or self-reflexivity, Holocaust art tends to be unreflectively reduced to how it can promote Holocaust education and Holocaust remembrance. Art, teaching and remembrance are thus collapsed without any sustained debate about the bond between these three cultural activities. In the context of Holocaust education and remembrance it is an unassailable axiom that historical genres and discourses, such as the documentary, the memoir, testimony, or the monument are much more effective and morally responsible in teaching the historical events than imaginative discourses. Accordingly, art in general is already problematic in and of itself, because it is imaginative, not documentary.[7]

7 For a more extensive argumentation on this, see above, in the first chapter and following, and Alphen, van, *Caught by History* (1997).

This objection to artistic engagement with the Holocaust holds much more strongly for toy art. Obviously, if art is not 'serious' enough in terms of historical reconstruction, it is clear that within the realm of the imaginative, toys represent the lowest and least respected activity. For they can be seen as doubly imaginative—as things to play with and to play out, as toys and as art. Fictional Holocaust novels are also problematic, as the controversies around Jerzy Kosinski's *The Painted Bird*, D.M. Thomas' *The White Hotel*, or Helen Darville's *The Hand that Signed the Paper* have shown. But at least such novels can teach something about the past, even though they are fictions. That is why the hybrid genre of the historical novel has gained respect and popularity.

Other hybrid genres are not so lucky. Roberto Benigni's film *Life is Beautiful* (1997), mixing the discourse of the Holocaust with that of fairy tales, caused great controversy; it was not historically engaged enough. The cardboard sets mocked realism; the script, the acting, and the filming itself emphasized that the mode of the film was a dramatic, slightly kitschy fairy-tale. Ignoring the cinematic genre that the film itself flaunted, it was judged on the basis of its truthfulness, a test it could only fail, and emphatically sought to fail. Hence, the play the father engaged in with his child to save him from the horror around him was not appreciated as pedagogically interesting, as a refusal to subject the child to events of his childhood entitled him to stay clear, but instead rejected as unrealistic.

Sander Gilman, for instance, dismissed Benigni's film on such realist grounds:

> Not purposeful action by adults but the accident of change allows children to survive, and this underpins the falsity of Roberto Benigni's *claim*. [...] Benigni's *promise* is that there are no accidents, that at the end of the comedy the gods in the machine will arrive to resolve the action and rescue those in danger.[8]

8 Gilman, 'Is Life Beautiful? Can the Shoah Be Funny?' (2000), 304, emphasis added.

I have emphasized words that demonstrate Gilman's unreflective attribution of a realistic intention (claim) as well as a childish attitude of expectation (promise). No other art would be subjected to such inappropriate criticism. As much as Benigni's film is already misread, this kind of reading is even more absurd for toy art. For, one of the remarkable features of toy art is that it cannot be compared to such representational genres as novels and films or other narrative material used for education. Toys do not tell. But how do they teach? Do they teach at all, or do they do something else?

Teaching as a Cultural Activity

In order to understand if and how toys teach, and what they teach if they do, it is necessary to reflect on teaching as a cultural activity, especially the role teaching plays in Holocaust remembrance. As Shoshana Felman has argued,

> Western pedagogy can be said to culminate in Hegel's philosophical didacticism: the Hegelian concept of 'Absolute knowledge' [...] is in effect what pedagogy has always aimed as its ideal: the exhaustion—through methodical investigation—of all there is to know; the absolute completion termination—of apprenticeship. Complete and totally appropriated knowledge will become—in all senses of the word—a *mastery*.[9]

Learning, according to this traditional conception she renders, is linear, cumulative and progressive, and leads to mastery of the subject studied. Mastery over the Holocaust is, indeed, one of the main motivations behind Holocaust education. In order to prevent something like the Holocaust from happening again, later generations have to have as much knowledge as possible about the Holocaust. It is through knowledge that one can 'master' the Holocaust. This conception of teaching assumes a collapse of two forms of mastery: to *know* and to *dominate*. If the past is known, the future can be dominated, kept under control.

But it is precisely that conception of learning as pursuing mastery over the object of study that seems to fail in the face of the Holocaust. Ram Katzir, for instance, noticed the over-familiarity with Nazi and anti-Nazi propaganda at the Israeli schools he attended. Even the most shocking images have been robbed of the power to move or to create serious attention by being turned into just another school subject.[10] In response to that education, he felt the need to revitalize Nazi photographs by using them as models for a colouring book. Boredom, not mastery, seems to be the result of the Holocaust education Katzir received.

9 Felman, 'Psychoanalysis and Education' (1982), 28.

10 Katzir, *Your Coloring Book* (1996–1998), 40.

11 Libera, 'Discussion' (1998), 225.

12 Derrida, *Dissemination* (1981).

13 Alphen, van, *Caught by History* (1997).

Holocaust teaching and remembrance in Poland had a similar effect on Zbigniew Libera. At the conference on contemporary art and the Holocaust organized by the Fondation Auschwitz in Brussels, he defended his art as follows:

> Of course, I was born fifteen years after the war and sometimes people call my art 'toxic' and actually it is toxic. But why? Because I am poisoned, I am poisoned of it. And that's all.[11]

Poisoning, like boredom, is the opposite of mastery, for it weakens a person. As a result, the weakened subject can no longer master himself or herself. Thus, the subject becomes unfit to master what is being studied. But as Plato, and later Jacques Derrida, show as they borrow a metaphor from medicine, poison can also heal by homeopathy.[12]

I completely sympathize with this negative assessment of Holocaust education. Elsewhere I have written about the effect Holocaust education in the Netherlands has had on me.[13] As someone born in the Netherlands in 1958, who attended primary and high school in the 1960s and early 1970s in the same country, I had the memory of World War II and the Holocaust drummed into my mind. Or rather, the Dutch school system tried to do so. But these efforts failed to have the required effect. I was bored to death by all the stories and images of that war, which were held out to me 'officially' as moral warnings. At school we were shown documentaries of the war. Our teachers encouraged us to read books that informed us in great detail of what had happened not so very long ago. But I avoided my society's official war narratives. Until decades later, for instance, I had refused to read Anne Frank's *Diary of a Young Girl*.

The kind of Holocaust teaching to which Katzir, Libera and myself have been exposed, fails because of two misconceptions. The first concerns the goal of teaching. That goal cannot be reduced exclusively to the mastery of a subject. Moreover, mastery as knowledge does not entail mastery as control. The second misconception concerns the nature of the Holocaust. The Holocaust is not just a history of memories that can be mastered by memorizing it. If that is impossible, the Holocaust cannot be taught along traditional pedagogical lines. For as we know, the traditional conception of learning implies first remembering and memorizing. The Holocaust, in contrast, is first and foremost a history of trauma, that is, a history of non-mastery and non-memory. Teaching a history of trauma means teaching knowledge that is not in mastery of itself. Felman's assessment of literary knowledge and its implications for teaching this knowledge, seems also a precise assessment of Holocaust teaching. This teaching '*knows it knows, but does not know the meaning of its knowledge*— does not know *what* it knows'.[14] In other words, Holocaust teaching confronts us with the problem of how to master by means of teaching a past which has not been mastered yet and cannot be mastered.

14 Felman, 'Psychoanalysis and Education' (1982), 41.

Felman analyzes the dominant conception of teaching within a framework that asks whether psychoanalysis has renewed the questions and the practice of teaching. Unlike traditional methods and assumptions of education, she sees psychoanalysis as a radically new pedagogy. But in light of the traumatic, hence non-masterable nature of the Holocaust, her remarks on psychoanalysis as a mode of teaching can also provide a model for Holocaust teaching. It can provide a model, that is, for teaching knowledge which is not in possession of itself:

> Psychoanalysis is thus a pedagogical experience: as a process which gives access to new knowledge hitherto

> denied to consciousness, it affords what might be called a lesson in cognition (and in miscognition), an epistemological instruction.[15]

The mode of learning practiced by psychoanalysis is radically different from the view that learning is a simple one-way road from ignorance to knowledge. It proceeds not through linear progression, but through 'breakthroughs, leaps, discontinuities, regressions, and deferred action'.[16] This teaching has nothing in common with the transmission of ready-made knowledge. It is rather the creation of a new condition of knowledge: the creation of an original learning-disposition.[17]

This disposition is 'new' in the ways it handles and structures repression. And, as those familiar with the psychology of child rearing know, repression is one of the most important strategies of traditional pedagogy. Freud understood how an excessive practice of such repressive pedagogy breeds mental illness. He wrote:

> The child must learn to control his instincts. It is impossible to give him liberty to carry out all his impulses without restriction... Accordingly, *education must inhibit, forbid and suppress* and this is abundantly seen in all periods of history. But we have learnt from analysis that precisely this suppression of instincts involves the risk of neurotic illness...That education has to find its way between the Scylla of non-interference and the Charybdis of frustration... An optimum must be discovered which will enable education to achieve the most and damage the least...A moment's reflection tells us that hitherto education has fulfilled its task very badly and has done children great damage.[18]

15 Felman, 'Psychoanalysis and Education' (1982), 27.

16 Felman, 'Psychoanalysis and Education' (1982), 27.

17 Felman, 'Psychoanalysis and Education' (1982), 31.

18 Quoted from Freud's *New Introductory lectures* in Felman, 'Psychoanalysis and Education' (1982), 23.

Freud's definition of over-repressive education, as structured by prohibitions and suppression, seems to have become also the explicit guideline or epigraph for Holocaust education. In the education of the Holocaust, prohibitions usually take the form of their binary opposite: They are articulated as orders or commands. Those orders together constitute a Holocaust 'etiquette', according to Sander Gilman.[19] But his own indignation in the face of a film like Benigni's that disobeys the 'etiquette' demonstrates that the rules also entail prohibitions.

The moral imperative of the prescriptions for 'respectable' Holocaust education and studies is more than explicit in the formulations of Terrence Des Pres. Appropriating, in a nice case of interdiscursive heterogeneity, the voice of God through his use of the 'genre' of the Commandments, he dictates:

> 1. The Holocaust shall be represented, in its totality, as a unique event, as a special case and kingdom of its own, above or below or apart from history.
> 2. Representations of the Holocaust shall be as accurate and faithful as possible to the facts and conditions of the event, without change or manipulation for any reason—artistic reasons included.
> 3. The Holocaust shall be approached as a solemn or even sacred event, with a seriousness admitting no response that might obscure its enormity or dishonor its dead.[20]

No wonder that later generations get a bit restless under such weight. The Holocaust art using toys may be a deliberate violation of these commandments and their complementary prohibitions.

First of all, Levinthal, Libera, and Katzir represent the Holocaust not as 'unique' but as a historical object that can be

19 Gilman, 'Is Life Beautiful? Can the Shoah Be Funny?' (2000), 282.

20 Des Pres, in Lang (ed.), *Writing and the Holocaust* (1988), 217.

toyed with, one that is exchangeable with, let's say, the Wild West, knights and medieval castles, pirates and pirate ships. Second, accuracy and faithful representation do not appear to have a high priority in their artworks. That lack of representational truthfulness does not imply that these toy artworks can be blamed for being the product of Holocaust denial. They are not untrue. In logical terms they are neither true nor false. For, they are not propositional statements. But something other than accuracy or historical truth is at stake. Third, the works actively seem to ignore the seriousness related to the Holocaust as a 'solemn or sacred event'. Instead, these artworks make us imagine (and feel) the pleasure certain toys can provide; affect roars its head. The toys imply pleasurable activities: identification, and impersonation or playacting. They run against the grain of traditional teaching. But then, is this art at fault, or is such teaching?

Identifying with the Perpetrator

To further probe the relationship between toy art and pedagogy, a tension must be acknowledged between the representation of documentation on the one hand, and (affective) identification on the other. Representation traditionally uses strategies that promote identification, but the relation is not reversible. Identification can be brought about outside the realm of representation. In the case of the artworks under discussion, indeed, identification is solicited while representation is at best mocked, or otherwise discarded. The issue of identification is ticklish in a double respect. First, identification predominates in the mode of looking that is stimulated by the works, at the expense of representation. Second, the target of identification has shifted in a drastic and rather shocking way, from that of the victim to that of the perpetrator. These two aspects of identification—its centrality and predominance over representation, and its shifted target—are inextricably bound together. They change Holocaust remembrance, art's role in it, and identification itself.

Presenting these artworks as toys (Libera, Katzir) or as images of toys (Levinthal) stimulates the viewer to envision herself or himself in a situation comparable to the 'real' situation. Identification replaces mastery. The toys (or images thereof) function as means that facilitate this envisioning oneself in the historical situation. So, the *distance* from the past required for mastery, which in Holocaust representation is so tenaciously guarded in the preference for historical genres and solemn tones—even, as we have seen, religiously so, speaking in a divine voice—is not respected but provocatively challenged. But the use of identification as a pedagogical tool is not problematic, or ticklish, as such. Recently, it has been applied in several Holocaust museums in order to make visitors imagine what it meant to be victimized. For instance, in the Holocaust Museum in Washington, D.C. the itinerary leads visitors through a cattle car. The experience of being transported to the camps by cattle cars is not being told about or shown at a distance but is thrusted upon the visitors. Inside a cattle car, identifying with those who were transported to the camps by those cars is almost unavoidable. In that museum, the kind of identification that is allowed, and even stimulated, is identification with the victims, not with the victimizers. But of course, in the context of an outing to a museum, such identification is not 'real', not total, but partial. Getting a small and short taste of the experience, a tiny bit of the poison, is the goal.

What if the object of identification consists of the victimizers instead, however? The toy artworks under discussion facilitate identification not with the victims, but with the perpetrators. This is, of course, much more difficult to do as well as to justify. How do the toy artworks accomplish this, and how can it be argued that this is helpful for the cultural remembrance of the Holocaust? In other words, how can this unsettling kind of identification be an effective form of pedagogy? One way to achieve this identification with an undesirable position is through making, shaping, forming the perpetrators. The visitors of Katzir's installations were invited to colour in images based on Nazi photography.[21] We, as visitors, are colouring Nazi leaders or members of the Nazi youth: we are giving them colour, form and substance, and in that process we 'generate' them. This making of the Nazis is a convoluted yet real form of identification. In creating the perpetrators, we as visitors become somewhat complicit in the possibility of the Nazis—not, of course, with *actual* Nazis.

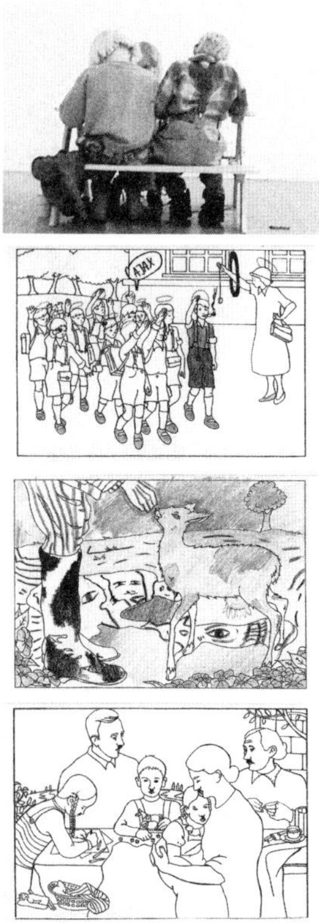

21 Ram Katzir, *Your Coloring Book* (1996–1998), audience participatory installation.

Libera deploys a different technique to make visitors get a small taste of identification with the perpetrators. His *LEGO Concentration Camp Set* stimulates visitors of the museum or the gallery to envision the possibility of *building your own concentration camp*. Again, viewers are put in the shoes of the victimizers, not of the victims. Here the identification concerns the acts perpetrated, conceiving of and constructing the physical tools of the Holocaust.[22] Levinthal's photographs are at first sight more ambiguous. His scenes of 'playing the Holocaust' seem to facilitate identification with victims as well as with perpetrators. But the moment we start to take the title of these photographs into consideration (*Mein Kampf*) the ambiguity evaporates, and we end up with an enforced identification with Hitler, the author of *Mein Kampf*.[23] We each have our own *Kampf*, our own ambitions that can be catastrophic. Here the identification triggers the ideological mindset out of which the historical disaster sprung.[24]

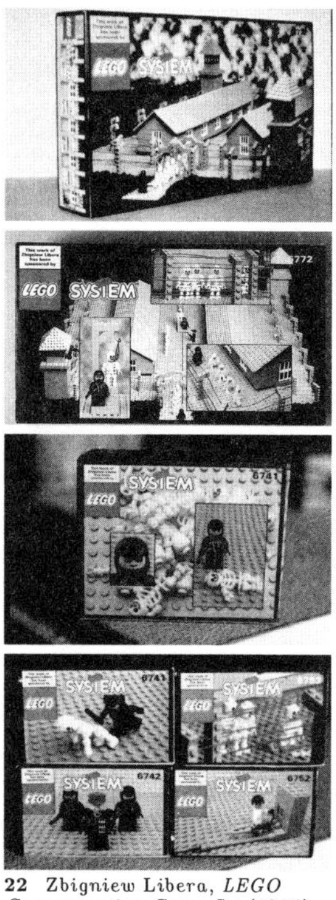

22 Zbigniew Libera, *LEGO Concentration Camp Set* (1996), installations.

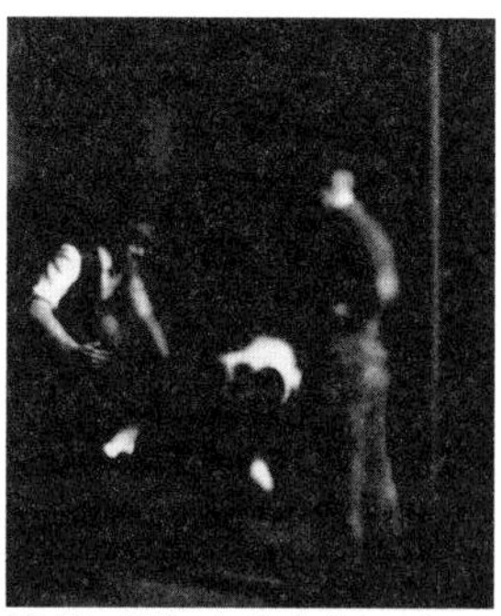

23 David Levinthal, from the series *Mein Kampf* (1993–1994), photograph.

This feature of the toy art calls for extending the genre or linking it to a neighbouring genre. Based on the artistic strategy of soliciting identification with the perpetrator, I claim a generic grouping on a much larger scale. Other art becomes understandable under the aegis of toy art. For example, the Israeli artist Roee Rosen's installation *Live and Die as Eva Braun* (1995) activates this mode of looking without the framework of toys and children and their emphatic relation to pedagogy. His installation consists of brief texts, printed in white letters on black column-like strips that run from floor to ceiling. Between the text columns hang black-and-white works on paper, sixty in total.[25] The texts are written in the second person. This is a powerful semiotic mode to entice the addressee to respond to and hence endorse a position. This 'message', although emanating from the first-person voice who is doing the addressing, may so strongly engage the second person—for example, for the first person to completely identify with the second—that endorsing the position put forward becomes hard to resist.[26]

This is the powerful rhetoric that Rosen deploys for the visitor to achieve identification—again, just a bit of it—with Eva Braun. The texts address the viewer. But they also address the historical figure Eva Braun, inviting the visitor to 'become' Hitler's mistress, Eva Braun:

> Excitement jolts through your body when you hear the steps outside. When he opens the door, you gasp at the sight of his small mustache. Because you are not only Eva it seems menacing, almost monstrous. But everything around the mustache is so congenial. He comes towards you with such warmth, his smile tired, his arms open to embrace you. Remember—you are Eva. When Hitler closes his arms around you, the view darkens and

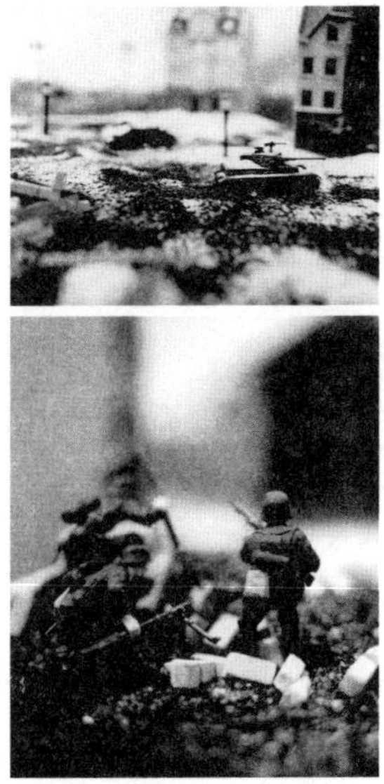

24 David Levinthal, from the series *Hitler Moves East* (1972–1975), photograph.

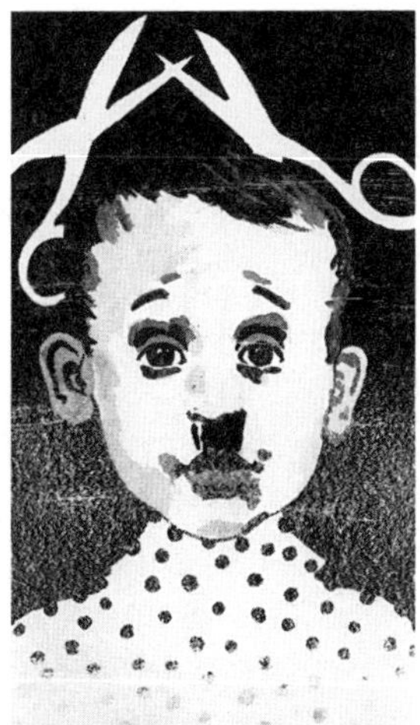

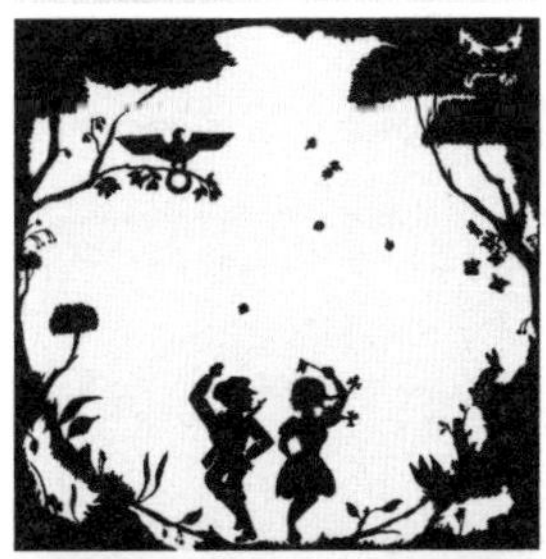

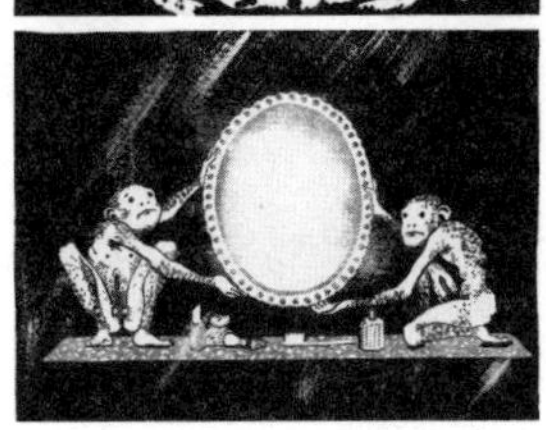

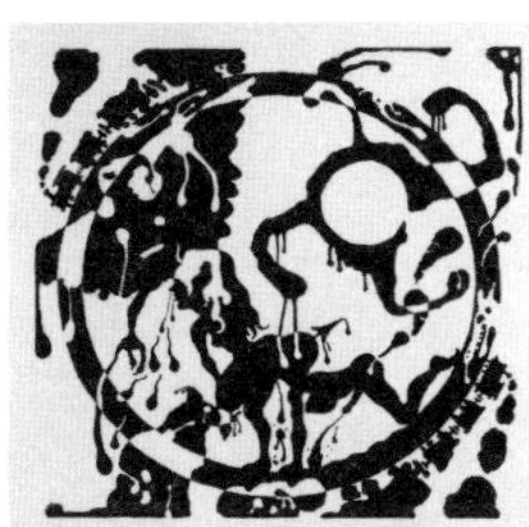

25 Roee Rosen, from the series *Live and Die as Eva Braun* (1995), installation.

26 See on the issues of second-person narrative Chapter 6 of Bal, *Quoting Caravaggio* (1999).

> you are almost overwhelmed with titillation when you feel the whiskers of that famous little facial tuft tickle your ear and the back of your neck.

Unlikely as it seems, this text so insists on humane qualities —warmth, a tired smile—that identification on the part of 'you', the second person, with the addressee of the text becomes quite plausible.

It should be noted that the identification programmed by this text is not blind. The viewer *is* Eva Braun and s/he *is not*: 'Because you are not only Eva it seems menacing.' What is menacing is precisely the schizophrenic identification with someone you really don't want to be. The threat of collapse of two incompatible positions that nevertheless coincide is unsettling. Like the identification with the victims triggered by the installations and rides in the Holocaust Museum, the identification is just a small taste of the actual experience. But unlike the cattle car, Rosen's work makes this restriction explicit. Moreover, focusing on Hitler's little moustache opens the story up to a rather heavy-handed irony. These two devices for portioning off a small, bearable measure of identification is Rosen's way of being a responsible educator. Nevertheless, identification and distance are being exchanged. This rhythm of alternation facilitates reflection on the experience of identifying with Eva Braun.

The texts follow a linear narrative. First, along with Eva Braun, the viewer experiences moments of romantic intimacy and sexual pleasure, then he or she is invited to co-experience Eva's suicide. The end of the story consists of a short trip to hell:

> There's no question, you are being led to hell—but why?
>
> As you wait for your tortures to be set, you view some of the other sinners. Particularly arresting is a

> group of two-dimensional people hanged by their sinning organs—hair, genitalia, breasts, tongues.
>
> You realize with some dismay that hell seems to be based on a famous painting.
>
> How would you be hanged? What of you should be minced, sliced, burnt? What, in your eager perfection, in your life dedicated to willful servitude, in your quiet harmony, is eternally punishable and damned?

All the events the viewer is asked to experience are totally set in the realm of affect and the physical: eroticism, sexual pleasure, suicide and torture. This is precisely the point.

An artwork based on the Holocaust like Rosen's cannot be dealt with simply in the framework of art and aestheticism; it inevitably activates the debate on Holocaust education and remembrance. This makes the cultural clichés acutely problematic. For, it can be argued that, regardless of that context, the texts are here and there straightforwardly obscene. This obscenity produces a clash, again, a challenge to the solemnity of Holocaust education. As Roger Rothman has pointed out, however, it is not in the context of art but in the context of Holocaust remembrance, that Rosen's *Live and Die as Eva Braun* is 'obscene':

> For we are *taught* how to mourn, just as we are taught how to paint. There is nothing 'real' or 'natural' about it. The language of our mourning is not our own, it is given to us. This perhaps the most repugnant of all the implications of *Live and Die*. Our Mourning is clichéd. It is not real. It is virtual. It is a game. A game we know how to play well by now. We are good at it and we know it. And we teach it to others so they will be good at it, too. This is the 'obscene' aspect of Rosen's work. But it is also the obscene aspect of Holocaust mourning, an

27 Rothman, in Rosen, *Live and Die as Eva Braun* (1997), n.p.

aspect all-too-often ignored or suppressed in mainstream memorials.[27]

Instead of rejecting the work for its obscenity, then, Rothman embraces that obscenity because of its relevance for Holocaust remembrance and mourning. Here, because of its mock dramatic style, but even more because of its second-person address that comes close to dramatic form, I consider Rosen's installation together with the artworks by Levinthal, Katzir and Libera within the framework of Holocaust remembrance through play. In this context, we are better off not jumping to conclusions. It is not necessary to conclude that in their provocative refusal of the 'commandments' of Holocaust education and representation, these artworks imply a wholesale refusal of the relation between art and education or art and remembrance. And Rosen's work, obscenity and all, is an instructive counterexample.

Rosen's insistence on the resonance between memory and painting retains a bond in the act that severs it. The bond with representations that are both imaginative and culturally commonplace, as well as recalled from the past—medieval paintings of Hell, for example—is simultaneously evoked, activated and severed, indicted for its loss of adequacy. For, following Freud and Felman, we can say that the artists install a new condition of knowledge that enables a new production of knowledge. This knowledge is first of all affective instead of cognitive. It is precisely this affective quality that is crucial in these Holocaust artworks. These artists need the concept of play and toys (or, in the case of Rosen, the reiteration of cultural commonplaces such as sexuality, suicide and torture) to replace cognition by *affect* on the agenda of Holocaust remembrance and its pedagogy.

Rosen's are ambiguous texts in terms of identification; they both entice and relativize identification with the evil side of the Holocaust. Unlike the identification provided by the Holocaust Museum, but equally partial, this work and the toy works solicit a form of identification that is not only different in target, but qualitatively different. As Kaja Silverman has argued, identification takes one of two forms.[28] One form involves taking the other into the self on the basis of a (projected) likeness, so that the other 'becomes' or 'becomes like' the self. Features that are similar are enhanced in the process; features that remain irreducibly other are cast aside or ignored. Silverman calls this idiopathic identification. The other form is heteropathic. Here, the self who is doing the identification takes the risk of temporarily and partially—'becoming' (like) the other. This is both exciting and risky, enriching and dangerous, but at any rate, affectively powerful.

In the case at hand, it can be argued that identification with the victims, although useful in realizing their horror, is also a way of reassuring visitors, perhaps unduly, of their fundamental innocence. To put the case strongly, this reassurance is unwarranted, and unhelpful in achieving the ultimate goal of Holocaust education: preventing history from repeating itself. Victimhood cannot control the future. In contrast, soliciting partial and temporary identification with the perpetrators makes one aware of the ease with which one can slide into a measure of complicity. To raise the possibility of such identification with the fundamentally cultural other, is appealing to heteropathic identification. Precisely because toys and play are not 'serious', toy art is so eminently suitable to solicit such heteropathic identification, which begins to blur overly rigid boundaries.

28 Silverman, *The Threshold of the Visible World* (1996).

Art and Pedagogy

So far, I have put forward the notion that the traditional, dogmatic 'rules' for Holocaust remembrance and education are inevitably a framing device for understanding the Holocaust art that challenges those rules. This frame is so powerful because when the Holocaust is concerned, education more than any other cultural practice is the transgenerational tool for remembrance. This view risks subjugating art to the pedagogical pursuit of Holocaust education. Through its reference to childhood, toy art endorses this subjugation but changes its terms. This antagonistic pedagogy as a major feature of the toys suggests that Holocaust art is a special, negative case of aesthetics in its 'interestedness'. It is not autonomous, as art since modernism likes to see itself, but subordinated, put in the service of another, inevitably 'higher' goal. In contrast, in the wake of Kant, art is usually seen as disinterested, that is, free from educational ideals. The toy art discussed here breaks through this opposition. Distinct from such a subjugation of Holocaust art to education, Libera's works seem to imply that Holocaust art and other kinds of art are not at all opposed. In this respect Holocaust art is not different, but perhaps only a stronger, more evident case of the pedagogical ambition of art in general. Hence, the shift this art brings to the pedagogy of remembrance also entails a change of aesthetics.

Libera's artistic interest is focused on those cultural products that serve to educate in the sense of forming the human being. To 'form', here, should be understood in the figurative as well as in the literal sense. The objects that he creates are made up of appliances that already exist in the contemporary cultural world, such as toys or machines used in fitness clubs or beauty salons. These are not related to the Holocaust. Besides the LEGO *Concentration Camp Set*, for example, he made *You Can Shave the Baby*. These are five pairs of baby dolls, with a shock of red hair emanating from their heads, and sprouting from their pubic areas, lower legs and underarms. *Ken's Aunt* is a barbie doll in the form of an overweight woman. These works have an upbeat tone to them that contrasts sharply with Rosen's suicide scene, yet in Rosen's work, the earlier, erotic fantasies have a similar artificial positivity to them. Libera's *Doll you can Undress* is a doll which reveals her stomach area and visible intestines. And *Eroica* is a set of fifty boxes of small bronze figurines that look like toy soldiers. But this time it is not the army but civilians, women, and the oppressed of society that are the toy-soldiers we play with. The tone here is more unsettling. Other works by Libera present themselves as 'correcting devices', such as: *Universal Penis Expander, Body Master* and *Placebo*. What matters in this non-Holocaust aspect of Libera's work is the emphasis on correction or 'forming'. 'Forming' takes on a multiple layered meaning. In light of this, the 'making' that underlies them all receives yet another nuance.

Libera's artistic *oeuvre* shows that although his LEGO *Concentration Camp Set* is unique in having the Holocaust as its subject matter, all of his works address, literally or figuratively, the education of body and of mind. In an illuminating essay, Andrew Boardman has argued that Libera challenges the contemporary belief that aesthetic values are disinterested, fluid or free-form. On the contrary, contemporary Western art is essentially a remnant from an indelible nineteenth-century construct according to which art and education go hand in hand with moral strength and prudence.

29 Boardman, *Zbigniew Libera* (1998), n.p.

> Although art produced today likes to believe that it has shed the majority of those stodgy 19th-century precepts, it has carefully disguised them in the fine-woven cloak of pedagogy. The built-in assumption of art today is that it acts to inform us, develop our faculties and therefore deliver us from a transgressive and earthly ignorance into the safe arms of civilization. [...] One might argue that Libera's work, because of its visual connection to child development and to learning, superficially epitomizes this 19th-century bourgeois outlook. In fact, by wrapping his work in this upright mode of educational discourse, Libera questions the sweet platitudes and patronizing certainties of art that adhere in our educational aspirations for visual culture.[29]

From this perspective, the target of Libera's LEGO *Concentration Camp Set* is twofold. In addition to exposing the repressions and inhibitions of Holocaust education and its conceptions of remembrance, he also exposes the moral rectitude of (contemporary) art.

These two conclusions make it clear that we cannot stop at the idea that in modern Western culture art unavoidably teaches and forms. The specificity of toy art remains *play*, which is also the tool for freedom from pedagogical lessons. The intricate relationship between art and teaching can neither be dismissed nor endorsed. No matter what art's pedagogical mission is, the function of play in relation both to art and to teaching needs to be considered. The question that is thrust upon us is also double: Does *play* teach, and how does play *teach* differently? Is the result or 'mastery' provided by play of a different order than the mastery resulting from cumulative and progressive learning?

Holocaust Narrative Versus Holocaust Drama

To understand how the mastery provided by toys differs from the mastery provided by 'learnable' knowledge, both modes of learning must be analyzed in terms of the generic discourse to which each belongs. 'Learnable knowledge' of the Holocaust takes the form of narrative. Personal narratives in the form of testimonies, diaries or memoirs are seen as especially instructive, teaching later generations not simply the facts of the Holocaust but its apocalyptic inhumanity. It is safe to assume that all Holocaust education, including the one that takes the form of art, shares this goal. But the artworks by Levinthal, Libera, Katzir or Rosen don't tell us much about the past. Like Boltanski's *Comic Sketches* before them, they envision playing the past. And I use the verb *envision* emphatically, because—with the possible exception of Katzir, who experimented with museum visitors actually colouring the books, on which more later—these works are not real toys. Instead, they are artworks in the form of toys.

These artworks are meant to be processed by adults, not by children. The distance between children playing and adults envisioning themselves as those children adds yet another layer of identification, in which adults act—or rather playact—like children. In the art under scrutiny, a shift in semiotic mode is at stake. The Holocaust is not represented by means of narration, but in the mode of drama or a script for a drama. This is, of course, more literally true in the cases of Katzir's installation and Libera's LEGO box than in the case of Levinthal's photographs. But I contend that Levinthal's photographs should also be understood as drama. It is as such that they solicit heteropathic identification and the possibility to identify with the other. In the case of the Holocaust the other is the moral other, no longer an inevitably

30 Young, in Levinthal, *Mein Kampf* (1996), 72.

abstract evil force from the beyond, but a person with whom one can even feel complicitous. Drama, then, becomes a centrally important semiotic mode of education.

James Young has remarked that the photographs of *Mein Kampf* generate a powerful sense of the past through a measured act of simulation. He uses the phrase 'a sense of the past' to distinguish an effect from an actuality.[30] What strikes me most, however, and in analogy to Young's view, is how these works generate a 'sense of the present'. This presentness points to their affective charge. I don't see fictional, narrativized images of a concentration camp. What I see, imagine, or even what I *am*, is a subject in post-Holocaust culture playing with a (fake) concentration camp. The narrative images are embedded in, or produced by, an act that should generically be defined as drama. And this difference between narrative and drama is of crucial importance in understanding what is at stake in the artworks under discussion.

You cannot actually play with Libera's LEGO boxes. But they evoke the possibility of a scene in which somebody in post-Holocaust culture performs Holocaust events within the setting of a camp. Constructing the setting, the artist facilitates the articulation of playacting Holocaust events. Katzir's work does not just envision the dramatic mode of representation, it really enacts it. In his installations of *Your Coloring Book*, realized in different ways in Utrecht, Enschede, Jerusalem, Vilnius, Krakow, Berlin, and Amsterdam, visitors were invited to sit on school benches and to colour or draw in the colouring books that had been placed on classrooms desks or tables. The visitors were drawn into a performance in which they actualized, shaped and coloured—in other words, generated—Nazi characters.

This dramatic aspect of the toy works is important in terms of both education and, specifically, Holocaust remembrance. For the difference between narrative and drama is particularly relevant for the understanding—a condition for curing—trauma. Drama is a very particular cultural form that is fundamentally different in form and effect from narrative. And this specificity of drama improves what toy art offers to Holocaust education and remembrance. In order to assess the crucial difference between works of art that narrate events from the Holocaust and those that perform or playact it, the distinctions the French psychiatrist Pierre Janet made between narrative memory and traumatic memory, already discussed, are again helpful. Because this distinction is also very important for an understanding of how the artworks under discussion relate to the history of the Holocaust, let me recall this argument, now in close connection to the art discussed in the present chapter.

As I explained, narrative memory consists of mental constructs that people use to make sense out of experience. Current and familiar experiences are automatically assimilated or integrated in existing mental structures. But some events resist integration: 'Frightening or novel experiences may not easily fit into existing cognitive schemes and either may be remembered with particular vividness or may totally resist integration.'[31] The memory of experiences which resist integration in existing meaning schemes are stored differently, and are not available for retrieval under ordinary conditions.

Trauma can be seen as failed experience. It is precisely this failure that makes it impossible to remember the event *voluntarily*. This is why traumatic reenactments take the form of drama, not narrative. Drama just presents itself, or so it seems; narrative implies some sort of mastery by the narrator. This is a fundamental difference. Bal sees this difference between narrative and drama as a matter of control over the

31 Kolk, van der & Van der Hart, 'The Intrusive Past' (1995), 160.

32 Bal, in Bal et al. (eds.), *Acts of Memory* (1999), ix.

33 Santner, in Friedlander (ed.), *Probing the Limits of Representation* (1992), 144.

events. Whereas the narrator of a story can always manipulate, expand and reduce, summarize, highlight, underscore, or minimize elements of the story at will, these options are inaccessible to the 'actor' who is bound to enact a drama.[32] This distinction between narrative memory and traumatic memory does not apply literally to the artworks under discussion. Although these works are not narrative, it is of little help to see them as instances of traumatic memory. These works are not involuntary re-enactments of the Holocaust, but rather purposeful attempts to shed the mastery that Holocaust narratives provide. Instead, they entice the viewer to enter into a relationship that is affective and emotional rather than cognitive. This is where the two parts of this book join forces.

Mastery is again the issue, but this time the method for obtaining this mastery is totally different: not mastery through knowledge, but mastery by admitting affect. This is by no means a passive opening up but an active countering of the foreclosure brought about by narrative mastery. To explain how these imaginative attempts to work through *work*, yet another distinction must be invoked. I am referring to the distinction made by Eric Santner between 'narrative fetishism' and mourning. He defines narrative fetishism as the construction and deployment of a narrative consciously or unconsciously designed to expunge the traces of the trauma or loss that called that narrative into being in the first place. The work of mourning, on the contrary, is a process of elaborating and integrating the reality of loss or traumatic shock by remembering and repeating it in symbolically and dialogically mediated doses. It is a process of translating, troping, and figuring loss.[33]

Santner uses Freud's discussion of the *fort/da* game in *Beyond the Pleasure Principle* to explain the mechanisms of mourning. Freud observed the fort/da game in the behaviour of his one-and-a-half-year-old grandson. In this game the child was able to master his grief over his separation from his mother by staging, playacting, his own performance of her disappearance. (She was gone—*fort*; then she was there—*da*.) This little boy, we can now see, was involved in heteropathic identification with the person who was, in his everyday drama, the 'perpetrator', the mother who left him. He did so by repetition, using props that D.W. Winnicott would call transitional objects. This game is based on a ritualized mechanism of dosing out and representing absence by means of substitutive figures. In the words of Santner:

> The dosing out of a certain negative—a thanatotic—element as a strategy of mastering a real and traumatic loss is a fundamentally homeopathic procedure. In a homeopathic procedure the controlled introduction of a negative element—a symbolic or, in medical contexts, real poison—helps to heal a system infected by a similar poisonous substance. The poison becomes a cure by empowering the individual to master the potentially traumatic effects of large doses of the morphologically related poison. In the fort/da game it is the rhythmic manipulation of signifiers and figures, objects and syllables instituting an absence that serves as the poison that cures.[34]

In the Holocaust toys, similarly, the poisonous—also Libera's word—stuff, needed in a carefully measured dose, is the 'Holocaust effect': to playact the camps instead of talking 'about' them or looking 'at' them.

This 'playing the Holocaust' does and does not distance the Holocaust to the past. It does not, because through the programmed identification the viewer is situated *inside* the camp, building and generating it. The heteropathic identification with the perpetrator, moreover, is effectuated

34 Santner, in Friedlander (ed.), *Probing the Limits of Representation* (1992), 146.

35 Hirsch, *Family Frames* (1997); see above, chapter 3.

through the role of the child. In the case of Freud's grandson, it was the child's own drama that was enacted. Here, the child stands for the next generations, who need to learn a trauma they have not directly lived, although, as Marianne Hirsch and others have emphasized, they may suffer from *postmemory*.[35] But at the same time, by the same gesture, a double distance is produced: play instead of reality, and art instead of real play, an institutional frame that sets these toys apart. To playact the Holocaust in this way is performed under the strict direction of a 'director', a *metteur en scène,* which is radically distinct from a 'revival' or 'repetition' of Nazism in the dangerous shape of neo-Nazism.

Touching Toys

Why is it that this trend of 'playing' the Holocaust by means of toys characterizes the art of this current second, third and fourth generation of post-Holocaust survivors and bystanders? How can this work contribute to the cultural necessity to shake loose the traumatic fixation in victim positions that might be partly responsible for the 'poisonous' boredom that risks jeopardizing all efforts to teach the Holocaust under the emblem 'never again'? In the face of the overdose of information and educational documentary material, there is clearly a need to complete a process of working-through not yet 'done' effectively. The overdose was counterproductive. In the face of that overdose, 'ignorance' is needed. An ignorance, not in terms of information about the Holocaust events, but of everything that stands in the way of a 'felt knowledge' of the emotions these events entailed. This is where affect is indispensable. Primarily, of the narrative mastery so predominant in traditional education.

In that perspective, the toys, with their childish connotations, 'fake' that ignorance that clears away the 'adult' overdose of information that raises obstacles to felt knowledge. 'Mastery', then, is no longer an epistemic mastery of what happened, but a performative mastery of the emotions triggered by the happenings. Only by working through knowledge that is not 'out there' to be passively consumed, but 'felt' anew every time again, by those who must keep in touch with the past, can art be effectively *touching*.

The Performativity of Provocation

The Case of Artur Żmijewski

Binding in the Present

Performativity occurs in, and on behalf of the present. This is where the two parts of this book collide and collude. This can be seen with special clarity in the speech act of provocation, which occurs in, and addresses, the present. True to my method of developing theoretical insights through 'thinking' artworks, in this chapter, I analyze the performative of provocation by focusing on two works by the Polish artist Artur Żmijewski: *Game of Tag* (1999) and *80064* (2005). Both works deal with the Holocaust in confrontational ways, and were highly controversial when they were exhibited. In their problematic nature, these works substantiate Slavoj Žižek's paradoxical statement that a coherent, truthful account of the traumatic past belies its own truthfulness. A narrative of trauma cannot be a clear narrative.[1] This requires a different artistic, semiotic posture: not representation but performativity, so that conventional prescriptive moral rules can be replaced by an effective, affect-based ethics. Żmijewski's videos shake up the fixed notions of Nazi victims and Holocaust

1 Žižek, 'Description Without a Place' (2009), 142.

survivors. And that is the first necessary step towards opening up the debate to a series of questions about the role of, in this case, Polish people, in the Holocaust. The importance and even necessity of these questions is demonstrated by the recent legislation in Poland that outlaws blaming Poles for the crimes of the Holocaust.

For decades now, we have learned the important distinction between constative and performative speech acts; the one that informs, tells, or represents, from the one that acts; that does what it says. J.L. Austin's philosophy of language, from 1962,[2] has drastically revised our conception of language, undermining the predominance of information. Jacques Derrida radicalized this view in 1988 with an emphasis on reiteration.[3] And Judith Butler made this new foregrounding of performativity socially productive by arguing for its production of sex and gender, and the reality of wounding by hate speech.[4] This is by now standard in interpretive practice. Strangely, however, in Holocaust-related art, that lesson still seems to have little effect. However, in what precedes in this book, performativity and performance have played an important, albeit under-illuminated part. In this final chapter I will argue what misunderstandings occur when in that field, we stick to an old, obsolete view of language. The primary consequence is tense; for performativity is rigorously an act in the present.

The performative speech act that often overshoots its target is the one of provocation—which is why I bring it center-stage here. First of all, its obscurity is due to the fact that frequently, such a speech act is not recognized as provocative: it is misunderstood as a constative speech act. But even acknowledged as performative, it is often not clear in what kind of situation or event the provocative speech-act should result—what perlocutive effect is meant to occur.

2 Austin, *How to Do Things With Words* (1975).

3 Derrida, 'Signature, Event, Context' (1988).

4 See Butler, *Excitable Speech* (1997); Butler, *Bodies that Matter* (1993); Butler, *Gender Trouble* (1990).

When provocation concerns the Holocaust, the risk of the misfiring that speech act theory calls 'infelicity', is even bigger. In the case of the Holocaust, a rather limited number of performatives are considered acceptable. Acceptable, because of the strong post-Holocaust morality I have cited above, which stipulates what we should and what we shouldn't do in relation to the Holocaust past and victims. The two performatives that are pre-scribed as morally responsible and necessary are those of teaching and commemoration. The performative of provocation is not primarily focused on the 'teachable' and 'commemorable' past, but on the present situation that is being challenged, and the present second persons who are being addressed. This displacement from the Holocaust past to the present is then seen as disrespect for the Holocaust past and its victims, because the conveyance of truthful accounts of that past is no longer the most important goal.

However, the stipulation of the performatives of teaching and commemorating, of what we should and what we shouldn't do, is only productive to a limited degree. It is especially a problem when accounts of the Holocaust are represented by means of literary and artistic practices. According to Walter Benn Michaels, the stipulation of the right moral attitude towards the Holocaust 'produces the dominant form of kitsch today—ethical kitsch'.[5] One can speak of ethical kitsch when artistic and literary representations of the Holocaust are not evaluated on the basis of their truthfulness, but on the right attitude towards the historical truth. In the case of Holocaust representation, truthfulness is usually seen as an important criterion because 'to know what happened' is an absolute precondition for political life in the present. That fact is proven by Holocaust denial as the most nefarious political practice we can imagine.

5 Michaels, 'Never Again, or Nevermore' (2015), 163.

6 Žižek, 'Description Without a Place' (2009), 142.

Literary texts or artworks, however, are usually not interested in teaching and commemorating the Holocaust, truthfully or not, although those performative speech acts can be part of literary and artistic projects. Their function tends to lie elsewhere. It is not the business of art and literature to represent what already occurred, to represent the truth of the Holocaust. Historical genres and discourses are much better equipped to represent the Holocaust as a history of events. The abundance of historical accounts of the Holocaust, of history books, documentaries, testimonies, witness accounts have inured the audiences. It is not just the abundance of historical accounts that is responsible for this effect, however, but as I have argued via Des Pres in the previous chapter, more specifically the framing of these accounts by the morality that prescribes the right attitude towards the Holocaust. Instead of promoting the right moral attitude, art and literature set up conditions for *relating* to the events.

For, how to relate to these events, that for many people are unimaginable: that is the problem. This is first of all the case for the survivors. Literary attempts to reproduce the facts about the Holocaust in a documentary way neutralize the traumatic impact of the described events. As Žižek has argued, the truth of the Holocaust can only be accepted in the guise of fiction. This is so because its truth is too traumatic to be confronted directly. Because of this mechanism, 'the pleasure of aesthetic fiction about the Holocaust is not a simple escape, but a mode of coping with traumatic memory: it is a survival mechanism.'[6] This resonates with the second chapter of the present book. And although the fiction of art and literature does not represent documentary truth, it can be completely truthful. As Žižek explains, what makes a narrative of trauma truthful, is its factual unreliability, confusion, inconsistency. He even proposes the following paradox:

'The witness who would be able to offer a clear narrative of his camp experiences would thereby disqualify himself.' Factual deficiencies in the report of a traumatized subject signal that the reported content has contaminated the very form of reporting on it. Žižek's conclusion is provocatively convincing:

> The aesthetic lesson of this paradox is clear. The horror of the Holocaust cannot be represented; but this excess of represented content over its aesthetic representation has to infect the aesthetic form itself. What cannot be *described* should be *inscribed* into the aesthetic form as its uncanny distortion.[7]

And when Žižek writes: 'The horror of the Holocaust cannot be represented', he may seem to vary on Adorno's famous, but usually misunderstood indictment that it is barbaric to write poetry after Auschwitz. However, Žižek is pointing at a semiotic, representational impossibility to represent the extreme horror of the Holocaust, whereas Adorno's statement implies a moral indictment.

But today, most Holocaust art and literature is no longer made by the survivors themselves. Later generations have problems of a different order to relate to the unimaginable events. They have this difficulty, because the events continue to be constantly framed by a fixed morality that prescribes the right attitude to them. An example of such a fixed morality is the article by Tanja Schult.[8] The facts are horrible, even unimaginable, which makes the problem of how to relate to them even more acute. The prescription of the right moral attitude has a counterproductive effect. It makes the events even more unimaginable. There is, most importantly, a significant consequence for the social behaviour of later generations to the way they relate to the Holocaust. Instead of 'the

7 Žižek, 'Description Without a Place' (2009), 145–146.

8 Schult, in Popescu & Schult (eds.), *Revisiting Holocaust Representation in the Post-Witness Era* (2015).

right' attitude, we, later generations, need affective investments in the Holocaust, but importantly, an understanding of our affective investments, because it is due to this understanding that we can be ethical instead of moral in our thinking. That is, only then can we be actively doing, or thinking, what is right instead of following conventional prescriptions. According to Jill Bennett it is precisely such an understanding that distinguishes ethical from moral art:

> An ethics is enabled and invigorated by the capacity for transformation; that is precisely by not assuming that there is a given outside to thinking. A morality on the other hand, operates within the bounds of a given set of conventions, within which social and political problems must be solved.[9]

The given set of conventions of how to adopt the right attitude towards the Holocaust stifles an effective ethics; it results in a Holocaust morality, or in the words of Michaels, 'ethical kitsch'. Instead, the ultimate goal of a sincere, effective ethics concerns our social behaviour, behaviour which might substantiate the conventional slogan 'never again'. This requires an affective effect in the present.[10]

9 Bennett, *Empathic Vision* (2005), 15.

10 On sincerity, and its distinction from its rhetoric, see Alphen, van et al. (eds.), *The Rhetoric of Sincerity* (2009).

Probing an Authentic Ethics Performatively

Some art and literature on the Holocaust do not obey uncritically the Holocaust etiquette, its commandments and taboos. Bypassing those conventions, such art is able to invigorate a new, live ethics. Especially such art and literature succeed in establishing affective investments in the events of the Holocaust by later generations. To make this more concrete, I will discuss two works by the Polish artist Artur Żmijewski as successful attempts of establishing an ethical and affective relationship to the Holocaust. He is able to do that because he refrains from the fixed morality that prescribes the right attitude towards the Holocaust. Although his works have been extremely controversial, precisely those aspects that make them controversial are, I will argue, those which activate an affective investment in the Holocaust.

Żmijewski's work can be best characterized through one of his own remarks about himself: 'I film situations I have provoked and set in motion.'[11] This describes what most of his films have in common. The artist sets up conditions in which individual people play out a trajectory of proceedings. The trajectories set in motion are fueled by curiosity and the desire to learn. This curiosity is enacted in the most radical way, because morality is suspended. This operating principle is inspired by the radical pedagogy of Żmijewski's teacher at the Academy of Fine Arts in Warsaw, Professor Grzegorz Kowalski. This influential teacher trained an entire generation of prominent artists among whom Katarzyna Kozyra, Pawel Althamer, and also Artur Żmijewski.

Żmijewski's artistic practice is the outcome of his theory of 'the applied social arts'. He introduced this term as the title of a manifesto he wrote in 2007 and published in the Polish journal *Krytyka Polityczna*. This journal is published by a group of artists, philosophers and political activists. Żmijewski is a pivotal member of this group. His theory of the applied social arts addresses the following issues:

> Does contemporary art have any visible social impact? Can the effects of an artist's work be seen and verified? Does art have any political significance—besides serving as a whipping boy for various populists? Is it possible to engage in a discussion with art—and is it worth doing

11 Żmijewski, 'A Storehouse of Limbs' (2005), 85.

so? Most of all, why are questions of this kind viewed as a blow against the very essence of art?[12]

In posing these questions Żmijewski seems to seek to reorient the relationship between art and politics as performative rather than constative (representational) and as 'away from being contradictory or mutually exclusive towards being complimentary and reciprocal'.[13] The impact of art on society is crucial for him. He is well aware of the fact that provocation can be the royal road to having an impact. In his own words:

> When, for instance, a radical cultural postulate expressed by an artist in the form of a visual action no longer antagonizes the public, does not evoke controversy, it means the message has become mainstream, entered into wide circulation, become part of elite knowledge, or even common knowledge.[14]

His provocations, instead, intend to disclose 'that which is hidden'.[15] His practice does not intend to inform, seduce or please the public.

Exorcizing Ghosts from a Haunted House

A prime example of Żmijewski's artistic practice of knowledge production through provocation is his video *Berek*, in English *Game of Tag*, made in 1999.[16] In this video we see a group of men and women, of different ages, play a kid's game, namely the game of tag. They are all naked; they run around chasing each other, laughing a lot. Sometimes they play the game fast and furiously, sometimes slowly. It takes place in an enclosed concrete space, which looks like a basement. But at the end we learn that there were two locations; one was the

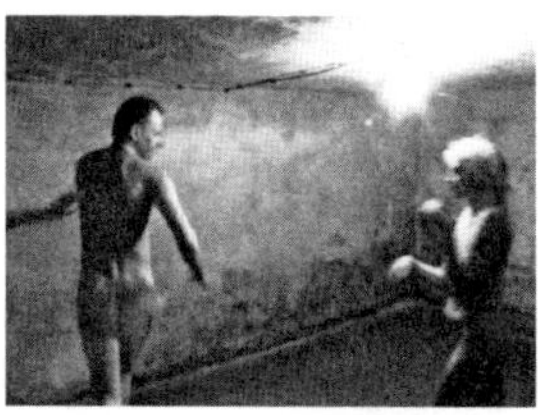
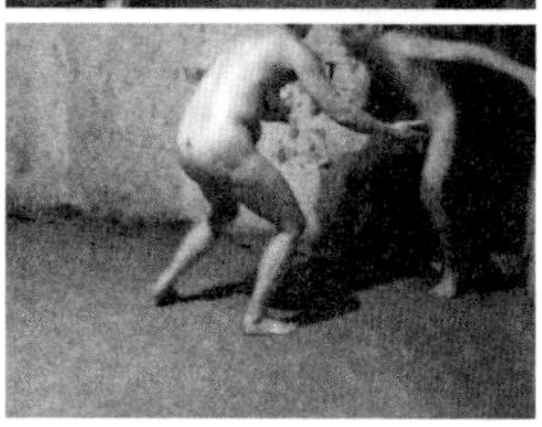
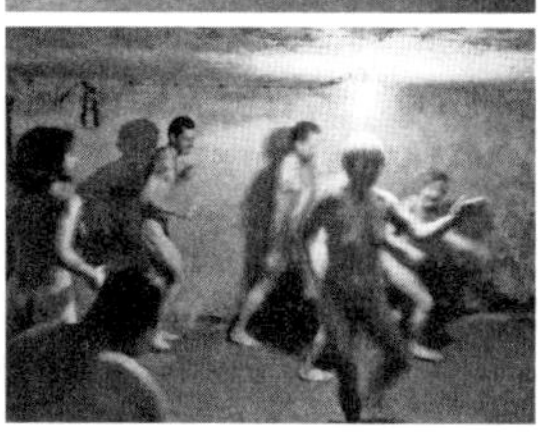
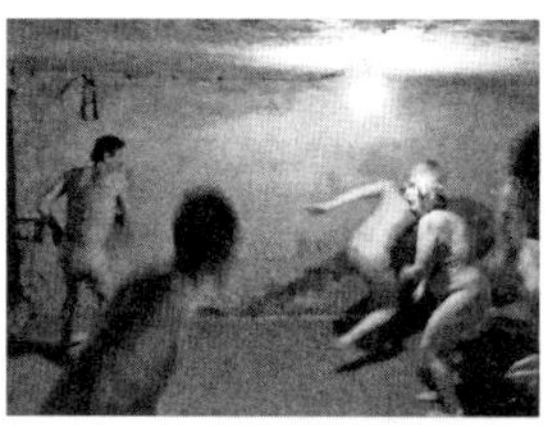
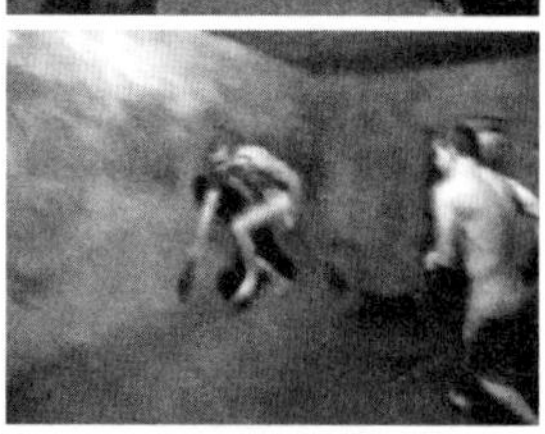
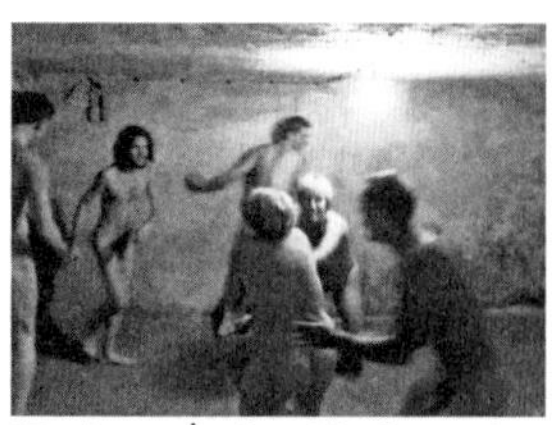

16 Artur Żmijewski, *Game of Tag* (1999), video stills.

12 Żmijewski, 'Applied Social Arts' (2007), 6.

13 Hlavajova, 'The Social Studio' (2008), 21.

14 Wolinski, 'Żmijewski' (2007).

15 Hlavajova, 'The Social Studio' (2008), 21.

basement of a private home, the other one was the gas chamber of a former Nazi extermination camp. Which camp it is, is not specified.

The controversies to which his video has led suggest that Żmijewski has violated the morality that prescribes the right attitude towards the Holocaust. When in 2012 the film was part of the exhibition 'Side by Side. Poland–Germany', curated by Anda Rottenberg, the director of the Martin-Gropius Bau, Gereon Sievernich, felt he had to remove it from the show, after protests that blamed Żmijewski for not respecting the dignity of the victims of the Holocaust. The director had taken this decision after Hermann Simon, the director of the New Synagogue Berlin and the Centrum Judaicum Foundation, had sent him a letter condemning the video. In 2015 the video was displayed in an art gallery in Estonia. Again, protests of the Jewish community led to the removal of the video from the show. When the film was included in 2015 in the show 'Poland–Israel–Germany: The Experience of Auschwitz' organized by the Museum of Contemporary Art in Krakow, several Jewish groups and officials called on the museum to remove the video installation from the show. Again, they blamed Żmijewski for a lack of respect for the victims. Although this time there were even international protests, especially from Israel, the director of the museum, Maria Anna Potocka, decided not to remove it, but she made changes in the display of it. Żmijewski's video was now presented with a warning and shielded off with added walls. She legitimized her decision to maintain the work by claiming that the intent of the exhibition was not to disrespect the memory of the Holocaust, but rather 'to awaken the young generation's empathy with the tragedy of the Holocaust by stirring their imagination'. In other words, to exert an effective ethical performativity.[17]

17 The protests this exhibition caused compelled the museum to produce a book, addressing the question how the Holocaust can be presented today, see Potocka (ed.), *Polyphonie des Holocaust* (2020).

Implicitly the protests stipulate what the right attitude toward the Holocaust is, and who is in charge of implementing this right attitude. First of all, former gas chambers should be treated as monuments; they stand symbolically for the victims who died there. Therefore, former gas chambers can only be allowed to be used as places of commemoration. Second, because of the fact that the majority of victims were Jewish, the memory of the Holocaust is owned by the Jewish people. That is why most protests came from Jewish organizations. Third, victims of the Holocaust are the people who died in the Holocaust, people who survived although they were supposed to be caught and killed in the Holocaust, and the offspring of people who were killed or who survived the Holocaust. That is the reason these organizations feel entitled to speak in the name of the murdered. This proprietary attitude strongly impedes the desired performativity that can make art socially activating.

Żmijewski clearly does not share these implications on which the right moral attitude is based, as we can see in in his description of his video project:

> In it a group of people play a kid's game. They are naked, they run around, they laugh a lot. But they are also very serious. They know where they are—in the gas chamber of a former extermination camp. *Berek* is about a part of history that is treated as untouchable and about overly painful memories, when the official commemorations of this history are not enough. The murdered people are victims—but we, the living, are also victims. And as such we need a kind of treatment or therapy, so we can create a symbolic alternative; instead of dead bodies we can see laughter and life. *Berek* is about how we can engage with this brutal history and work with imposed

> memory. It's possible to have active access to history, and to attempt to emancipate ourselves from the trauma.[18]

18 Sienkiewicz, 'Artur Żmijewski' (2009).

This statement answers a number of questions implied in the protests against Żmijewski's video. First of all, the category of victims is not restricted to the people who died in the Holocaust or who were meant to die there. Also, those who are 'living' after the Holocaust are in one way or another, victims of the Holocaust. One could ask oneself if this applies especially to those living in Poland, the country where some of the most notorious concentration camps of the Holocaust were located, and where most of the victims of the Holocaust died. Later generations in Poland are much more directly and intensely confronted with the legacies of the Holocaust than people in most other European countries, such as the Netherlands.

Secondly, those who came after, the living, do not have memories of the past of the Holocaust themselves; therefore, the memories they have, have been imposed on them. As discussed in in the chapter 'Explosions of Information, Implosions of Meaning: The Release of Affects' in the case of children and grandchildren who do not have their own memories of the Holocaust, the term 'post-memory' is often used to describe their imaginative efforts to relate to the past of the (grand)parents. But post-memories are not only the result of imaginative efforts of later generations. They are also imposed on later generations by means of morality. The memories do not come from within, but are internalized. Thirdly, because of the fact that those who are living also have to cope with a traumatic past, the official commemorations of the past of the Holocaust are not enough, because they do not focus on the living but on the dead. The past has to be worked through: 'We need a kind of therapy', in order

19 'Working through' as the alternative for a repetitive 'acting out' is Dominick LaCapra's Freud-based proposal in *Writing History, Writing Trauma* (2001).

'to attempt to emancipate ourselves from the trauma.' The therapy for the living is performed in the video; they, the living, play tag, 'they are naked, they run around, they laugh a lot'. The enacted situation should not be understood in terms of commemoration or a perverse violation of it, but in terms of therapy, in the sense of the psychoanalytic term 'working through'. Working through is the task for the younger generations; it is what the artwork's performativity provokes them to do. Clearly, 'representation' is the wrong category here. And 'respect' for the victims is not at issue. Activating the later audiences is the goal of the provocation.[19]

The notion of therapy is foregrounded by the playing of a game. It makes clear that it is not 'reality' or a representation of it; the ontological world into which the viewer is allowed, is different. The viewer is drawn into the imaginative world of play. In this sense, Żmijewski's video resonates with the toy art, discussed in the previous chapter. This crucial element of play and imagination is also suggested by the location where the game playing takes place. The credits of the video begin with the following statement:

> The film was shot in two different locations: in the basement of a private home and in a gas chamber of one of the former concentration camps.

It is, however, not specified in which concentration camp this gas chamber is located. In the many protests against Żmijewski's video the exact gas chamber is not identified either. The provocative statement about the location is puzzling in yet another respect. If the authenticity of the location, a real former gas chamber, is of any importance to Żmijewski's provocative therapeutic project, why then is half of the video filmed in the basement of a private home? This is especially puzzling because of the fact that the basement of the private home and the so-called gas chamber of a former concentration camp are very similar. They are so similar that I only became aware of the fact that two locations had been used after having read the credits. It is less and less plausible that Żmijewski filmed his video in an actual Nazi extermination camp; he seems to have filmed it in a space intended to resemble one.

The juxtaposition of an ordinary basement and a fictional gas chamber introduces the ontological dimension of play and imagination in yet another way. It suggests to imagine your own basement as a gas chamber. And to use it for something else, not for the enactment of death, but for the enactment of life: laugh and play; and laugh and play seriously. In Żmijewski's video this playful therapy is an effective working through of the trauma of the living. The living re-appropriate the place where they are living, a place which is haunted by the spectre of the Holocaust. It is not too far-fetched to identify this imaginary location as Poland. This re-appropriation is necessary because one of the effects of official commemorations is the continuation of this haunting spectre. This spectral effect is due to the fact that the Holocaust is more readily identified with the location of Poland than with Germany as its agent.

Something should also be said about the nakedness of the people playing tag. Victims who were sent into actual gas chambers were also naked. Does this mean that the naked people playing tag 'represent' those who were killed in gas chambers? I do not think so, because in all other respects the people playing tag look completely different. Their behaviour is the opposite of what we imagine the behaviour of people dying in gas chambers was like. In Żmijewski's work nakedness and playfulness are intimately related, not only in *Game of Tag*, but also in some of his other videos in which his actors are naked—for example, *Oko za Oko* (An Eye for an Eye), from 1998. The meaning of nakedness in his work is suggested by Żmijewski himself in one of his theoretical texts. In 'A Favorite Theory of Art' he declares the following: 'I am interested in mental space, the space of human contact, i.e., contact with another person'.[20] Later in the same text he explains how he understands mental space:

> Mental space is related to a superior order of the world, somewhat different for each individual, an order whose existence allows us to live. The violation of that order requires defense and defense, in turn, reveals the spans upon which the order was built. This is our normal nakedness, and is the most authentic encounter of all, although it can have little in common with pleasure or mutual ardour or warmth.[21]

Nakedness refers to authentic encounters with other persons, encounters which are mental, but can be best imagined and visualized by the contact of naked bodies. In *Game of Tag* the encounters with other persons take place within the imaginative situation of therapeutic working through the relation to a haunted house: Poland.[22]

20 Żmijewski, 'A Favorite Theory of Art' (2006), 68.

21 Żmijewski, 'A Favorite Theory of Art' (2006), 73.

22 About Holocaust representation in Poland, see Borowicz, in Popescu & Schult (eds.), *Revisiting Holocaust Representation in the Post-Witness Era* (2015).

Re-enacting Conformism

Another kind of provocation constitutes the performative heart of the next work by Żmijewski I will briefly discuss. In his video *80064*[23] from 2005 Żmijewski persuaded Józef Tarnawa, a 92-year-old former prisoner of Auschwitz to 'renew' his prisoner number tattooed on his arm. As one can imagine, this video also triggered controversy. The film was rejected by the Fritz Bauer Institute in Frankfurt, which

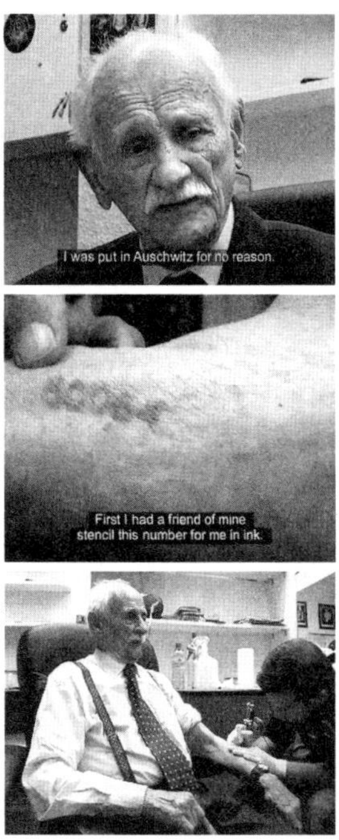

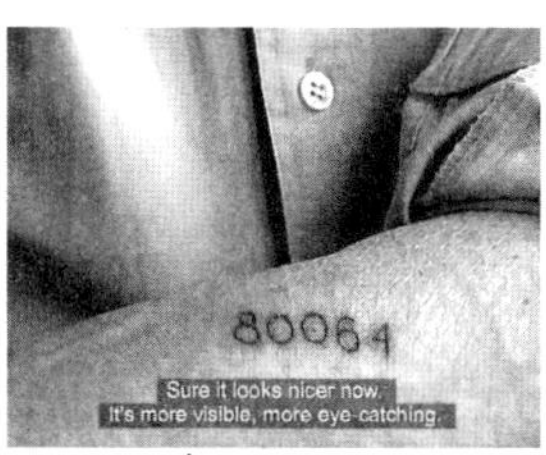

23 Artur Żmijewski, *80064* (2005), film stills.

commissioned it for an exhibition about forty years of trials against Nazi war criminals. The work Żmijewski had made did not meet the expectations of the Institute. This film too should be understood within a performative-therapeutic framework. According to Żmijewski's website it is a film experiment with memory. 'I expected that under the effect of the tattooing, the doors of memory would open.' In this respect the experiment resembles Lanzmann's *Shoah*. Lanzmann also tried to re-enact the trauma of survivors by interviewing them in situations similar to those in which the trauma originated. The barber in charge of shaving the new inmates arriving in Auschwitz was interviewed by Lanzmann in a barbershop. Lanzmann has been criticized for how he used traumatized survivors of Auschwitz for his own cinematic project.[24] His ambition to make an authentic documentary about the Holocaust was not the result of empathy for the survivors. On the contrary, according to some of his critics he exploited the survivors mercilessly to make his point about authenticity, truthfulness and the Holocaust, fiction film and documentary.[25] The re-enactment of the trauma of the survivor was not pursued within a therapeutic framework, but in a documentary one. In other words, it was not performatively effective, but only representational.

This question of performative vs. constative is precisely the sore point of Żmijewski's video *80064*. Is his film experiment at the same time a therapeutic experiment, or is a cinematic experiment performed under the pretext of therapy? In other words, is the therapeutic framework only *mise-en-scène*, or does it legitimize his cinematic experiment? In the case of Żmijewski's art practice this question is difficult to answer. This is so because his notion of art is thoroughly therapeutic and political as such. He radically opposes the idea that the so-called autonomy of art implies that all kinds

24 E.g. LaCapra, *Writing History, Writing Trauma* (2001).

25 See Hansen, 'Schindler's List Is Not *Shoah*' (1996).

26 Żmijewski, 'A Favorite Theory of Art' (2006), 69.

of excesses in art are by definition legitimized. In his own words:

> The artist is a product of the repulsion caused by acute reality, though the way its elements affect each of us is a personal matter. The artist levitates over that reality, lowering cognitive tentacles into it. Consequently, being an artist is a secure position, a justification for all kinds of excesses, and certainly artistic ones (the work). However, if we abolish the privileges that come with the title 'artist', those justifications disappear. The bandage is removed, and convention no longer offers asylum. This can be quite dangerous and painful, since the encounter with life without a 'life-proof' suit can hurt, especially when you touch swollen sore points.[26]

But who has been hurt in the case of *80064*? Is it the former prisoner of Auschwitz Józef Tarnawa, who is persuaded to renew his tattoo? Or is it the artist Artur Żmijewski, whose provocative artwork was rejected by the institution that commissioned him to make the work, and whose experiment to open the doors of memory of the viewers was successful in only a modest degree?

In order to answer these questions, we should look at what exactly happens when the old man is persuaded to refresh his tattoo. The man acknowledges that he agreed beforehand to have this done. But while being filmed he is having second thoughts. He likes his tattoo the way it is and does not see the point of renewing it. He worries what other people will think of it. But Żmijewski urges him implacably, and eventually the old man surrenders. The tattooist retraces the digits and a perfectly neat fresh tattoo is the result. The old man is, however, ambivalent; it is hard to tell what he feels after he surrendered.

There are two painful moments in the video that stand out. The first one is at the beginning when the old man is telling about Auschwitz. Whereas the exact identity of the man is so far unclear, he suggests implicitly that he was not sent to Auschwitz because of being Jewish:

> I ended up over there for no reason. I hadn't done anything. I was put in Auschwitz for no reason.

His clumsy way of expressing himself implies that other inmates of Auschwitz had 'done' things which explained and legitimized their transportation to Auschwitz. He, however, 'hadn't done anything'. Immediately after making this bizarre distinction between people who have and who have not done anything before ending up in Auschwitz, he tells about his arrival in Auschwitz:

> JÓZEF TARNAWA: Holy cow, we had no idea it was Auschwitz.
> ARTUR ŻMIJEWSKI: You hadn't known anything about Auschwitz before?
> JÓZEF TARNAWA: I knew that such a place existed, but I had no idea where. I wasn't interested, no one was.

Here, the conventional idea of the typical Holocaust victim is radically undermined. This man seems not to be Jewish but ethnically Polish. Another conventional idea is activated and seems to be confirmed, namely that the Polish population was largely indifferent to what happened to the Jewish population in their country, and in many cases even complicit.

The second painful moment comes after this and consists of Żmijewski's implacable urging. He does not show any empathy with the survivor when the latter has second thoughts about his earlier agreement to have his tattoo refreshed. He wants to proceed with the original script for this filmic experiment. Probably he insists because he expects that the renewal of the tattoo will release traumatic memories in the old man. But this never really happens. Whereas before the refreshing of the tattoo the man tells a few things about his experiences in Auschwitz, during the re-making of the tattoo and after it, the conversation only concerns this event in the present, nothing in the past.

The controversy about *80064* highlights only the second painful moment: the artist Żmijewski's implacable urging. Critics and viewers identify with the man as victim and have a blind spot for his possibly more ambiguous position in the past. The old, fragile man is victimized a second time, this time for an artistic, filmic experiment. Żmijewski's urging is, however, put in a completely different perspective when we take the remarks of the victim-survivor Józef Tarnawa into consideration. The conversation and confrontation in this video are not between a Jew and a Pole, but between two Polish people from two different generations. The younger Pole puts pressure on the older one and wants him to explain his indifference about the Holocaust. An indifference that is hard to understand, since he ended up in Auschwitz.

Our listening to Józef Tarnawa is a good example of the fixed morality that came into place after the Holocaust. He survived Auschwitz and is a victim of Nazi atrocities. This implies that our empathy with him should be total, should be without any reservation. This is the norm, because in the case of the conventional image of the Holocaust there are only two positions: victims and perpetrators. Yes, there were also bystanders, quite a number even, but because of the fact that Józef Tarnawa ended up in Auschwitz, he is just a victim. In the case of *80064* the prescription of the right moral attitude has clearly a counterproductive effect. It limits the video to a filmic experiment, intending to release traumatic memories in a survivor, very much like Lanzmann did in *Shoah*. Suspending this imposed morality makes it possible to look at this video differently, however. When we really listen to Józef Tarnawa the constellation in the video is very different: two Polish people, of two different generations. The younger Pole has set up this experimental situation in order to interrogate the older one about his ambiguous, conflicted role in World War II and the Holocaust. From this perspective Żmijewski's urging is no longer just implacable, but responsible and politically highly relevant. This relevance lies in his enactment of conformism in the Polish victim Józef Tarnawa. His indifference during World War II about the Holocaust shows its face in the video in the form of conformism. He gives in to a situation that asks for resistance. He gives in to the tyrannical artist and has his tattoo refreshed.

In the context of *Game of Tag*, I described Poland as a haunted house. Poland is not only a haunted house because a major part of the Holocaust took place on its soil. More importantly, it is haunted because it is far from clear what its involvement in and responsibility for the Holocaust was. The fixed morality makes it impossible to explore those questions. Żmijewski, however, who puts provocation at the heart of his artistic practice, is not afraid of this morality; he dares to explore these questions, even if the results in *80064* are disturbing. Józef Tarnawa testifies to his indifference to the Holocaust during the War, but that is all. But providing all kind of detailed information about his position and role in World War II, or re-enacting traumas contracted during his imprisonment in Auschwitz, is not the real issue. This video shakes up the fixed notions of Nazi victims and Holocaust survivors. And that is the first necessary step towards opening up the debate to a series of questions about the role of Polish people in the Holocaust.

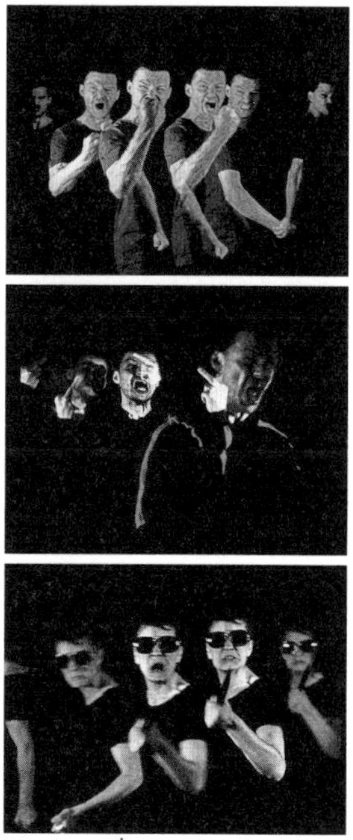
27 Artur Żmijewski, *Gestures* (2019), chronophotograph.

The importance of this debate has become even more urgent after the Lower House of the Polish Parliament passed legislation that would make it illegal to suggest Poland bore responsibility for atrocities committed on its soil by Nazi Germany during the occupation in World War II. Although Żmijewski made his *Game of Tag* and *80064* before the conservative Polish government had imposed this legislation, these new political circumstances renew the importance of Żmijewski's provocation to open up reflection and debate about the role of Polish people in the Holocaust. The ways these videos stir the imagination enacts effective ethical performativity, which is needed in debates about the Holocaust, at the present moment especially in Poland.

As an artist working in the now, and after having encountered rejections and other forms of contempt, it seems no coincidence that more recently, Żmijewski has made a series of photographs showing gestures of contempt, hatred, and exclusion. They express the hate-speech slogan 'shame on you!' in the most explicit way. Shame is a powerful affect. Żmijewski has taken these photographs using the classic technique of chronophotography, which captures human movement through multiple exposure. We know this kind of photography especially from nineteenth-century photographers like Étienne-Jules Marey. Each of Żmijewski's images is a study of a specific confrontation aimed at the viewer. Instead of recording actual public scenes, Żmijewski has them enacted in a studio using professional actors, thus neither analyzing the roots of the violence nor ascribing them to any particular identity. He looks at the gestures themselves and their morphology, beyond context or ideology. A range of aggressive gestures becomes a synthesis of behaviours.[27]

Those behaviours exist as a means of expression both in

private and public spaces where they constitute social relationships based on domination and exclusion. Taking the moment when Żmijewski made these images into consideration, namely 2019, two more specific contexts for the slogan 'Shame on You!' impose themselves. First of all, the international outcry against sexual abuse and intimidation of the #MeToo movement; secondly the Polish context of an extreme right-wing government. Those two together suggest that the object on which shame is bestowed in Żmijewski's images, is male sexuality and male authority, both abusive. It is of course also the context of this itinerary through art that activates these two elements as objects of shame on top of, but also through that framing, the two historical contexts. This is how Żmijewski's affective art can resonate with the traumatic re-enactments in the aftermath of disaster, to which the first part of his book was devoted, while compelling a realization that affective transmission happens in the present. Thus, both past and present, and the impact of the former on the latter but importantly, also, vice versa, cannot be ignored in (visual) culture today.

Contemporary Iconoclasm and Affect

Contesting Public History

In recent years, all over the world statues have been removed from their plinths, as an act of destruction, as a total refusal and negation of the historical past embodied by the removed statues. Already some years ago, the Cecil John Rhodes statue at the university of Cape Town[1] was removed by the university on 9 April 2015, after ongoing protests of the black student population. More recently, on 7 June 2020, the statue of Edward Colston in Bristol was destroyed[2] and thrown into the water; this time, however, not by officials, but by the protesters themselves. As we now know, Edward Colston was not only an English merchant, philanthropist and Tory and Member of Parliament, but also an Atlantic slave trader. After Black Lives Matter protests in the wake of the murder of George Floyd, many statues in American cities were removed or are going to be removed or adapted soon. In the Netherlands, too, there are many controversies around statues and other kinds of historical places. The most important one concerns the statue of Jan Pieterszoon Coen,[3] in his birthplace Hoorn. Let me quote what can be found on him on Wikipedia:

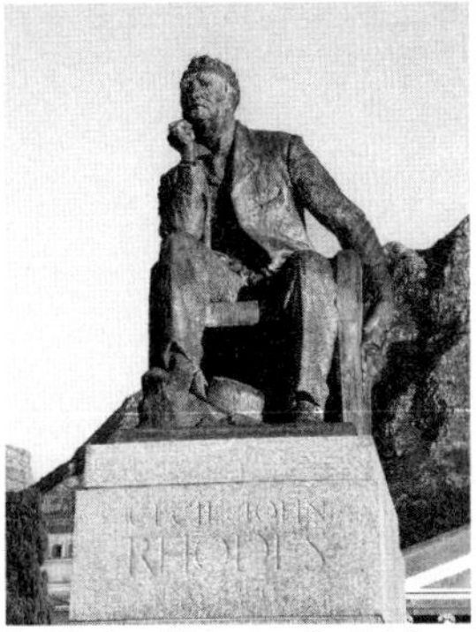

1 Marion Walgate, *Cecil John Rhodes*, Capetown (1934), sculpture.

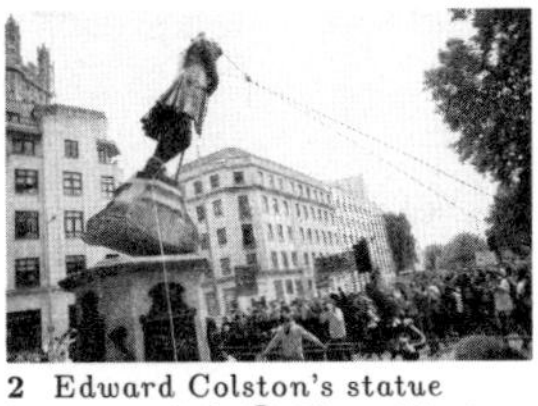

2 Edward Colston's statue being toppled. © Photo Marton Gosztonyi.

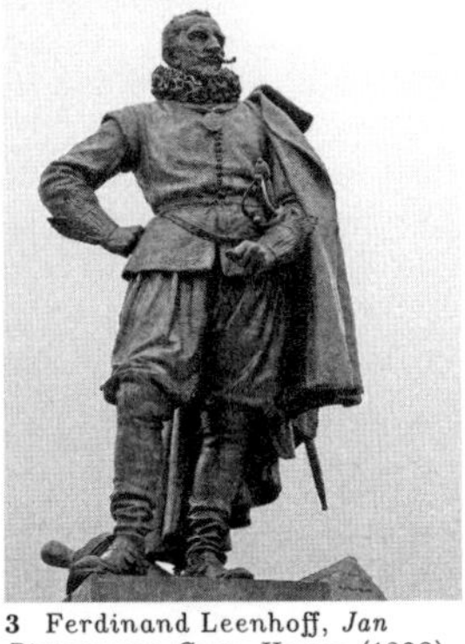

3 Ferdinand Leenhoff, *Jan Pieterszoon Coen*, Hoorn (1893), sculpture.

> Jan Pieterszoon Coen was an officer of the Dutch East India Company in the early 17th century, holding two terms as Governor-General of the Dutch East Indies. He was the founder of Batavia, capital of the Dutch East Indies. Renowned for providing the impulse that set the VOC on the path to dominance in the Dutch East Indies, he was long considered a national hero in the Netherlands. Since the nineteenth century, his legacy has become controversial due to the violence he employed, especially during the last stage of the Dutch conquest of the Banda Islands, in order to secure a trade monopoly on nutmeg, mace and clove.

Many protests have taken place to get this statue removed from the place where it was originally established at the end of the nineteenth century, the central square of the town of Hoorn. But it is still there, although it was accidentally toppled a few years ago by a crane removing Christmas lighting.

What all the above examples have in common is that the famous, illustrious men elevated on their pedestals had an involvement in slavery, in an imperialist, colonial-racist past. People who are critical of the destruction of these historical sites or *lieux de mémoire* tend to have a very rational way of thinking about solving the problem embodied by these historical markers. Instead of removing the statue and destroying the historical site, the site should be reframed. For example, Cecil John Rhodes should not be remembered as the founder of the South African territory of Rhodesia, but also as a British colonialist responsible for the racial segregation under Apartheid. When we destroy this historical site by removing the statue, we lose and repress important historical knowledge. So, the meaning embodied in these statues should not be repressed but reframed by adding the problematic, that is, the racist, colonial background of these figures. This, it is argued, stimulates the historical understanding of the world we live in.

But it is indeed a paradox that in times in which people consider history more and more important, people do not want to *see* history anymore in the public space, in the neighbourhoods or cities they live in. We are less and less future oriented and as compensation for that more and more past oriented. But our interest in history is first of all personal; public history is contested.

At first, and only at first sight, I can follow the kind of rational argumentation set out above, and I even agree with it, insofar as we do not gain much by making historical knowledge we do not like invisible. But this mode of thinking also leaves an important dimension of these historical sites and statues undiscussed, namely how they work affectively.[4] These statues are not just about the historical meanings they embody or repress, but also about the affects they trigger. Let me explain what I mean with the affective power of these colonial, racist historical sites by the example of the affect of shame and how these statues, depending on who looks at them, do not just activate feelings of admiration, but also of shame. This shame does not concern the venerated figure, but the person who watches it.

4 For a critical assessment of the different uses of the term affect, see Alphen, van, 'Affective Operations of Art and Literature' (2008); for a mapping of different affective transmissions, see Alphen, van & Jirsa (eds.), *How to Do Things With Affects* (2019).

The Painfulness of History

After having made the film *12 Years a Slave,* Steve McQueen was interviewed by Decca Aitkenhead for *The Guardian*. The title of the interview was 'Steve McQueen: My Hidden Shame'. The painful secret behind his shame is the history of slavery. When the interviewer asks him if he feels angry

5 Aitkenhead, 'Steve McQueen' (2014).

6 Long, in Van Alphen (ed.), *Shame! And Masculinity* (2020), 154, emphasis in original.

about this history of black people, he is puzzled and baffled by this question and answers:

> Angry? No. You feel hurt that someone did such things, but angry? No. Painful, sure. Hurt, absolutely. I do not know if that can be seen as anger. Not to say that I am not angry with injustice, of course—and slavery is a huge injustice. But thinking about it that way? No.[5]

McQueen makes a distinction between slavery as injustice and slavery as a painful past experience that still hurts him personally. This painfulness makes him shameful.

Although slavery officially, that is politically and juridically, belongs to the past, it remains part of our societies. In his contribution to the book *Shame! and Masculinity*, which I edited, South African psychoanalyst Wahbie Long explains well in what sense slavery continues to hurt people and to make them shameful. He stresses the importance of a universal quality that the ancient Greeks called *thymos*: 'the part of the soul that craves recognition of dignity'. Long writes:

> Human beings, that is, seek recognition from their peers, and when they do not receive it, one of two things happens. If they feel undervalued, they become resentful, and if they reckon within themselves a failure to meet the standards of others, they feel ashamed. Human beings are not satisfied with only food and shelter; they also want *respect*.[6]

The reason why Steve McQueen feels shameful and hurt by the history of slavery can thus be explained by the fact that this past implies the denial of respect to black people. And since racism is still a structural element of our societies, many black people also keep feeling shameful about how they fail to meet the white standards of our society. Slavery was an extreme phenomenon which, however, continues to exist as a structural, systemic invalidating of marginalized groups.

In recent years, we have seen two societal outcries that can be explained by shame and the denial of respect to certain people or groups. First of all, the MeToo movement, initiated by women, joined by men, who finally refused to be silent about having been and being made shameful by sexual violence and abuse. Second, the very recent anti-racism protests after George Floyd, a black man, died when a white policeman kneeled on his neck for nearly nine minutes. Although this violent death happened in the American city of Minneapolis (Minnesota), the protests were worldwide and continued for several weeks. The Black Lives Matter movement already existed long before George Floyd was killed, but was fueled by new energy. The name of this movement is first of all a response to the systematic violence of the American police against black people. This violence is performed by killing them. But Black Lives Matter can also be read as a request for respect: black people are asking for the respect and dignity that has so far been denied to them. This is, in fact, the precondition for not being killed anymore.

When Black Lives Matter is read as a request for respect and dignity, it becomes understandable that the anti-racism protests happened worldwide. These protests are not just acts of solidarity with the black victims of police violence in the United States. After all, the police practices in most European countries and in Australia are not as extremely violently racist as they are in the United States. This difference suggests that the anger expressed by the protests all over the world is motivated by solidarity with a societal injustice that characterizes the United States. But it is a relative difference. Although this extreme structural racist violence is perhaps first of all

7 Jaeger, 'Nieuwe beeldenstorm zorgt voor reflectie en verandering' (2020), n.p.

characteristic of the US, the denial of respect and dignity to black people is a worldwide structural phenomenon. The anger was therefore not just motivated by solidarity with others in another country, although that was certainly also the case, but also by the feeling of being shameful because of the continuous denial of respect to black people everywhere, personally and collectively.

The attacks on the statues of Edward Colston in Bristol and of Cecil Rhodes in Cape Town were not just motivated by what these statues signify or repress, but also by what they do affectively. They release feelings of shame in many of the people who have to live with these historical figures. They feel shameful, because the statues remind them of the past in which their people were enslaved. And although they are themselves not enslaved anymore, they still experience that no dignity is bestowed on them, even as black students at a prestigious South African university. In addition, as I just said, the attacks as such should be understood not in only terms of what they mean but also in terms of what they do affectively. As has been argued before, these attacks were 'political and emotional events where people danced, chanted and became visibly moved'.[7] The unveiling of a statue is much less impressive than the removal of a statue. Toef Jaeger describes these removals as having the same impact as the most interesting performance art, referring also to the removal of the statue of Saddam Hussein in 2003. And, as I contend, good performance art is of importance, not just for what it represents or means, but for what it does, performatively and affectively.

Iconoclasm in Byzantium

But first I would like to reflect on how these present performances of iconoclasm can be compared to former practices of iconoclasm and how the latter can illuminate the former. I will focus on Marie José Mondzain's brilliant analysis of one of the most (in)famous iconoclast times, those of Byzantinism. In her book *Image, Icon, Economy,*[8] she describes the problems of the visible world in Byzantine and present times as follows:

> Consideration of the image is still a sacred cause today only because the fate of thought and liberty are at stake in it. The visible world, the one that is given to us to see: is it liberty or enslavement? In order to be able to envisage a world radically founded on visibility, and starting from the conviction that whatever constitutes its essence and meaning is itself invisible, it proved to be essential to establish a system of thought that set the visible and invisible in relation to each other. This relation was based on the distinction between the image and the icon. The image is invisible, the icon is visible. The economy was the concept of their *living* linkage. The image is an enigma. The economy was the concept of their *relation* and their *intimacy*. The image is eternal similitude, the icon is temporal resemblance. The economy was the theory of the *transfiguration of history*.[9]

Although we now have a very different notion of economy (and of image), in Byzantine discourse it concerned the transfiguration of history, of a visible icon to an invisible image. Today, we would call this signification, the process that links a signifier to a signified or meaning. And in Byzantine times, the eternal similitude on which the invisible image was based

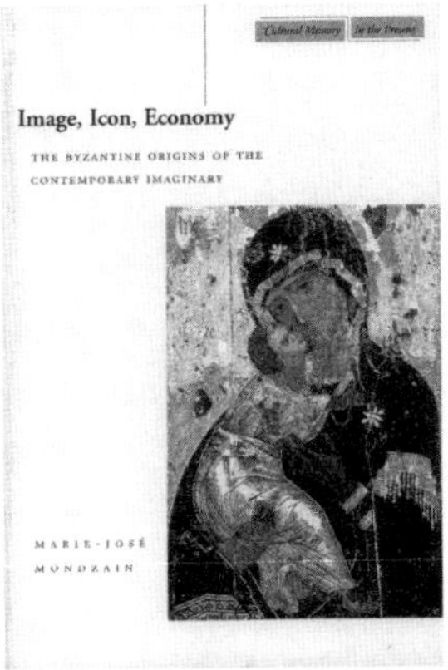

8 Marie José Mondzain, *Image, Icon, Economy* (2004), book cover, transl. from French.

9 Mondzain, *Image, Icon, Economy* (2004), 3, emphasis in original.

was thought to be transcendental, whereas in semiotic discourse it is just called conceptual, which is certainly not eternal but bound in and by history. In spite of these differences, Mondzain's understanding of Byzantine iconoclasm helps us to better understand present-day iconoclast conflicts.

The protesters against the statues of colonialist/racist/imperialist heroes refuse to transfigure the historical facts about these figures into the eternal value, meaning, or sublimation of them, which makes them heroes. By that refusal, they are not defending an eternal truth of the invisible image, but a historical truth. The people who defend these statues, in contrast, stick to the so-called transfiguration of history that has already taken place, and that has transfigured the characters into eternal, universal role models. The question that has not been answered yet is *why* the protesters refuse to transfigure history into eternal values and truth. Is it only because their view of history is more complex than that of the admirers of these statues, or is there more at stake?

Symbolic Violence and Shame

Again, I contend that we have to take affect into consideration, not only the affects triggered by these statues, but also those triggered by the destruction of these historical sites. Wahbie Long, whom I already quoted at the beginning of my text, has argued that shame and envy, when framed at the societal level, are not

> only among the principle *drivers* of violence in South Africa, they are also *responses* to violence in the broadest sense of the term, that is violence as a manifestation of power that denies people their humanity.[10]

10 Long, in Van Alphen (ed.), *Shame! And Masculinity* (2020), 154, emphasis in original.

Shame as a response to the power that denies people their humanity is a response to symbolic violence. This symbolic violence pervades institutions of higher education in South Africa, and hence also the University of Cape Town, where after years of black student protests the statue of Cecil John Rhodes was finally removed in 2015. The response of this black student elite should be understood as shame transformed into resentment. Referring to Bourdieu's ideas about symbolic violence, Long argues that symbolic violence designates the intimate encounter in which the oppressed cannot help but assess their predicament through the terms of reference provided by the oppressor and thereby participate unwittingly in their own subjugation.[11]

> The protests that have shaken university campuses over the last four years, that is, signal a conscientization about the workings of symbolic violence. All the talk of intellectual colonization, Eurocentrism, whiteness privilege, epistemic violence and so on is university speak for a perceived system of knowledge and an encompassing institutional culture that make it impossible for black students and academics to participate as their white counterparts' equals in intellectual life.[12]

The South African student movement promotes what is called 'Fallism' and the students are called 'Fallists'. The idea of Fallism first emerged as a collective noun to describe student movements at universities in South Africa that used the 'Must Fall' hashtag, including #RhodesMustFall and #FeesMustFall.[13] Although the Fallists were responsible for the removal of the Rhodes statue, it is clear that Fallism involves much more; that it is the institutional culture of South African Universities that has to 'fall'. The Fallist movements argue that the universities' epistemic architecture is

11 Bourdieu, 'Social Space and Symbolic Power' (1989).

12 Long, in Van Alphen (ed.), *Shame! And Masculinity* (2020), 161.

13 Long, in Van Alphen (ed.), *Shame! And Masculinity* (2020), 162.

14 Long, in Van Alphen (ed.), *Shame! And Masculinity* (2020), 162, emphasis in original.

15 Long, in Van Alphen (ed.), *Shame! And Masculinity* (2020), 163.

16 Long, in Van Alphen (ed.), *Shame! And Masculinity* (2020), 163.

deeply rooted in coloniality, and that, consequently, the university as we know it must fall.

Long also argues that the 'Fallist fury' has a touch of drama to it, that it is a 'politics of spectacle' that should be understood for its affective and performative power. As a result,

> no matter how far backwards university management bent, students could never feel satisfied. It was as if they *had* to be angry—regardless of the actual deal on the negotiating table.[14]

They will continue their anger, because for the Fallists the internal logic of the institution is white and whatever deal is put on the negotiation table, that will not change. They feel they are being deprived of the fruits they imagined a university education would confer, which triggers for many familiar feelings of deprivation:

> They feel persecuted by an institution experienced as massively shaming, and as they begin to compare themselves to more privileged students, their shame turns to envy. In a literal display of anal sadism, they set about spoiling the university, unloading bins of human feces into lecture halls. Haunted by a relentless sense of grievance, they set fire to life-affirming artworks and shut down life-giving classes of knowledge. 'If we cannot enjoy this place', then no one will, they may as well be saying.[15]

The affective, performative dynamic that is now at play is described by Long in psychoanalytic discourse: 'The more the Fallists destroy the institution, the more impoverished the collective ego feels. Their envy grows stronger still and the protests spiral out of control.'[16]

Long's analysis of Fallism in the context of South African Universities is of great importance also for understanding the toppling of statues in other parts of the world. For, the fact that South Africa has a dysfunctional school system for the majority of the black population that does not prepare for the university and the Enlightenment values it espouses is not fundamentally different from the situation in which migrants in the UK and the Netherlands, and black people in the US, live and grow up. Their living conditions, too, are massively shaming, because they cannot meet the white standards of the societies they live in. It is only when the shaming of groups of people in our societies stops that statues will no longer be toppled. Ultimately, the agents behind the destruction of these statues are the affects of shame, resentment and anger of people upon whom no dignity is bestowed. This explains why, in most of these cases, re-framing the statues is not enough, because it does not take into account that people feel ashamed by the knowledge the statues embody. The shame will only increase, even when the provided historical information is finally more up-to-date.

Notes on the Texts

This book consists of texts that have been published before in journals, catalogues or books. In some case the original text is published here, in some other cases the original text has been slightly adapted.

The second part of the 'Introduction' on affect is partly based on: 'Introduction: Mapping the Affective Operations', in Ernst van Alphen & Tomáš Jirsa, *How to Do Things with Affects*, Leiden: Brill, 2019, pp. 1–16 (co-author Tomáš Jirsa)

Chapter 1 'The Limits and the Need of Representing the Holocaust; Redefining the Notion of Experience' has been published as: 'Symptoms of Discursivity: Experience, Memory, Trauma' in *Acts of Memory: Cultural Recall in the Present,* eds. Mieke Bal, Jonathan Crewe, Leo Spitzer. Hanover NH: University of New England Press, 1999, pp. 24–38

Chapter 2 'Caught by Images: On the Role of Visual Imprints in Holocaust Testimonies' has been published as: 'Caught by Images: on the Role of Visual Imprints in Holocaust Testimonies', *Journal of Visual Culture* 1, 2, 2002, pp. 201–17

Chapter 3 'Neither "Post-" nor Memory: Second Generation Testimony, Transmission of Trauma and the Concept of Postmemory' has been published as: 'Second-Generation Testimony, Transmission of Trauma, and Postmemory', *Poetics Today* 27, 2, 2006, pp. 473–88

Chapter 4 'Legacies of Stalinism and the Gulag: Shame and Nostalgia' has been published as: 'Legacies of Stalinism and the Gulag: Manifestations of Trauma and Post Memory', in: *After Memory. World War II in Contemporary Eastern European Literatures,* eds. Matthias Schwartz, Nina Weller and Heike Winkel. Berlin: De Gruyter, 2021, pp. 111–31

Chapter 5 'Explosions of Information, Implosions of Meaning: The Release of Affects' has been published in two different versions: 'Affective Operations of Art and Literature', in *RES: Journal of Anthropology and Aesthetics* 53/54, Spring/Autumn, 2008, pp. 20–30; and 'Explosions of Information, Implosions of Meaning, and the Release of Affects', in *Images that Move,* eds. Patricia Spyer & Mary Steedly. Santa Fe: SAR, 2013, pp. 219–236

Chapter 6 'Francis Bacon and the Work of Sensation: Formal and Structural Dimensions' has been published in a catalogue as 'Making Sense of Affect', in *Francis Bacon: Five Decades*, ed. Tony Bond. Sydney: Museum of New South Wales, 2012, pp. 65–73

Chapter 7 'Legible Affects: The Melodramatic Imagination in Painting' has been published as: 'Legible Affects: The Melodramatic Imagination in Painting', in *Legibility in the Age of Signs and Machines*, eds. Pepita Hesslberth, Janna Houwen, Esther Peeren, Ruby de Vos. Leiden: Brill-Rodopi, 2018, pp. 21–34

Chapter 8 'Playing the Holocaust: Playacting and Toys' has been published in a catalogue as: 'Playing the Holocaust', in *Mirroring Evil: Nazi Imagery/Recent Art*, ed. Norman L. Kleeblatt. New York: The Jewish Museum/New Brunswick: Rutgers University Press, 2001, pp. 65–84

Chapter 9 'The Performativity of Provocation: The Case of Artur Żmijewski' has been published as: 'The Performativity of Provocation: The Case of Artur Żmijewski', *The Journal of Visual Culture,* 18–1 (2019), pp. 81–96 and a different version in: 'Toys and Affect: Identifying with the Perpetrator in Contemporary Holocaust Art', *Australian and New Zealand Journal of Art*, 2&3, 2, 1, 2001–2, pp. 159–190.

Bibliography

Abraham, Jugu. 2006. 'Andrei Zvyagenitsev's "Vozvrashcheniye" (The Return)' in *Movies Sans Frontiers* 31 August. www.moviessansfrontiers.blogspot.com/2006/08/2-andrei-zvyagenitsevs-vozvrashcheniye.html

Abrams, M.H. 1953. *The Mirror and the Lamp: Romantic Theory and the Critical Tradition*. Oxford: Oxford University Press

Ahmed, Sara. 2012. *On Being Included: Racism and Diversity in Institutional Life*. Durham: Duke University Press

——. 2004. *The Cultural Politics of Emotion*. New York: Routledge

Aitkenhead, Decca. 2014. 'Steve McQueen: My Hidden Shame', in *The Guardian* 4 January

Aksyonov, Vasily. 1994. *Generations of Winter*. New York: Random House

Alexievich, Svetlana. 2016. *Second Hand Time: The Last of the Soviets*. Transl. Bela Shayevich. New York: Random House

Alphen, Ernst van. 2008. 'Affective Operations of Art and Literature', 21–30 in *Res: Anthropology and Aesthetics* 53/54

——. 1997. *Caught by History: Holocaust Effects in Contemporary Art, Literature and Theory*. Stanford, CA: Stanford University Press

——. 1992. *Francis Bacon and the Loss of Self*. London: Reaktion Books/Cambridge, MA: Harvard University Press

Alphen, Ernst van (ed.). 2020. *Shame! And Masculinity*. Amsterdam: Valiz

Alphen, Ernst van & Tomáš Jirsa (eds.). 2019. *How to Do Things With Affects: Affective Triggers in Aesthetic Forms and Cultural Practices*. Leiden: Brill Press

Alphen, Ernst van, Mieke Bal & Carel Smith (eds.). 2009. *The Rhetoric of Sincerity*. Stanford, CA: Stanford University Press

Altman, Morris (ed.). 2015. *Handbook of Contemporary Behavioral Economics: Foundations and Developments*. London: Routledge

Appelfeld, Aharon. 1994. *Beyond Despair: Three Lectures and a Conversation with Philip Roth*. New York: Fromm International

Archimbaud, Michel. 1993. *Francis Bacon in Conversation with Michel Archimbaud*. London: Phaidon

Armando. 1992. 'An International Primeur', *Gard Sivik* 33, Jan./Feb.

——. 1988. *De straat en het struikgewas (The Street and the Undergrowth)*. Amsterdam: De Bezige Bij

——. 1985. (interview *NRC Handelsblad)*

——. 1980. *Aantekeningen over de vijand (Notes about the Enemy)*. Amsterdam: De Bezige Bij

——. 1973. *Dagboek van een dader (Diary of a Perpetrator)*. Leiden: Tango

Armando & Hans Sleutelaar. 1990 [1967]. *De SS'ers. Nederlandse vrijwilligers in de tweede wereldoorlog (The SS-ers: Dutch Volunteers in the Second World War)*. Amsterdam: De Bezige Bij

Austin, J.L. 1975 [1962]. *How to Do Things with Words*. Cambridge, MA: Harvard University Press

Bal, Mieke. 2021. *Figuraciones. Cómo la literature crea imagines*. Murcia: Editum

——. 2017. *Narratology: Introduction to the Theory of Narrative*. Toronto: University of Toronto Press

——. 2010. *Of What One Cannot Speak: Doris Salcedo's Political Art*. Chicago: University of Chicago Press

——. 2002. *Travelling Concepts in the Humanities: A Rough Guide*. Toronto: University of Toronto Press

——. 1999a. 'Introduction', vii–xvii in *Acts of Memory: Cultural Recall in the Present*,

eds. Mieke Bal, Jonathan Crewe & Leo Spitzer. Hanover, NH: University of New England Press
——. 1999b. *Quoting Caravaggio: Contemporary Art, Preposterous History*. Chicago: University of Chicago Press
——. 1991. *Reading 'Rembrandt': Beyond the Word-Image Opposition*. Cambridge, UK and New York: Cambridge University Press
Bañón, María Luz. 2021. *Tiempos Instalados*. Tésis doctoral, Universidad de Murcia, facultad de Bellas Artes
Barthes, Roland. 1981. *Camera Lucida: Reflections on Photography*. Transl. Richard Howard. New York: Hill and Wang
Benigni, Roberto. 1997. *Life is Beautiful* (*La vita è bella*). Prod. Melampo Cinematografica
Benjamin, Andrew. 1994. 'Installed Memory: Christian Boltanski', 54–69 in *Object, Painting*. London: Academy Editions
Bennett, Jill. 2009. 'A Feeling of Insincerity: Politics, Ventriloquy and the Dialectics of Gesture', 195–213 in *The Rhetoric of Sincerity*, eds. Ernst van Alphen, Mieke Bal & Carel Smith. Stanford, CA: Stanford University Press
——. 2005. *Empathic Vision: Affect, Trauma, and Contemporary Art*. Stanford, CA: Stanford University Press
Benveniste, Émile. 1966. *Problèmes de linguistique générale*. Paris: Gallimard
Berlant, Lauren. 2011. *Cruel Optimism*. Durham, NC: Duke University Press
Bernstein, Michael André. 1994. *Foregone Conclusions: Against Apocalyptic History*. Berkeley: University of California Press
Blackman, Lisa. 2012. *Immaterial Bodies: Affect, Embodiment, Mediation*. London: Sage
Blanchot, Maurice. 1985. *Vicious Circles: Two Fictions and 'After the Fact'*. Barrytown, NY: Stationhill Press
Blotkamp, Carel. 1989. 'Past Imperfect: Armando's Theme' in *Armando, Damnable Beauty, or Resonance of the Past* (exhib. cat.). Edinburgh: Fruitmarket Gallery
Boardman, Andrew. 1998. *Zbigniew Libera*. Warsaw
Boletsi, Maria. 2016. 'From the Subject of the Crisis to the Subject in Crisis: Middle Voice on Greek Walls', 328 in *The Journal of Greek Media and Culture* 2, 1; reprinted 2017, 431–468 in *The documenta 14 Reader*, eds. Quin Latimer & Adam Szymczyk. München: Prestel
Boltanski, Christian. 1994. *Christian Boltanski: Lost*. Glasgow, Dublin: CCA—Tramway Douglas Hyde Gallery—Glasgow School of Art
——. 1984. *Boltanski* (exhib. cat.) Paris: Musée National d'Art Moderne
Borowicz, Jan. 2015. 'Holocaust Zombies: Mourning and Memory in Polish Contemporary Culture', 132–148 in *Revisiting Holocaust Representation in the Post-Witness Era*, eds. Diana I. Popescu & Tanja Schult. London: Palgrave
Bourdieu, Pierre. 1989. 'Social Space and Symbolic Power', 14–25 in *Sociological Theory* 7, 1
Borowski, Tadeusz. 1976 [1967]. *This Way for the Gas, Ladies and Gentlemen*. Selected and transl. Barbara Vedder. Introduction by Jan Kott. New York: Penguin Books
Brennan, Teresa. 2004. *The Transmission of Affect*. Ithaca, NY: Cornell University Press
Brinkema, Eugenie. 2014. *The Forms of the Affects*. Durham and London: Duke University Press
Brooks, Peter. 1995 [1976]. *The Melodramatic Imagination: Balzac, Henry James, Melodrama, and the Mode of Excess*. New Haven: Yale University Press
——. 1984. *Reading for the Plot: Design and Intention in Narrative*. New York: Alfred A. Knopf
Browning, Christopher R. 1992. *Ordinary Men: Reserve Battalion 101 and the Final Solution in Poland*. New York: Harper Collins
Butler, Judith. 1997. *Excitable Speech: A Politics of the Performative*. New York: Routledge
——. 1993. *Bodies that Matter: On the Discursive Limits of 'Sex'*. New York: Routledge
——. 1990. *Gender Trouble: Feminism and the Subversion of Identity*. New York: Routledge
Bykov, Dmitry. 2005. *Justification* (*Оправдание*). Moscow: Wagrius

Carroll, Noël. 1999. 'Film, Emotion, and Genre', in *Passionate Views: Film, Cognition, and Emotion*, eds. Carl Plantinga & Greg M. Smith. Baltimore: Johns Hopkins University Press
Celan, Paul. 1986. *Collected Prose*. Transl. Rosemarie Waldrop. Riverdale-on-Hudson, NY: Sheep Meadow Press
Clough, Patricia T. & Jean O. M. Halley. 2007. *The Affective Turn*. Durham: Duke University Press
Culler, Jonathan. 1988. *Framing the Sign: Criticism and Its Institutions*. Norman and London: University of Oklahoma Press

Damasio, Antonio. 1994. *Descartes' Error: Emotion, Reason and the Human Brain*. New York: Avo Books
Darville, Helen [Demidenko]. 1995. *The Hand that Signed the Paper*. Sydney: Allen and Unwin
Davies, Hugh & Sally Yard. 1986. *Francis Bacon*. New York: Abbeville Press
DeKoven Ezrahi, Sidra. 1996. 'Representing Auschwitz', 121–154 in *History and Memory* 7, 2 (Fall/Winter)
——. 1980. *By Words Alone: The Holocaust in Literature*. Chicago: The University of Chicago Press
De Lauretis, Teresa. 1983. 'Semiotics and Experience', 158–186 in *Alice Doesn't: Feminism, Semiotics, Cinema*. London: MacMillan
Delbo, Charlotte. 1995. *Auschwitz and After*. Transl. Rosette C. Lamont. Introduction by Lawrence L. Langer. New Haven and London: Yale University Press
Deleuze, Gilles. 2002 [1981]. *Francis Bacon:*

The Logic of Sensation. Transl. and introduction by Daniel W. Smith. Minneapolis: University of Minnesota Press

——. 1983. 'What Is a Minor Literature?', 13–33 in *Mississippi Review* 11, 3 (Winter/Spring)

——. 1971. 'Proust y los signos' en *Ideas y Valores*. Revista del Departamento de Filosofía y Humanidades de la Facultad de Ciencias Humanas de la Universidad Nacional, nº 38 y 39, 326, 15 y 20. Traducción de Mary Mora de Ducay

——. 1964. *Proust and Signs*. Transl. Richard Howard. New York: Braziller

De Nijs, Pieter. 1990. 'Ik heb iets vreselijks gezien. De stoere gevoeligheid van Armando', 820 in *Bzzlletin* 173

Derrida, Jacques. 1988. 'Signature, Event, Context', 123 in *Limited Inc*. Transl. Samuel Weber. Evanston, IL: Northwestern University Press

——. 1982. 'Différance', 3–27 in *Margins of Philosophy*. Transl. Alan Bass. Chicago: University of Chicago Press

——. 1981. *Dissemination*. Transl. Barbara Johnson. London: The Athlone Press

Des Pres, Terrence. 1988. 'Holocaust Laughter', 216–233 in *Writing and The Holocaust*, ed. Berel Lang. New York: Holmes & Meier

——. 1976. *The Survivor: An Anatomy of Life in the Death Camps*. Oxford: Oxford University Press

Didi-Huberman, Georges. 2005. *Confronting Images: Questioning the Ends of a Certain History of Art*. Transl. John Goodman. Philadelphia: Penn State University Press

Dijck, José van. 2007. *Mediated Memories: Personal Cultural Memory in the Digital Age*. Stanford, CA: Stanford University Press

Dresden, Samuel. 1992 [1963]. 'Souvenir inoubliable', 7–12 in *Raster* 57

Duncan, Pansy. 2016. *The Emotional Life of Postmodern Film: Affect Theory's Other*. New York: Routledge

Elsaesser, Thomas. 1991. 'Tales of Sound and Fury: Observations on the Family Melodrama', 68–91 in *Imitation of Life: A Reader on Film and Television Melodrama*, ed. Marcia Landy. Detroit: Wayne State University Press

Epstein, Helen. 1979. *Children of the Holocaust: Conversations with Sons and Daughters of Survivors*. New York: G.P. Putman's Sons

Etkind, Alexander. 2013. *Warped Mourning: Stories of the Undead in the Land of the Unburied*. Stanford, CA: Stanford University Press

Felman, Shoshana. 1982. 'Psychoanalysis and Education: Teaching Terminable and Interminable', 21–44 in *Yale French Studies* 63

Felman, Shoshana & Dori Laub. 1992. *Testimony: Crises of Witnessing in Literature, Psychoanalysis and History*. New York: Routledge

Fokkema, R.L.K. 1965. 'De dichter als nuchtere romanticus', 63–67 in *Armando, schilder-schrijver*. Weesp: De Haan

Fresco, Nadine. 1984. 'Remembering the Unknown', 417–428 in *The International Review of Psycho-Analysis* 11

Frey, Bruno S. & Alois Stutzer. 2002. *Happiness and Economics: How the Economy and Institutions Affect Human Well-Being*. Princeton and Oxford: Princeton University Press

Friedlander, Saul. 1993a. [1982] *Reflections on Nazism: An Essay on Kitsch and Death*. Transl. Thomas Weyr. Bloomington, IN: Indiana University Press

——. 1993b. *Memory, History, and the Extermination of the Jews of Europe*. Bloomington, IN: Indiana University Press

Friedlander, Saul (ed.). 1992. *Probing the Limits of Interpretation: Nazism and the 'Final Solution'*. Cambridge, MA: Harvard University Press

Friedman, Carl. 1994. *Nightfather*. Transl. Arnold Pomeran & Erica Pomerans. New York: Persea Books

Ginzburg, Yevgenia. 1995 [1967]. *Journey into the Whirlwind*. New York: Harcourt

Gilman, Sander L. 2000. 'Is Life Beautiful? Can the Shoah Be Funny? Some Thoughts on Recent and Older Films', 279–308 in *Critical Inquiry* 26

Gjessing, Steinar. 1994. 'Christian Boltanski: An Interview, November 1993', 41–50 in *Treskel/Threshold* 11

Goldenberg, Myrna. 1990. 'Different Horrors, Same Hell: Women Remembering the Holocaust', 150–166 in *Thinking the Unthinkable: Meanings of the Holocaust*, ed. Roger S. Gottlieb. New York: Paulist Press

González-Torres, Félix. 2006. 'The Gold Field', in *Félix González-Torres*, ed. Julie Ault. New York: Steidl Publishers

Gregg, Melissa & Gregory J. Seigworth. 2010. 'An inventory of Shimmers', 1–25 in *The Affect Theory Reader*, eds. Melissa Gregg & Gregory J. Seigworth. Durham: Duke University Press

Gribling, Frank. 1985. 'Armando en de romantische traditie', 49–61 in *Armando, schrijver-schilder*. Weesp: De Haan

Griffin, Randall C. 2014. 'Andrew Wyeth's *Christina's World*: Normalizing the 'Abnormal' Body', 113–127 in *Rethinking Andrew Wyeth*, ed. David Cateforis. Berkeley: University of California Press

Gumbrecht, Hans Ulrich. 2012. *Atmosphere, Mood, Stimmung: On a Hidden Potential of Literature*. Transl. Erik Butler. Stanford, CA: Stanford University Press

Gumpert, Lynn. 1994. *Christian Boltanski*. Paris: Flammarion

Hansen, Miriam. 1996. 'Schindler's List Is Not *Shoah*: The Second Commandment, Popular Modernism, and Public Memory', 292–312 in *Critical Inquiry* 22, 2 (Winter)

Hardt, Michael. 1999. 'Affective Labor', 89–100 in *boundary 2* 26, 2 (Summer)

Hartman, Geoffrey H. 1996. *The Longest Shadow: In the Aftermath of the Holocaust*. Bloomington, IN: Indiana University Press

——. 1995. 'Learning from Survivors: The Yale Testimony Project', 192–207 in *Holocaust and Genocide Studies* 9, 2
——. 1994. 'Public Memory and Its Discontents', 24–40 in *Raritan* 13, 4
Hirsch, Marianne. 2012. *The Generation of Post-Memory: Writing and Visual Culture After the Holocaust*. New York: Columbia University Press
——. 2008. 'The Generation of Postmemory', 103–128 in *Poetics Today* 29, 1
——. 1997. *Family Frames: Photography, Narrative, and Postmemory*. Cambridge, MA: Harvard University Press
Hlavajova, Maria. 2008. 'The Social Studio', in *Arthur Żmijewski: The Social Studio*. Utrecht: BAK
Hoffman, Eva. 2004. *After Such Knowledge: Memory, History, and the Legacy of the Holocaust*. New York: PublicAffairs
Hogan, Patrick Colm. 2011. *Affective Narratology: The Emotional Structures of Stories*. Lincoln and London: University of Nebraska Press

Jaeger, Toef. 2020. 'Nieuwe beeldenstorm zorgt voor reflectie en verandering', in *NRC Handelsblad* 29 December. www.nrc.nl/nieuws/2020/12/29/was-dit-het-jaar-van-blijvende-veranderingen-in-de-kunsten-a4025387
'Jan Pieterszoon Coen'. *Wikipedia*. en.wikipedia.org/wiki/Jan_Pieterszoon_Coen
Jakobson, Roman. 1960. 'Linguistics and Poetics' (fragment), 350–358 in *Style in Language*, ed. Thomas A. Sebeok. Cambridge, MA: MIT press

Kacandes, Irene. 1994. 'You Who Live Safe in Your Warm Houses: Your Role in the Production of Holocaust Testimony', 189–213 in *Insiders and Ousiders: Jewish and Gentile Culture in Germany and Austria*, eds. Dagmar Lorenz & Gabriela Weinberger. Detroit: Wayne State University
Kant, Immanuel. 1983 [1790]. *Kritik der Urteilskraft*. Vol. 5 of *Werke*. Darmstadt: Wissenschaftliche Buchgesellschaft
Karatzogianni, Athina, & Adi Kuntsman (eds.). 2012. *Digital Cultures and the Politics of Emotion: Feelings, Affect and Technological Change*. Basingstoke: Palgrave Macmillan
Katzir, Ram. 1998. *Your Coloring Book: A Wandering Installation*. Amsterdam: Stedelijk Museum
Koerner, Joseph Leo.1990. *Caspar David Friedrich and the Subject of Landscape*. London: Reaktion Books
Kolk, Bessel A. van der & Onno van der Hart. 1995. 'The Intrusive Past: The Flexibility of Memory and the Engraving of Trauma', 158–182 in *Trauma: Explorations in Memory*, ed. Cathy Caruth. Baltimore: Johns Hopkins University Press
Kosinski, Jerzy. 1965. *The Painted Bird*. Boston, MA: Houghton Mifflin Harcourt
Krauss, Rosalind E. 1999. *'A voyage on the North Sea': Art in the Age of the Post-Medium Condition*. London: Thames and Hudson
——. 1985. 'Notes on the Index' (parts 1 and 2), 196–209 and 210–220 in *The Originality of the Avant-Garde and Other Modernist Myths*. Cambridge, MA: MIT Press
——. 1977. *Passages in Modern Sculpture*. Cambridge, MA: MIT Press

LaCapra, Dominick. 2004. *History in Transit: Experience, Identity, Critical Theory*. Ithaca, NY: Cornell University Press
——. 2001. *Writing History, Writing Trauma*. Baltimore, MD: The Johns Hopkins University Press
——. 2001. 'Interview with Yad Vashem (June 9, 1998)', in *Writing History, Writing Trauma*. Baltimore, MD: The John Hopkins University Press
——. 1994. *Representing the Holocaust: History, Theory, Trauma*. Ithaca, NY: Cornell University Press.
Lam, Janneke. 2002. *Whose Pain? Childhood, Trauma, Imagination*. Amsterdam: ASCA
Lang, Berel. 1990. *Act and Idea in the Nazi Genocide*. Chicago: The University of Chicago Press
Langer, Lawrence L. 1991. *Holocaust Testimonies: The Ruins of Memory*. New Haven: Yale University Press
Lascault, Gilbert. 1971. 'Boltanski au Musée municipal d'art moderne', 143 in *XXe Siècle* 33, 7
Laub, Dori. 1992. 'An Event Without a Witness: Truth, Testimony and Survival', 75–92 in *Testimony: Crises of Witnessing in Literature, Psychoanalysis and History*, eds. Shoshana Felman & Dori Laub. New York: Routledge
Leiris, Michel. 1983. *Francis Bacon. Full and in Profile*. Oxford: Phaidon
Libera, Zbigniew. 1998. 'Discussion', 225–240 in *Bulletin Trimestriel de la Fondation Auschwitz* 60
Lifton, Robert Jay. 1991. *Death in Life: Survivors of Hiroshima*. Chapel Hill, NC: University of North Carolina Press
Long, Wahbie. 2020. 'Shame, Envy, Impasse and Hope: The Psychopolitics of Violence in South Africa', 153–175 in *Shame! And Masculinity*, ed. Ernst van Alphen. Amsterdam: Valiz
Lothe, Jakob. 2017. *Time's Witnesses: Women's* Voices from the *Holocaust*. Edinburgh: Fledgling Press
Lotman, Juri. 1977. *The Structure of the Artistic Text*. Transl. Gail Lenkoff & Ronald Varson. Ann Arbor, MI: University of Michigan Press

Marsh, Georgia. 1990. 'Christian, Carrion, Clown and Jew; Christian Boltanski interviewed by Georgia Marsh, Revised by Christian Boltanski', in *Reconstruction* (exhib. cat.). London: White Chapel Gallery
Massumi, Brian. 2002a. *A Shock to Thought: Expression after Deleuze and Guattari*. London: Routledge
——. 2002b. *Parables for the Virtual: Movement, Affect, Sensation*. Durham: Duke University Press
——. 1996. 'The Autonomy of Affect', in

Deleuze: A Critical Reader, ed. Paul Patton. Oxford: Blackwell
——. 1993. 'Everyone You Want to Be: Introduction to Fear', 3–37 in *The Politics of Everyday Fear*, ed. Brian Massumi. Minneapolis: University of Minnesota Press
Michaels, Walter Benn. 2015. 'Never Again, or Nevermore', in *The Beauty of a Social Problem*. Chicago: University of Chicago Press
Mitchell, W.J.T. 2021. 'Present Tense: An Iconology of the Epoch', 370–406 in *Critical Inquiry* 47 (Winter)
Mondzain, Marie José. 2004. *Image, Icon, Economy*. Transl. Rico Frances. Stanford, CA: Stanford University Press
Morrison, Toni. 1987a *Beloved*. New York: Alfred A. Knopf
——. 1987b. Toni Morrison 'Site of Memory', 111–112 in *Inventing the Truth: The Art and Craft of Memoir*, ed. William Zinsser. Boston: Houghton-Mifflin
Mühlhoff, Rainer. 2015. 'Affective Resonance and Social Interaction', 1001–1019 in *Phenomenology and the Cognitive Sciences* 14, 4

Newman, Michaell. 1992. 'Suffering from Reminiscences', 84–114 in *Postmodernism and the Re-Reading of Modernity*, eds. Francis Barker, Peter Hulme & Margaret Iversen. Manchester: Manchester University Press
Ngai, Sianne. 2012. *Our Aesthetic Categories: Zany, Cute, Interesting*. Cambridge, MA: Harvard University Press
Nickas, Robert. 2006. 'Félix González-Torres: All the Time in the World', in *Félix González-Torres*, ed. Julie Ault. New York: Steidl Publishers
Noordenbos, Boris. 2016. *Messages from the Black Hole: Post-Soviet Literature and the Search of a Russian Identity*. New York: Palgrave Macmillan
Novick, Peter. 2000. *The Holocaust in American Life*. Boston: Mariner Books

Oxford English Dictionary, 3rd edition (2010), s.v. 'trigger'. Web, accessed 20 June 2018
Oxford Russian Life History Archive (n.d.), www.digital.humanities.ox.ac.uk/project/oxford-russian-life-history-archive

Panksepp, Jaak. 1998. *Affective Neuroscience: The Foundation of Human and Animal Emotions*. Oxford: Oxford University Press
Papacharissi, Zizi. 2015. *Affective Publics: Sentiment, Technology, and Politics*. Oxford: Oxford University Press
Peirce, Charles Sanders. 1984. 'Logic as Semiotic', 3–11 in *Semiotics: An Introductory Anthology*, ed. Robert E. Innis. Bloomington. IN: Indiana University Press
Potocka, Maria Anna (ed.). 2020. *Polyphonie des Holocaust*. Wallstein Verlag & Centre for Persecuted Arts Solingen

Raczymow, Henri. 1994. 'Memory Shot Through with Holes', 98–105 in *Discourses of Jewish Identity in Twentieth Century France*, ed. Alan Astro. *Yale French Studies* 85
Rajchman, John. 1995. 'Another view of Abstraction', 16–25 in *Journal of Philosophy and the Arts* 5
Randle, Judith. 2004. 'Deaths, Disasters, and Traumas: Changing Meanings of the Word "Survivor", 1850–present'. PhD paper, Rhetoric Department, UC Berkeley
Ringelheim, Joan. 1990. 'Thoughts About Women and the Holocaust', 141–149 in *Thinking the Unthinkable: Meanings of the Holocaust*, ed. Roger S. Gotlieb. New York: Paulist Press
Rose, Julian. 2012. 'Trading Spaces: "A Roundtable on Art and Architecture"' 201–211 in *Artforum* 51, 2
Rossi, Paolo. 1995. 'The Scientist', 263–289 in *Baroque Personae*, ed. Rosario Villari. Chicago: The University of Chicago Press
Rothman, Roger. 1997. 'Mourning and Mania: Roee Rosen's Live and Die as Eva Braun', n.p. in Roee Rosen, *Live and Die as Eva Braun: Hitler's Mistress, in the Berlin Bunker and Beyond——An Illustrated Proposal for a Virtual-Reality Scenario, Not to Be Realized*. Jeruzalem: Israel Museum

Sanders, Martijn. 1985. 'De galm van het verleden. Martijn Sanders in gesprek met Armando', in *Armando. 100 tekeningen, 1952–1984* (exhib. cat.) Rotterdam: Museum Boymans van Beuningen
Santner, Eric. 1992. 'History Beyond the Pleasure Principle: Some Thoughts on the Representation of Trauma', 143–154 in *Probing the Limits of Representation: Nazism and the Final Solution*', ed. Saul Friedlander. Cambridge, MA: Harvard University Press
Schmitz, Hermann, Rudolf Owen Müllan, & Jan Slaby. 2011. 'Emotions Outside the Box——the New Phenomenology of Feeling and Corporeality', 241–259 in *Phenomenology and the Cognitive Sciences* 10, 2
Schult, Tanja. 2015. 'To Go or Not to Go? Reflections on the Iconic Status of Auschwitz, Its Increasing Distance and Prevailing Urgency', 107–131 in *Revisiting Holocaust Representation in the Post-Witness Era*, eds. Diana I. Popescu & Tanja Schult. London: Palgrave
Shaviro, Steven. 2010. *Post-Cinematic Affect*. Winchester: Zero
Sienkiewicz, Karol. 2009. 'Artur Żmijewski', in *Culture.pl*. www.culture.pl/en/artist/artur-zmijewski, accessed 28 July 2016
Sedgwick, Eve Kosofsky. 2003. *Touching Feeling: Affect, Pedagogy, Performativity*. Durham: Duke University Press
Silverman, Kaja. 1996. *The Threshold of the Visible World*. New York: Routledge
Sontag, Susan. 1967. 'Against Interpretation', in *Against Interpretation and Other Essays*. London: Eyre and Spottiswoode
Spinoza, Baruch. 1994. *A Spinoza Reader: The Ethics and Other Works*, ed. and transl. Edwin Curley. Princeton: Prince-

ton University Press
Spyer, Patricia. 2016. 'Images without Borders' in *Images that Move*, eds. Patricia Spyer & Mary Margaret Steedly. Santa Fe, NM: SAR Press
Stewart, Kathleen. 2007. *Ordinary Affects*. Durham: Duke University Press
Stigter, Bianca. 2008. 'Staren naar een stuk kaas', 4 in *NRC Handelsblad* 2 May
Sylvester, David. 1987. *The Brutality of Fact: Interviews with Francis Bacon*. London: Thames and Hudson

Theweleit, Klaus. 1985. 'The Politics of Orpheus, Between Women, Hades, Political Power, and the Media: Some Thoughts on the Configuration of the European Artist, Staring with the Figure of Gottfried Benn. Or: What Happens to Euricide?', 133–156 in *New German Critique* 36
Thomas, D.M. 1981. *The White Hotel*. New York: Viking Press
Tomkins, Silvan S. 1992. *Affect, Imagery, Consciousness*. New York: Springer
Tomkins, Silvan S. & Elaine Virginia Demos (eds.). 1995. *Exploring Affect: The Selected Writings of Silvan S. Tomkins*. Cambridge, UK: Cambridge University Press

Warhol, Andy. 1965. *Empire*. Prod. Andy Warhol
——. 1964. *Sleep*. Prod. Andy Warhol
Wehrs, Donald R. & Thomas Blake. 2017. *The Palgrave Handbook of Affect Studies and Textual Criticism*. Cham: Springer
Wetherell, Margaret. 2012. *Affect and Emotion: A New Social Science Understanding*. London: Sage
White, Hayden. 1992. 'Writing in the Middle Voice', 179–187 in *Stanford Literary Review* 9
——. 1972. 'The Structure of Historical Narrative', in *Clio Journal* 1, 3
Williams, Linda. 1989. *Hard Core: Power, Pleasure and the Frenzy of the Visible*. Berkeley: University of California Press
Winnicott, D.W. 1971. 'Transitional Objects and Transitional Phenomena', 125 in *Playing and Reality*. New York: Basic Books
Wolinski, Michal. 2007. 'Interview with Żmijewski', 104–106 in *Metropolis M*, 5

Young, James. 1996. 'David Levinthal's *Mein Kampf*: Memory, Toys, and the Play of History', 67–82 in *Mein Kampf*, David Levinthal. Santa Fe, NM: Twin Palms Publishers
——. 1993. *The Texture of Memory: Holocaust Memorials and Meaning*. New Haven, CT: Yale University Press

Žižek, Slavoj. 2009 [1997]. 'Description Without a Place: On Holocaust and Art', 141–161 in *Inaesthetik: Politics of Art* 1
——. 1989. *The Sublime Object of Ideology*. London: Verso
Żmijewski, Artur. 2008. *Artur Żmijewski: The Social Studio*. Utrecht: BAK
——. 2007. 'Żmijewski: Applied Social Arts' in *Krytyka Polityczna* 11–12
——. 2006. 'A Favorite Theory of Art', in *Das unmögliche Theater/The Impossible Theater: Performativity in the Works of Pawel Althamer, Tadeusz Kantor, Katarzyna Kozyra, Robert Kusmirowski, and Artur Żmijewski*. Nürnberg: Verlag für moderne Kunst
——. 2005. 'A Storehouse of Limbs', Artur Żmijewski Speaks with Katarzyna Bielas and Dorota Jarecka, n.p. in *Artur Żmijewski. If it happened only once it's as if it never happened* (exhib. cat.). Warsaw: Zachęta National Gallery of Art
Zvyagintsev, Andrey. 2003. *The Return* (*Vozvrashchenie*). Prod. Dmitri Lesnevski

Index of Names

Index of Terms

About the Author

Ernst van Alphen is professor emeritus of Literary Studies at Leiden University. Before that, he was Queen Beatrix Professor of Dutch Studies at UC Berkeley. His publications include:

Seven Logics of Sculpture: Encountering Objects Through the Senses (Valiz 2023), *Productive Archiving: Artistic Strategies, Future Memories, Fluid Identities* (ed. Valiz 2023), *Shame and Masculinity* (ed. Valiz 2021), *Failed Images: Photography and Its Counter-Practices* (Valiz 2018); *Staging the Archive: Art and Photography in the Age of New Media* (Reaktion Books 2015); *Art in Mind: How Contemporary Images Shape Thought* (University of Chicago Press 2005); *Francis Bacon and the Loss of Self* (Harvard University Press 1992); *Caught by History: Holocaust Effects in Contemporary Art, Literature and Theory* (Stanford University Presss 1997).

Author: Ernst van Alphen
Project editor: Mirna Vrdoljak/Valiz
Proofreading: Jacinta van de Ven
Index: Simone Wegman, Jacinta van de Ven
Design: Sam de Groot
Typefaces: Eldorado (William Addison Dwiggins, 1953),
Computer Modern (Donald Knuth, 1984),
SKI DATA (Tariq Heijboer, 2014)
Paper: Munken Print White, 100 g/m² 1.5 (inside),
Munken Lynx Rough, 300 g/m² (cover)
Lithography: Gaëlle van den Dool, Wilco Art Books
Printing and binding: Wilco Art Books, Amersfoort
Publisher: Valiz, Amsterdam, 2026, www.valiz.nl
Astrid Vorstermans

This publication has been printed on FSC-certified paper by an FSC-certified printer. The FSC, Forest Stewardship Council, promotes environmentally appropriate, socially beneficial, and economically viable management of the world's forests. www.fsc.org

Distribution
NL/BE/LU: Centraal Boekhuis, www.cb.nl
Europe/Asia: Idea Books, www.ideabooks.nl
GB/IE: Central Books, www.centralbooks.com
USA/Canada/Latin America: D.A.P., www.artbook.com
Australia: Perimeter Books, www.perimeterbooks.com
Individual orders: www.valiz.nl; info@valiz.nl

Amsterdam, 2026
ISBN 978-94-93246-56-0
Printed and bound in the EU

Graphic Design
Sam de Groot designs in close collaboration with artists, publishers and art institutions. Alongside this, he co-develops typefaces and he frequently writes, publishes and performs self-initiated projects. He has taught typography at the graphic design department of the Gerrit Rietveld Academie since 2011.
www.samdegroot.nl

Publisher
Valiz is an independent international publisher that addresses contemporary developments in art, design, urban affairs, and visual culture. Our books offer critical reflection and interdisciplinary inspiration in a broad-based and imaginative way, often establishing a connection between cultural disciplines and socio-economic questions. Valiz is based in Amsterdam, and connects with authors, artists, designers, institutes, bookshops, distributors and readers worldwide.
www.valiz.nl

The vis-à-vis series provides a platform to stimulating and relevant subjects in recent and emerging visual arts, architecture and design. The authors relate to history and art history, to other authors, to recent topics and to the reader. Most are academic researchers. What binds them is a visual way of thinking, an undaunted treatment of the subject matter and a skilful, creative style of writing.

2015

Sophie Berrebi, *The Shape of Evidence: Contemporary Art and the Document*, ISBN 978-90-78088-98-1

Janneke Wesseling, *De volmaakte beschouwer: De ervaring van het kunstwerk en receptie-esthetica*, ISBN 978-94-92095-09-1 (e-book)

2016

Janneke Wesseling, *Of Sponge, Stone and the Intertwinement with the Here and Now: A Methodology of Artistic Research*, ISBN 78-94-92095-21-3

2017

Janneke Wesseling, *The Perfect Spectator: The Experience of the Art Work and Reception Aesthetics*, ISBN 978-90-80818-50-7

Wouter Davidts, *Triple Bond: Essays on Art, Architecture, and Museums*, ISBN 978-90-78088-49-3

Sandra Kisters, *The Lure of the Biographical: On the (Self-)Representation of Artists*, ISBN 978-94-92095-25-1

Christa-Maria Lerm Hayes (ed.), *Brian O'Doherty/Patrick Ireland: Word, Image and Institutional Critique*, ISBN 978-94-92095-24-4

2018

John Macarthur, Susan Holden, Ashley Paine, Wouter Davidts, *Pavilion Propositions: Nine Points on an Architectural Phenomenon*, ISBN 978-94-92095-50-3

Jeroen Lutters, *The Trade of the Teacher: Visual Thinking with Mieke Bal*, ISBN 978-94-92095-56-5

Ernst van Alphen, *Failed Images: Photography and its Counter-Practices*, ISBN 978-94-92095-45-9

Paul Kempers, *'Het gaat om heel eenvoudige dingen': Jean Leering en de kunst*, ISBN 978-94-92095-07-7

Eva Wittocx, Ann Demeester, Melanie Bühler, *The Transhistorical Museum: Mapping the Field*, ISBN 978-94-92095-52-7

2019

Nathalie Zonnenberg, *Conceptual Art in a Curatorial Perspective: Between Dematerialization and Documentation*, ISBN 978-90-78088-76-9

Wouter Davidts, Susan Holden, Ashley Paine (eds.), *Trading between Architecture and Art: Strategies and Practices of Exchange*, ISBN 978-94-92095-67-1

Jeroen Lutters, *In the Shadow of the Art Work: Art-Based Learning in Practice*, ISBN 978-94-92095-66-4

2020

Jeroen Lutters, *Creative Theories of (Just About) Everything: A Journey into Origins and Imaginations*, ISBN 978-94-92095-74-9

Ashley Paine, Susan Holden, John Macarthur (eds.), *Valuing Architecture: Heritage and the Economics of Culture*, ISBN 978-94-92095-93-0

2021

Florian Göttke, *Burning Images: A History of Effigy Protests*, ISBN 978-94-92095-96-1

2023

Ernst van Alphen, *Seven Logics of Sculpture: Encountering Objects Through the Senses*, ISBN 978-94-93246-15-7

2025

Mark Kremer, *Beautiful Madness: Art Writing as Art Curating*, ISBN 978-94-93246-36-2